A VOLUNTEER'S ADVENTURES

J. W. De Forest, 1868

A

VOLUNTEER'S ADVENTURES

*A UNION CAPTAIN'S RECORD
OF THE CIVIL WAR*

BY

John William De Forest

Edited, with Notes, by
JAMES H. CROUSHORE

LOUISIANA STATE UNIVERSITY PRESS
BATON ROUGE AND LONDON

Louisiana Paperback Edition, 1996
05 04 03 02 01 00 99 98 97 96   5 4 3 2 1

Library of Congress Cataloging-in-Publication Data

De Forest, John William, 1826–1906.
    A volunteer's adventures : a Union captain's record of the Civil
War / by John William De Forest ; edited, with notes, by James H.
Croushore. — Louisiana paperback ed.
        p.   cm.
    Originally published: New Haven, Conn. : Yale University, 1946.
    Includes index.
    ISBN 0-8071-2084-7 (p : alk. paper)
    1. De Forest, John William, 1826–1906—Correspondence. 2. United
States—History—Civil War, 1861–1865—Personal narratives.
    3. Connecticut—History—Civil War, 1861–1865—Personal narratives.
    4. Soldiers—Connecticut—Correspondence.   I. Croushore, James H.
E601.D32 1996
973.7'81—dc20   95-50684
                                                                      CIP

The paper in this book meets the guidelines for permanence and durability of the
Committee on Production Guidelines for Book Longevity of the Council on
Library Resources. ⬤

EDITOR'S PREFACE

IN September, 1861, Major General Benjamin F. Butler of Massachusetts received authority to raise for special service a division consisting of one regiment from each New England state. In the recruiting of troops that ensued, Connecticut prepared to contribute a unit to be known as the Charter Oak Regiment, with Henry C. Deming, former mayor of Hartford, as colonel and Ledyard Colburn, formerly major in the Second Connecticut, as lieutenant colonel. John William De Forest received a commission as captain in this regiment.

Though volunteers, once formed into military commands, were under the immediate jurisdiction of the War Department, the governor of the state furnishing recruits for the Union armies was empowered to appoint the field, staff, and company officers of the organization. Thus commissions in new units were often awarded to men entirely on the basis of their ability to secure enlistments. The examinations to determine the successful applicant were, according to De Forest, shams. "My own," he wrote later, "consisted of a few minutes of genial conversation about the chances of European interference."

In November a nucleus of four companies reported for training at Camp Lyon, two miles from Hartford; and in December the Twelfth Connecticut Volunteers was formally mustered into Federal service. After a period of preparation and training the unit left camp for New York on February 24, 1862. Three days later it sailed from that port for an unknown destination. While he was at sea De Forest wrote his wife the first of the letters which were later to form a part of *A Volunteer's Adventures*.

The story begins with the expedition against New Orleans in March and April of 1862, and ends with the battle of Cedar Creek in the Shenandoah Valley on October 19, 1864. There is a gap in the action from January to June, 1864, six months during which De Forest's regiment returned to Connecticut on furlough.

The six chapters of the book that deal chiefly with camp life are composed of letters De Forest wrote to his wife at the time. The narrative descriptions of battles and forced marches were written in the field immediately after the event or were prepared later from notes made then. In October, 1864, De Forest was given the assignment of writing about the Nineteenth Army Corps, and the accounts of the battles of the Opequon and of Cedar Creek were in all probability part of this assignment. The narrative sections, "The First Time under Fire," "Forced Marches," "Port Hudson," "Sheridan's Victory of the Opequon," and "The Battle of Cedar Creek," all appeared in *Harper's New Monthly Magazine* or *Galaxy* between 1864 and 1868. Later De Forest revised the published articles, added new material selected from his letters to his wife, and prepared a complete history of his army career under the title "Military Life." Then, as a final step toward publication, about 1890 he rewrote the account and gave it its present title. This is its first publication.

The text of this book follows the manuscript in the De Forest papers which Mr. L. Effingham de Forest has deposited in the Yale University Library and which he has most kindly allowed me to use. A few minor changes in capitalization and punctuation have been made and obvious misspellings have been corrected. In addition, the names of towns and rivers have been made consistent with the spellings in present-day atlases, and in two or three instances the spelling of the names of officers and men has been revised to agree with War Department records. Introductory notes have been added by the editor to most of the chapters. Unsigned footnotes are De Forest's own.

The letter from De Forest to William Dean Howells on page 204 is cited by permission of the Houghton Library, Harvard University, which owns the original.

I wish to thank Professor David M. Potter for his advice while I was preparing the volume for publication; and I gratefully acknowledge the help which I received from members of the staff of the Yale University Press.

JAMES H. CROUSHORE

CONTENTS

ILLUSTRATIONS

The maps were drawn by Jean Day Zallinger

AUTOBIOGRAPHICAL PREFACE

NOT long after the close of the Bull Run campaign I commenced recruiting a company for the Twelfth Connecticut Volunteers. During the autumn of that year (1861) the regiment went into camp at Hartford, and passed nearly the whole winter there in assiduous drill, being meanwhile assigned to the "New England Division" for service under Major General Benjamin F. Butler.*

In the latter part of February, 1862, we left Hartford for New York, and sailed by transport *Fulton* for Ship Island in the Gulf of Mexico to take part in the expedition against New Orleans. The military life which ensued is narrated in the following letters and narratives.†

On the 2ᵈ of December, 1864, I was discharged "by reason of termination of period of service," and went home with what then seemed a totally ruined constitution. My former chief, Major General Godfrey Weitzel, at that time in command of the Ninth Corps, urged me to take a field position in one of his regiments. "The finest I can get for you," he explained; "it shall be a majority, at the least. I consider you one of the best volunteer officers that I ever had under me."

But I was then far too weak for active service, and I felt obliged to decline this flattering offer. It was during this period of invalidism that I wrote *Miss Ravenel,* a novel subsequently published by Harpers.

* My commission, as captain of Company I, was dated January 1, 1862. I was ninth captain in rank by date of commission, and third in rank when I was mustered out three years later.

In a separate summary of his own military record (page 106 f.) De Forest wrote that he was mustered out of the Twelfth Connecticut Volunteers as fourth captain by seniority. On December 2, 1864, William Berry, whose date of enlistment was April 18, 1861, was promoted to captain and was discharged on the same day. Thus De Forest became the fourth captain in length of service, but he remained third captain in date of commission. (Ed.)

† I was made inspector general of the first division, Nineteenth Corps, in December, 1863; chief of ordnance in the same division, October, 1864; aide on Nineteenth Corps' staff a few days later.

On the 10th of February, 1865, upon recommendation of Generals Sheridan, Weitzel, Emory and McMillan, I was commissioned captain in the Veteran Reserve Corps and assigned to Company I, 14th Regiment, stationed at Washington. After a few months of garrison duty I became chief of the Veteran Reserve Corps' office (under Major General Fry, Provost-Marshal General) with the title of Acting Assistant Adjutant General.* In 1866, May 15, I was commissioned major by brevet, dating from March 13, 1865, "for gallant and meritorious services during the war."

In July, 1866, the Veteran Reserve Corps having been disbanded, I was assigned to the Bureau of Freedmen and Refugees, under Major General O. O. Howard. My first duty was on a board to revise regulations for the Bureau. Then came a furlough home; then orders to South Carolina. In October I took charge of the Bureau district of Greenville and Pickens counties, subsequently increased by the addition of Anderson. While here I received the offer of a first lieutenantcy in a colored infantry regiment of the regular army, but declined it because I wished to return home and resume my literary life. I was finally mustered out of military service in January, 1868.

The letters printed in this volume were mostly to my wife. Of course many more were written, but a certain number have naturally disappeared, and others were mere scraps on ammunition paper, etc. Those here included might have been reduced to a narrative; but it seems to me that they show camp life clearly and naturally; hence I leave them as they are.

* Orders dated September 13, 1865.

A VOLUNTEER'S ADVENTURES

Chapter I

CAMP LIFE AT SHIP ISLAND

Steam transport Fulton, March 6, 1862.

DID you receive the note which I sent you by the pilot? If so you know that the *Fulton* carries five companies of the Fourteenth Maine besides the ten companies of the Twelfth Connecticut, in all some fifteen hundred military greenhorns.

We are still rolling and splashing southward without a chance to mail you a letter. I was disappointed when we passed Fortress Monroe, and surprised as well as disappointed when we passed Charleston. It became clear then that we were to go to Ship Island or some other point in the Gulf, far from you and from all possibility of learning promptly of your welfare.

With the exception of one moderate gale, lasting barely eighteen hours, the passage has been a smooth one, and since we reached the latitude of Georgia, delightful. Light breezes, a calm sea, a bright sun, a temperature which makes the men take off their coats have accompanied us around Florida and into the Gulf. The coughs and colds that worried us in camp at Hartford have disappeared. Not one of the swarming men on board has died or seems likely to for a good while to come.

Personally I am more comfortably situated than I expected to be. I have got out of the hole where I was lodged at first, and am in a tolerable stateroom beside the stairway, only objectionable as being too near the boiler and also not quite large enough for three. Even the soldiers are much better accommodated than I supposed when I last wrote you; there is room enough below for every man to stretch himself at full length in his blanket or overcoat. Some of them were comically surprised and indignant when they learned that they were not to be made free of the after part of the ship. "That's a pooty way to treat a poor soldier!" whined one gawky lout as the sergeant of the guard, an old regular, routed him out of a seat on the quarter-deck and hustled him forward.

Not a woman on board; the ship is as the world was before Eve was created; the most jealous of wives need not be afraid to have her husband here. I am as indolent as passengers usually are; I cannot even study my drill book and the regulations. I smoke like a Turk; I walk the deck till the broiling sun sends me up to the breezy top of the wheelhouse; I load my revolver and shoot at gulls or floating tufts of seaweed; in my best estate I play at checkers on the quarter-deck. The cabin is so hot and close that it is not pleasant to linger there.

The general indifference to our future is curious and makes me wonder if we are beginning to be heroes. Nobody knows where we are ultimately going, and nobody appears to care. We vaguely expect to follow Porter's mortar fleet and occupy some place which has been shelled into submission. It seems impossible as yet to believe that we peaceful burghers are going to fight. You must not suppose that this tremulous handwriting results from terror of coming battle. It is merely the ship's engine shaking the table.

March 7th. We are running northerly in the teeth of a norther; the weather is as cold as latter March in Connecticut. The officers have on their heavy overcoats, and the men are hiding below from the bitter wind. It is blowing half a gale and something to spare, with a short cross sea which makes the novices ill again. They are somewhat comforted by a rumor that Ship Island will shelter us under its lee some time tomorrow. The smoke of a steamer, dimly visible in the landward distance, frightens us with the thought of capture. We have not a cannon on board, and our muskets are coming out on another transport, so that we should fall an easy prey to a swift Rebel gunboat.

March 8th. Here we are, at seven in the morning, dropping anchor within a mile or two of Ship Island. The water is smooth, the sky grey and lowering, the air damp but not cold. Around us are three or four navy steamers and several sailing vessels which are probably transports. The island is a low stretch of sand, almost as white as snow, with no discernible vegetation except something which looks like pine underwood. A few board shanties are visible, two or three encampments of white tents, and a ghostly lighthouse. Five or six miles away is what seems to be another island, scattered with trees which remind me of palmettos, though they may be tufted pines.

Officers and men are joking over our new home. One wants to know where the best hotel is; another says he is going ashore to shake the orange trees; another counsels his friends not to eat too much fruit. On the main deck a private berates a gasconading comrade who had yarned to him about a previous visit to Ship Island and its abundant groves of lemons.

Ship Island, March 10, 1862.

SHIP ISLAND is the sandiest region this side of the Great Sahara. Sullivan's Island,* which you know so well, is a spot of verdure in comparison. Here the sand is of a dazzling white which glitters in the moonlight like snow, and by day dazzles and fatigues the eyes unless the weather be cloudy.

We made a long, stupid, tedious job of landing. The *Fulton* lay far out from the northern shore of the island, between it and the dim, cloudlike mainland a dozen miles away. There were steam ferryboats at the anchorage; but for some mysterious reason, perhaps because they belonged to the navy, we could not have the use of them; hence the first day passed in getting two companies of our regiment ashore. These two (mine and Company D) clambered down into a steam tug which had been brought alongside the *Fulton*. The steam was simmering in the boilers, but we could not use it because the rudder had disappeared, how and where no one knew. So the men were set to warping us up to the beach by means of a windlass and hawser. Erelong the hawser snapped, and we came to anchor for two hours, during which we heard the dinner gong sound on the steamer, and of course did some hungry grumbling. Finally we

* Near Charleston, South Carolina. (Ed.)

got a small boat, bent on a fresh hawser and reached land. There the sergeant major detailed nearly half of my company to guard regimental stores. With the rest I marched to the ground which had been assigned us for a camp. Our instructions were simple and embarrassing; we were to "go right out there and get to work"; such were the luminous words of the lieutenant colonel. Following a plank road, we made our way through a city of tents, meeting scores of neat soldiers who touched their hats to officers like regulars. These were the fellows of the Ninth Connecticut and Twenty-sixth Massachusetts, who had been for months under General Phelps and had learned military manners. Our greenhorns stared at them with a mixture of wonder, envy and gloomy foreboding. "Has it come to this!" they seemed to be thinking. "Are freeborn Americans to be made slaves of in this fashion! And yet, what if those men should whip the Rebels, and we should run away!"

Our campground proved to be a distracted rabble of sand hills on the southern side of the island. Here and there sprouted giant grasses, twisted and writhed like vines. No other herbage was visible except the dank bulrushes of two marshy ponds, one on either flank. Here was the sergeant major, an exceedingly perplexed young man, standing between a herd of wheelbarrows and a pile of shovels. What were we to do?

"Why, level the campground, of course."

"But isn't Company D to help us?"

"Oh, the quartermaster has stopped that to guard baggage."

My fifty men seized their shovels and set to work at filling up hollows. But the camp had not been staked out, and erelong we learned that we were digging outside our limits, so that there was a deal of lost labor. The lieutenant colonel had sent the quartermaster back to the ship, promising to arrange the camp himself, and then had not done it. The tents came: but there were no tent pins: they had been left at Boston. The lieutenant colonel went to General Phelps and asked for tent pins.

"Make them," drawled the general, who is a Vermonter and proud of it.

"Give me the material," suggested the lieutenant colonel.

"Find it," squalled the general.

I succeeded in pitching one tent, and used it for a guard post whence to watch the others, which were sprawled about in all directions. By this time it was nightfall, and we draggled back to the steamer, having done near upon nothing.

The next day brought rather more to pass. By means of lifeboats we landed about two thirds of the regiment. But even yet the camp was not set up till four in the afternoon. I could not get my baggage, and slept in my tent on the sand with a rubber coat for bed and my cloak for coverlet. The result is that I am quite cured of a troublesome sore throat which I caught on board the *Fulton.* Or was my recovery attributable to a delicious dinner of fat pork cut up into dice and stewed with scraps of hard bread? How is it that I never tried that savory and wholesome dish before? When I get home we will have it frequently.

There has been a skirmish at Mississippi City on the mainland, between two companies of Massachusetts men on a gunboat and a considerable force of Rebels. Our people wanted cattle, but came back without beef and with one man wounded. They do not pretend that the engagement will change the result of the war.

Ship Island, March 15, 1862.

WHY were we born! Just imagine a regiment landing on a desert island without baggage wagons and horses, without tents enough, and without even a tent pin to kindle a fire with! Every day I detail from a quarter to three quarters of my company to collect wood for cooking; and this wood they must bring on their backs a distance of two, three, and four miles. We have no cook-tent, and no lumber wherewith to build cookhouses, so that I must store all the rations of my company in my own tent.* Consequently I am encumbered with boxes of hardbread, and dispense a nutritious perfume of salt pork, salt beef, onions, potatoes, vinegar, sugar and coffee.

Yesterday I sent off my crack soldier, Sergeant Weber, with a squad of twenty-four men to bring logs from the eastern end of

* In time we learned to do without any tents at all.

the island for the building of a cookhouse. They cut several dozen young pines, dragged them to the nearest beach, lashed them into a raft and floated it three miles along the shore, wading knee-deep and waist-deep, though the seawater is still quite chilly. Meantime a southerly gale commenced and by afternoon blew violently, driving the surf clean over the sandy neck which unites the two ends of the island. About four o'clock one of the squad reached me and reported that Weber was getting on with difficulty, and likely to lose his raft.

I had already sent thirty of my men to collect firewood, and nearly all the remainder were on police work or guard duty. But I got together about a dozen and marched a mile or so to help Weber. He had fought his way through the roughest water, and we saved the precious raft. But it was on the northern side of the island, and our camp lies on the southern side. So after the logs were landed, the men had to drag them or shoulder them for nearly half a mile across a puddly morass, midleg-deep in some places. But the glorious final result is that we have material for both a cookhouse and a storehouse.

By nightfall the gale became a thunderstorm which deluged the camp and upset many tents. The pins of mine pulled out of the wet sand as if it had been butter, and the whole thing went prostrate with a hateful soft *swish*. As raising it in that tempest was out of the question, I plunged into the tent of a neighboring captain and slept on his floor. No harm resulted to health and very little to property. This reminds me to say that the general sanitary condition on the island is wonderfully good. The Ninth and the Twenty-sixth have not had a death during their four-months' stay, so that if we hold on here and let the Rebs alone we may all become centenarians.

Three Western regiments joined us lately, making ten regiments now on the island besides a troop of cavalry and a battery of artillery, in all above nine thousand men. Nearly every day there are arrivals of transports, mortar boats, gunboats and ships of war. The naval officers tell us that this is to be a large expedition, and that there will be fully twenty-two thousand men of the land forces alone. If this is true, I infer that we are going to New Orleans, and that we are not likely to start immediately.

Today we have for the first time seen the mainland distinctly; it is a low, far-stretching coast, apparently covered with forests. A mirage lifts it in the air so that there is a bar of steel-color between the verdure and the yellow waters of the Sound; and this same atmospheric magic must enable the Mississippians to study our array of masts and smoke funnels; all the same we are twenty miles asunder.

We are in the rainy season now, and the mornings are chilly. I have a chance to know this, for we get up at sunrise. Then the *reveillé* beats; the men turn out under arms; the three commissioned officers look on while the first sergeant calls the roll; the muskets are stacked and the men break ranks. At half past six we breakfast; from seven to eight there is company drill; from half past nine to half past ten, more company drill; at twelve, dinner, which means soup and hardtack; from four to six, battalion drill; at half past six, hardtack, pork and coffee; at nine, another roll call; at a quarter past nine, lights out. It is a healthy, monotonous, stupid life, and makes one long to go somewhere, even at the risk of being shot.

Ship Island, April 6, 1862.

ABOUT a week ago we had a day of martial expectancy. After morning drill the lieutenant colonel called the officers together, congratulated us on the fact that we were soon to see fighting, and directed us to report to the colonel's tent for orders.

The men were marched to quarters and dismissed, hurrahing with excitement. Our instructions were to pack up, inspect arms, distribute forty rounds of ball cartridge per man, send trunks and extra baggage to the quartermaster, and hold ourselves ready to move at a minute's notice. The Twelfth was to embark on the sailing transport *E. W. Farley* and be towed by a gunboat to the South Pass of the Mississippi. Other troops, including cavalry and artillery, were assigned to other vessels.

Man is a brave animal, at least when danger is distant. Nine out of ten of our invalids got well as soon as they heard that we were to fight. None of my company wanted to stay behind, although five were on the sick list and one of them could scarcely hobble. As for myself, my only fear was lest my men should disgrace me and the regiment by running away; and I loaded my revolver with the grim intention of shooting the first dastard who should start for the rear. Of course, if ever the bullets begin to whistle about me, I may set the example of poltroonery. That suspicion really alarms me more than anything else. "Let not him that putteth on his armor boast himself."

All that Saturday, all Sunday and until noon on Monday we waited for marching orders, sleeping in our blankets on the ground with our arms by our sides. At the sound of the long roll the regiment fell in with slung knapsacks, canteens filled, and four days' rations in the havresacks. The officers carried their blankets and rubber blankets in a long roll (not a musical one) hanging diagonally from the right shoulder. We were all heavy laden enough as we trudged under a hot sun through nearly a mile of deep sand to the dock. There we stood in close column of companies until a flat-bottomed tug could be brought up to transfer us to the *Farley*. How luxurious it seemed to sit at a table once more, eating hot biscuit, butter, pickles and applesauce!

But there our campaign ended. News came that the fighting fleet was detained by the bar at the mouth of the Mississippi, and would not be ready to open upon the forts for ten days. We lingered twenty-four hours upon the transport and then draggled back to camp. Meantime, however, we witnessed a naval battle, though at a safe distance.

It seems that Butler's adjutant general, Major Strong, had steamed over to the mainland in a tugboat, carrying with him a little girl who had been picked up adrift in a skiff. He showed a flag of truce, but all the same he was fired on; so the next day an expedition sailed for Biloxi to avenge the insult. A ferryboat bearing six hundred of the Ninth Connecticut went with the three gunboats. Next morning there was a lively *bang! bang!* to the north of us, while flashes of cannonade gleamed through the hazy miragic distance, and faraway black motes of steamers chased to and fro. All day we were somewhat anxious, for only two gunboats remained at the island, and if the enemy should win we might get shelled.

But evening brought glory; first one gunboat in charge of a captured steamer; then another with a schooner, and so on. Later came the Ninth, loaded with a whimsical variety of spoil and bubbling over with blatherskite. They had been fired on by a shore battery, and two men had been scratched by splinters. They had landed, marched six miles into the country and broken up a camp of militia, part infantry and part cavalry. The enemy had fired two rounds without hitting anybody, and then emigrated due north at the top of their speed. We Twelfth fellows envy the Ninth their victory, and meekly besiege them for particulars and trophies. The most valued of these are Southern newspapers, for we scarcely get any Northern ones.

You would perhaps like a sketch of General Butler. Three of us Twelfth officers called upon him apropos of rations, and in my character of novelist I made a study of him. He is not the grossly fat and altogether ugly man who is presented in the illustrated weeklies. He is stoutish but not clumsily so; he squints badly, but his eyes are very clear and bright; his complexion is fair, smooth and delicately flushed; his teeth are white and his smile is ingratiating. You need not understand that he is pretty; only that he is better looking than his published portraits.

He treated us very courteously and entered into the merits of our affair at length, stating the *pros* and *cons* from the army regulations like a judge delivering a charge, and smiling from time to time after the mechanical fashion of Edward Everett, as if he meant to make things pleasant to us and also to show his handsome teeth. On the whole he seemed less like a major general than like a politician who was coaxing for votes. The result of the interview was that we got the desired order and departed with a sense of having been flattered.

Yesterday I called on General Phelps, the chief of our brigade. He is a swarthy, grizzled six-footer, who looks all the more giant-like because of a loose build and a shambling carriage, and says unexpected things in a slow, solemn humoristic way.

"Come in, Captain; what's the news?" he drawled, rather satirically as I thought; for how can a captain tell a general anything?

When I replied that I had heard nothing but vague and absurd reports about possible movements, he smiled as if approving my incredulity, or my reticence, and said, "Sit down, Captain; what do you want?"

I explained that I merely wanted some blanks for property returns from the brigade quartermaster; but he kept me nearly half an hour, talking much about drill and discipline and more about the South. He hates the Rebels bitterly, not so much because they are rebellious as because they are slaveholders, for he is a fervid abolitionist. He would not hearken with patience to the faint praise which I accorded them for their audacity and courage. His face flushed, and he replied in an angry snarl, "What have they done? They brag enormously and perform next to nothing. Their deeds fall so far below their words that they are nothing less than ridiculous."

On the drill ground the general is instructive and amusing. He gives his orders in a high-keyed, penetrating, tranquil drawl which makes the men titter, partly because the tone is funny in itself, and partly because the commands follow each other so continuously. At the close of each movement the colonel shouts, "Order arms!—in place, rest!"

The soldiers think they are going to have a moment's peace; but scarcely have the muskets struck earth when they come up again. The general squalls, "Ten—shun!—Shoulder arrums! —Right—shoulder—shift arrums! On first de—vees—yun of first be—tal—yun, left in front, deploy masses! Queeck ma— arch!"

If things go wrong, especially if an officer blunders, the general tumbles all to pieces with distress. His body jerks forward; his elbows flap up and down like wings; he seems to trot several feet ahead of his horse; he arrives at the scene of confusion with a face of anguish. Sometimes he instructs; sometimes he scoffs; sometimes he swears.

"Why don't you dress, men!" he yells. "Come up! come up into line, I say! There! did it hurt ye? What the hell are you abeout? Why can't you dress at once?"

To one of our officers he said, "Cap—tain, I've been takin' notice of ye all this afternoon." (The captain straightens up and looks extremely flattered.) "Yes, I've noticed ye," the general proceeds. "You've been attendin', Captain, to everything but your business. You are there to dress that comp—ny, and instead of doing it you are staring all over the island. Let everything else alone and 'tend to your comp—ny."

The captain subsides into his boots, and the general recommences on the brigade. "Ten—shun!—Shoul—der arrums!—Countermarch, by file right and file left.—Queeck ma—arch!'"

It is a fine sight to see the brigade in his hands; the five great regiments moving together like an enormous machine; folding into column, forming square, recovering column, deploying into line; everything going at once in a sublimely smooth, sure, massive fashion. The general is much respected here for his knowledge of martial matters, and for his simplicity, earnestness and uprightness of character. The soldiers laugh over his oddities and like him the more for them.

Re-enforcements arrive fast, and we number about fifteen thousand men, mostly infantry. But there is no telling when we shall move: probably not till the fleet is ready to smash the forts: perhaps not till they have been smashed. The land forces, we suspect, will have no great share in the fighting.

Ship Island, April 13, 1862.

THE colonel has just given us news with regard to our future movements. We are to pack again, fill cartridge boxes and havresacks, draw extra shoes and stockings for the men, and in short get ready to start for New Orleans. We volunteers, he thought, might have to do some digging, but probably no battling. The forts, he added, were venerable brick affairs with some earthwork additions. They would surely be ruined by Porter's mortars, and then the city would surrender to the first gunboat. But if the fleet failed to take them, we should quietly return to Ship Island, the country of the lower Mississippi being impassable to land forces. We should move, he supposed, on Tuesday, that is day after tomorrow.

If I am not greatly mistaken the colonel was coaxing us not

to be scared. Well, we must put up with such imputations until we have fought, and have done it creditably.

I am regimental officer of the day. My duties consist largely in wearing a sash diagonally and in keeping quiet. Also I am solemnly bound to go twice a day to the guard tent. At sight of my sublime approach the lieutenant or sergeant of the guard roars, "Officer of the day!—Turn out the guard!"

Immediately the guard bustles forth, seizes the guns from the stocks in front of the tent, and comes to a shoulder. When I am within a few feet the sergeant commands, "Present arms!"

I raise the forefinger of my right hand to my cap and then drop it in an impressive manner which it would terrify you to see.

Again the sergeant shouts, "Shoulder arms! Order arms! Stack arms! Without doubling, right face! Break ranks, march!"

The soldiers struggle back into the tent, and I give an order about something, if I can think of one. This ceremony must be performed twice a day, or the nation would go to the bowwows.

CHAPTER II

THE high command of the North early recognized the strategic importance of New Orleans. By seizing the river port, Union forces could use it as a base for future operations in Mississippi and Louisiana and, in addition, could prevent the supplies of Texas and the West from reaching the eastern states of the Confederacy. In accordance with this strategy, David G. Farragut was sent with a naval force to undertake the capture of the city. In April, 1862, having reduced the forts guarding the mouth of the Mississippi, he steamed up the river and forced New Orleans to surrender.

The capture of New Orleans was only one of a series of Union successes in the winter and spring of 1862. Northern armies had achieved major triumphs in taking Forts Henry and Donelson. The crumbling of the Confederate line of defense in the West had forced Southern troops to evacuate Nashville. Later Union forces pushed still more deeply into Tennessee and finally gained, at Shiloh, a costly victory over Beauregard's army. In other theaters of operations, McClellan was approaching Richmond; McDowell was guarding Washington; and Frémont and Banks had temporary control of the Shenandoah Valley. The North, therefore, was encouraged to believe that the war would be over before the end of the year.

During the summer of 1862 reports were current that Brigadier General John W. Phelps would be ordered North because he differed with his immediate superior, General Butler, on the slavery question; and that Colonel Deming, commanding officer of the Twelfth Connecticut, would be chosen to fill his place. There would then be a vacancy in De Forest's regiment. In an attempt to secure the colonelcy for her husband, Mrs. De Forest sent several letters from influential friends to William A. Buckingham, governor of Connecticut. General Phelps, however, was succeeded by Brigadier General Thomas W. Sherman and not by Colonel Deming. De Forest meanwhile had been sent to Camp Parapet, some miles up the river from New Orleans, and he remained there with his company during the disagreeable months of July and August and suffered from the ill effects of the humid weather. He later admitted in "Military Life," an early draft of *A Volunteer's Adventures,* that he "had been more seriously ill—with a touch of country fever—than is confessed in this letter [July 31, 1862]." (Ed.)

CAMP LIFE IN LOUISIANA

New Orleans, April 30, 1862.*

WELL, the forts have been captured, and New Orleans also. But the Louisianians cannot lay it to us innocent land forces. We feel very poor in spirit when we remember that we have as yet done no fighting, while the sailors have done so much and done it so splendidly. We are very respectful to the naval officers, when we chance to meet them, because they have been under fire, and we not.

And yet we expected to fight and were willing to fight. Before we left Ship Island fugitives and prisoners arrived from the mainland who said that New Orleans was covered by one hundred thousand men. We did not believe that, but we thought there might be twenty thousand. My supposition was that we might storm the forts, and afterwards skirmish our way to New Orleans by land, scouring forests, turning fieldworks, and ending off with a street fight. Some cowards, among them one officer, took fright, shammed sickness and obtained their discharges. But the great majority soon got used to the idea of battle, and awaited it day after day with singular indifference and incuriosity. I suspect that it is thus with most fairly trained soldiers until peril is actually present.

I shall probably astonish you when I say that we did not find the bombardment magnificent nor even continuously interesting. It was too distant from us to startle the senses and too protracted to hold our attention. We could hear a continuous uproar of distant artillery; we could see clouds of smoke curling up from behind the leafage which fringed the river;

* The letter which described the bombardment having been lost, I introduce here a later one (to another correspondent) which alludes to it.

and on the first day, when we were near the scene of action, we could see vessels lying along the low banks. Also, if we climbed up to the crosstrees, the forts were visible beyond a forested bend. Then we were ordered to the head of the passes, seven miles below; and there we lay for a week, gradually losing our interest in the combat.

We smoked and read novels; we yawned often and slept a great deal; in short, we behaved as people do in the tediums of peace; anything to kill time. Once or twice a day we got a rumor from above that the bombing was doing wonders, or that it was doing nothing at all. Now and then a blazing fireship floated by us, lighting red the broad, swift, sublime river, and glowing away southward.

At last came a story that Farragut had run the forts, and we had one day of excitement, expectation, anxiety. During the late evening a submerged hulk, which some one guessed was the Rebel ram *Manassas,* drove against our iron cable, tearing it down through the hawsehole and its timber casement, and making the *Farley* plunge and quiver. If the wreck had not been fended off by the cable, if it had struck one of its angles into our wooden bows, we should have gone to the bottom through one hundred and fifty feet of water. This was our one noteworthy alarum and danger during the whole siege.

Some days later, the forts having been abandoned, we were towed up to them, and I got a chance to go ashore. The long, green, moundlike earthworks of Fort St. Philip were quite un-injured. The mouldy old brickwork of Fort Jackson showed no damage beside some broad scales knocked off the facings, and a few enormous holes bored in the summits of the ramparts by the eleven-inch bombs. The barracks, however, were a curiosity of ruin, shattered into miscellaneous tatters and splinters. If the garrison had remained in them it would have been made mince-meat of; but it had the casemates for shelter, and it suffered but moderate damage.

General Phelps, whom I met in Fort Jackson, seemed as much interested in the spectacle as I, and told me that he had never before seen anything of the sort.

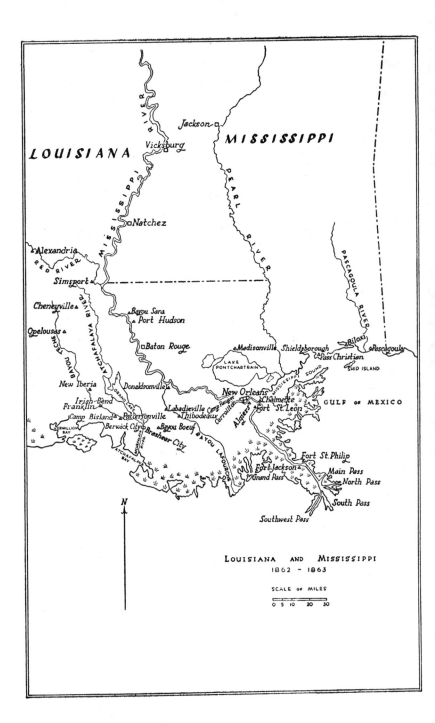

LOUISIANA AND MISSISSIPPI
1862 - 1863

SCALE OF MILES
0 5 10   20   30

New Orleans, May 2, 1862.

WE had a charming sail from Fort Jackson to New Orleans through scenery which surpasses the Connecticut River valley and is not inferior to that of the Hudson, though quite different in character.

It is a continuous flat, generally below the level of the Mississippi, but richly beautiful and full of variety. The windings of the mighty river, the endless cypress forests in the background, the vast fields of cane and corn, the abundant magnolias and orange groves and bananas, the plantation houses showing white through dark-green foliage furnished an uninterrupted succession of lovely pictures. Of course the verdure was a fascinating novelty to men who came last from the white sands of Ship Island, and previously from the snows of New England.

Apparently this paradise had been nearly deserted by its inhabitants. Between Fort Jackson and Chalmette, a few miles below New Orleans, we saw hardly fifty white people on the banks, and the houses had the look of having been closed and abandoned. Even the Negroes were far from being as numerous as we had expected. None of the whites signalled to us, or took any other notice of us, or seemed to see us. One elderly man, driving northward with a rockaway full of women, kept along with us for a quarter of a mile or so, without once turning his white-bearded face toward us.

The blacks, as might be expected, were more communicative and more friendly. They gathered to stare at us, and when there were no whites near, they gave enthusiastic evidence of good will, dancing at us, waving hats or branches and shouting welcome. One old mauma, who spoke English and had perhaps once been "sold down de ribber," capered vigorously on the levee, screaming, "Bress de Lawd! I knows dat ar flag. I knew it would come. Praise de Lawd!"

Perhaps some of the planters had fled the region in fear of a slave insurrection; but, as we had learned at Fort Jackson, they had another reason for seeking a place of safety. The fleet had come up the river like an angel of destruction, hurling shells and broadsides into thickets which sheltered ambuscades, and knocking to pieces dwellings occupied by guerrillas. Seventeen miles below New Orleans it pitched into Fort Leon, and sent the garrison flying across the flats to the cypress forest. Then the town surrendered, and with it all the fortifications in the vicinity, while the Rebel troops scurried up the river.

Our tug dragged the *Farley* to dock during the evening of April 30th. The city was dark and quiet; not a soul came near us; we slept on board. During the following morning we were towed further up the levee to make a landing. Thousands of people gathered along the docks to stare in silence at the passing transports. The first troops ashore were the Fourth Wisconsin, Thirty-first Massachusetts, Ninth Connecticut and part of a battery. Then came the turn of the Twelfth Connecticut. Company by company we formed on the quarter-deck, each man carrying his arms, knapsack, havresack and canteen, the whole kit weighing near fifty pounds.

Down the ladder we crept and fell into line fronting the city, surrounded by male and female roughs and ragged urchins, who hooted and sneered and swore. Some of them stared angrily at Weber, my veteran first sergeant, as his monotonous orders cracked out, "Lhoad at will, lhoad! Order aharms! Carry aharms! Pr's'nt aharms!"

Thereupon, as the presentation is to me, I shout, "Shoulder arms! Order arms! In place, rest!"

The regimental line forms slowly, for the transport towers high above the low wharf, and it is uneasy work descending the long, slippery ladder. The roughs, the low women and the ragged urchins continue to hoot, jeer, swear and call us evil names. The soldiers (who had learned discipline at Ship Island) stand like statues, without replying by word or look. The mob becomes more excited when it learns that we have really loaded with ball. A red-nosed man, addressing me personally, declares with many oaths, "We don't want you here, damn it! You haven't come among friends, not by a damn sight. We don't want you, d'ye understand? We wouldn't give you a cup of water."

I don't want a cup of water, and I make no reply. But a ragged

Irishman emerges from the crowd with a shillelah four feet long, which he holds by the middle and whirls around his wolfish head, meanwhile damning and God-damning and God-damning-to-hell the red-nosed man, who hastily departs around the nearest corner. Then the Irishman salutes me in military style, takes off his shabby hat to the colors and makes them a low bow.

Other and better dressed people follow his example. One man gives Lieutenant Potter an *Evening Delta*, begging him in a whisper not to mention it. Another mutters to Captain Dickinson that, if we want recruits, there will be plenty. A handsome, grey-whiskered gentleman and a very handsome young lady, evidently his daughter, study our faces sympathetically and then salute the flag with an expression of solemn joy.

Obviously there are two parties in the city, and for aught we yet know, ours may be the strongest. In any case there is no danger of a popular insurrection. Our fleet, with guns run out and howitzers in the tops, commands various points along the levee and could suppress New Orleans without help from the army.

Carrollton, Louisiana, May 14, 1862.

My last gave you an account of our arrival in the Crescent City. We passed one night on the dock, sleeping in our ranks, musket and sabre within reach and sentries out.

· Next morning we marched a mile or more to Lafayette Square, a pretty little park well turfed and shaded, where we went into bivouac. Very few people, and those only of the baser sort, turned out to watch our passing. There was no welcome, but there was no hooting. The ragged boys and girls, who the day before hurrahed for Jeff Davis and sang Rebel songs, were absent or silent. The mayor has issued a proclamation calling on the citizens to be peaceable and civil. On the other hand, our colonel has been emphatic in commanding the soldiers to abstain from violence and verbal squabbling.

But once we were inside the iron fence of Lafayette Square, the crowd became numerous, bold and insolent. The civilest remark that I heard was from a little boy who stared in amazement at our huge knapsacks, and said, "I don't wonder the Yankees can't fight; they have such big loads to carry." There was an almost continual mutter of "Damn Yankees" from the row of ugly, dirty, vicious faces which surrounded our pen. Meantime the sentries marched up and down their beats, driving back every soldier who offered to respond to these insults. My own feeling was and is that the men were held too close. Our colonel, an amiable and gentlemanly man, is too fat and gouty and elderly to command troops. He is, I think, afraid of a street fight; hence the repressive nature of his orders.

We bivouacked for three nights in the square. Then we took the steam transport *Mississippi* and came to Carrollton, some few miles up the river. Here there is a large Rebel fortification, facing northward and stretching from the levee on the west to a cypress swamp on the east. It is an earthwork nearly twelve feet high and protected by a ditch fifteen feet broad. The twenty large iron guns which lately defended it are lying on the ground, their carriages having been burned by the rabble after the garrison left. At present our sole artillery consists of four brass pieces belonging to a Massachusetts battery.

We, the Twelfth Connecticut, are encamped next the levee, while the Ninth holds the flank near the swamp. It is reported that the rest of the brigade will soon be here, and we earnestly hope so, for the front is long and the guard duty heavy. Williams' brigade has gone up the river, though how far I cannot tell you. Shepley's, including the Thirteenth Connecticut, garrisons New Orleans. This is all that I know, and more than must be printed; when officers are not discreet, officers' wives must be.

The country about seems beautiful to wanderers from Ship Island. It is mere flat plain, but picturesque with groves and wonderfully fertile. The eastern vista is closed by an endless, sombre cypress forest; near at hand are plantations of cane, clumps of orange trees and thickets of bananas; here and there rise evergreen oaks and magnolias. But there is no fruit; the orange season is over; the figs and melons are to come.

Besides the few rich planters who live near us, the population consists of poor Germans, poorer French Creoles and ragged slaves. The Germans are the most industrious, and are not yet altogether poverty stricken. The Creoles, dressed in tatters and extremely dirty, are as miserable a race as the peasantry of southern Italy. Wealthy Creoles exist, I understand; but they have not yet come under my notice. By the way, when I speak of Creoles I do not mean half-breeds, but people of pure French descent born in Louisiana.

The poverty of the once flourishing city of New Orleans is astonishing. I have seen nothing like its desolation since I quitted the deserted streets of Venice, Ferrara and Pisa. Almost the only people visible are shabby roughs and ragged beggars. Many poor Irish and Germans hang about our regiments begging for the refuse of our rations. The town is fairly and squarely on the point of starvation. No one denies now that our blockade has been effective; it kept out everything, even to the yellow fever. General Butler has commenced distributions of food; and it is possible that industry will recover within a few weeks from the fright of the threatened bombardment; but it will be years before it quite recovers from all the effects of this stupid rebellion.

Unless work is soon found for these people, I do not see how famine can be averted. Flour ranges from twenty-three to thirty dollars a barrel; Irish potatoes, eight dollars a bushel; sweet potatoes, undiscoverable. Mess beef, which the quartermaster holds at thirteen dollars a barrel, sells in the city at thirty. The country people charge us ten cents a quart for milk and seventy-five cents a dozen for eggs. A common broom, worth a quarter of a dollar at the North, fetches here a quarter of an eagle; a tin teapot, worth sixteen cents in Connecticut, costs seventy-five cents in Louisiana. Apparently, if the South should be corked up and left to itself, it would very soon turn savage and go naked. Already it is verging on the barefooted stage; common soldiers' shoes sell for eight dollars; cavalry half-boots for twenty and thirty.

Of course these prices represent the depreciation of Confederate money as well as the scarcity of merchandise. Specie there was none before we arrived; nothing but shinplasters of fifty contemptible descriptions; a worse state of things than in bankrupt Austria. Louisiana small change consists of five-cent tickets for omnibuses, barrooms and shaving shops. Shortly after our landing my first sergeant bought some tobacco for the company and paid in gold and silver.* The shopkeeper, a German woman, caught up a quarter of a dollar, kissed the eagle on it and said, "That's the bird for me. Why didn't you men come long ago?"

Negroes have depreciated as much as any other Southern circulating medium. They straggle into camp daily, more than we know what to do with. I have one named Charley Weeks, a bright and well-mannered mulatto, evidently a pet household servant, and lately chattel to one General Thompson of the departed Rebel army. He has a trunk and two suits of broadcloth, besides his workaday clothes. I have established him in my cooking tent and promised him my sublime protection, which is more effective here now than it would have been three weeks ago.

His master would have a deuce of a time in reclaiming him from the brigade commander, who clutches with delight at every chance of humiliating slaveholders and Rebels. The other day he sent our Lieutenant Potter with a file of men to search a planter's house for arms. "Don't take any sauce," he said. "If they are impudent, arrest 'em. If they fight, shoot 'em."

Camp Parapet, May 23, 1862.†

OFFICERS who have visited New Orleans report that the citizens have dropped their surly air, and show a willingness to talk civilly if not cordially. For the present General Butler is rather popular with them than otherwise. If they ever feel disposed to grumble at him, they have only to remember the grim old abolitionist who commands our brigade, and their mouths are shut. General Phelps tells me that in his opinion New Orleans ought to be confiscated and brought to the hammer; also that we owe

* Our last previous payment had been in gold.
† Camp Parapet was the camp above Carrollton.

it to justice and humanity to proclaim the immediate abolition of slavery throughout the South.

The Twelfth has lately had a compliment from the grizzled martinet; he told the lieutenant colonel that our dress parade of day before yesterday was the finest he had ever seen. This from a veteran regular officer is great praise, and flatters us more than you can probably imagine. He is rarely so gracious; he says that we are as lacking in discipline as we are praiseworthy for drill; and alas! he is right.

Not that our men are mutinous or disorderly; on the contrary they are as obedient and quiet as sheep. But they don't touch their caps when they meet an officer; they don't salute promptly and stylishly when on guard; in short, they are deficient in soldierly etiquette. For such sins as these the brigadier comes down upon offenders in a style which scares them half out of their wits. Two days ago he fell afoul of a gawky lieutenant who was lately promoted from a sergeantcy. The lieutenant, dressed in trousers and a red shirt, and barefoot, was seated on the head of a barrel, eating an apple and gossiping with a sentry. The general, who was taking a stroll, halted in front of him and glared at him. The lieutenant, without rising, and still munching his apple, saluted.

"Who are *you?*" snarled the general.

The lieutenant gave his name, title, company and regiment.

"What business had you talking to a guard? What are you dressed in that style for? Don't you know any better?"

The lieutenant dismounted from his barrel and tremulously entered upon a defence of his costume and behavior.

The general interrupted him: "What's your business at home?"

"General, I was a carpenter."

"I should think as much! You'd better go home and get to carpentering again. You may be a good carpenter, but you're a damn poor officer. Be off now, and don't let me catch you talking to a guard again, except when it's your duty to give him instructions."

And with an expression of disgusted despair the general stalked away to blow up a sentry whom he found sitting down on post. "I wouldn't have been so mad with that fool lieutenant," he afterwards explained, "if he hadn't saluted me with his apple core."

Camp Parapet, June 3, 1862.

A GREAT misfortune has befallen me. I had a perfect first sergeant, and I have him no longer. About a fortnight ago I noticed that Weber, the model and mentor and regulator of my company, was taking to drink. One evening he came to my tent, saluted more obsequiously than usual, drew himself up with hands down and heels together, and in a high, tremulous voice discoursed as follows:

"Captain, I am virst sergeant of I Gumpanee. But, Captain, if the virst sergeant of I Gumpanee cannot be respected, den, Captain, I will resign with your bermission, and be a brivate in your gumpanee, Captain."

His grievance was that the cook had refused to give him his supper. But the testimony of various men showed that Weber had got drunk, had eaten his supper, had fallen asleep, and now wanted supper over again, apparently forgetful that he had had it. I sent him to his quarters, and next day admonished him. He promised reformation, and erelong obtained a pass to the city. On the way down he confided to a comrade that he "meant to have one good drunk and done with it." Later he was seen staggering about town, still in his uniform, but minus sword and sash. He has been gone a week now, and may have been murdered, or deserted to the enemy. If he returns, he must of course lose his position and become "a brivate in I Gumpanee."

If we had lost two or three generals, I should not feel so badly. He had brought me great glory; he had made "I Gumpanee" one of the best companies in the regiment; he had drawn praise for its elegantly packed knapsacks from General Phelps himself; every one of my brother captains envied me Sergeant Weber. Naturally and unavoidably he knew his glorious and laborious duty. He had been a regular in his native land of Hanover, and a regular in our army during the Seminole War.

I had expected that, if we ever met the Rebels, Weber would show me how to whip them, or at least how to get away from them.

If he had had sense enough to keep sober, he would soon have been a lieutenant with a good chance of further promotion. Of course a mere unmilitary woman like yourself cannot understand how valuable a trained first sergeant is to a company. Let me meekly assure you that he is better worth his salt than a greenhorn of a captain, although he wears plainer clothes and gets smaller pay.

In this connection I mention with pleasure a rumor that a paymaster will soon visit us. I shall be mortal glad to see him, for we have not been paid in nearly four months, and I have not a dollar in my pocket, not even a dime wherewith to buy a cigar.

Camp Parapet, June 15, 1862.

SINCE we have been here regiment after regiment has arrived from below and sailed up the river. Where they go the general does not bother himself to inform us; but we learn that there are troops at Baton Rouge and that others are said to have started for Vicksburg. It would seem that we of the Twelfth Connecticut, one of the healthiest, largest and best drilled regiments in the division, are destined to stay in peaceful possession of this earthwork, guarding New Orleans against a foe which cannot get near it. I begin to despair of finding a chance to fight unless there is another war after this one.

Singular as it may seem, this is a disappointment. Nearly every officer and the majority of the men would prefer to go up the river, taking the certainty of hard fare and hard times generally, with a fair likelihood of being killed or wounded, rather than stay here drilling and guard mounting in peace. When the long roll beat for the Seventh Vermont to start foeward, they hurrahed for ten minutes while we sulked over their luck and their exultation, not even giving them a cheer as they marched by us to embark. Meanwhile we sniff at the Thirteenth Connec-

ticut as a dandy corps which has never lived out of doors and is
only fit to stand guard around General Butler. We believe that
we could whip it in a fight, and we know that we could beat it in
battalion drill. And so on, through a series of grumblings and
snarlings, all illustrative of human nature.

The colonel of the Thirteenth met me lately in the city and
asked me to dinner. You would have considered it a decent meal,
and I marvelled at it as a luxurious one. Just think of claret;
also of sparkling Isabella, served in coffee cups for lack of
glasses; also wine sauce on the pudding, and *café noir* as a final.
The Thirteenth is a terrible regiment in the way of spoiling the
Egyptians and letting the oppressed go free. General Butler pets
it because of its fine clothes, its bright outfit of Springfield and
Sharpe rifles, and its dandy officers whose uniforms are as yet
unsoiled by field service.

But it worries him much (or so he makes believe) by its hostility to the patriarchal institution. It has forty Negro laun-
dresses, all belonging to men whom he is trying to pacificate.
The owners go to the general and beg for their ebony chattels.
The general sends for the captains of the Thirteenth and re-
quests them to let the people go. The captains argue that the
girls want to wash and get paid for it, and that the regulations
allow forty washerwomen to a battalion of ten companies. There
the matter invariably ends, as the story is told to me. Meantime
the quartermaster has seventy Negro men, regularly enrolled
and rationed, who clean and repair the customhouse, which is
the regimental barrack.

The Twelfth also has contrabands, fully sixty in number,
some of them nurses and laborers at the hospital, others servants
to officers, the remainder company cooks. Two of them carry
my written protections in their pockets. Who said John Brown
was dead? There are six hundred thousand John Browns now
in the South. The old enthusiast is terribly avenged. The rotten
post of slavery is getting a rousing shake.

The officer of the guard tells me that outside of his picket
there is a camp, or rather bivouac, of one hundred and fifty
Negroes, lately arrived from the other bank of the river. Their
owner (a thousand-hogshead man) got into a rage about something, perhaps their insubordination, ordered them off the plan-

tation and bade them go to the devil. Also there is a great floating population of blacks; men and women and pickaninnies
streaming daily into the camp and sticking there until they are
expelled as "unemployed persons"; a burden to the soul of our
brigade provost marshal and a subject of intense commiseration
to our general.

We have at last established an officers' mess. We dine in a
small house inside camp limits, waited on at table by our own
servants, and cooked for by artists borrowed from neighboring
plantations. Our crockery we were also obliged to borrow from
the deserted dwelling of a gentleman who is absent as captain in
the Rebel army. As the paymaster has not yet arrived we cannot
indulge in luxuries; but our steward draws army stores on our
account from the regimental commissary and barters them for
fish, chickens, eggs and vegetables; these delicacies being mostly
brought in by nocturnal darkies who perhaps stole them from
"Masr." The living is not exceptionally fine, but is far above
our former barbarous style.

Did you get my letter mentioning the death of my first lieutenant, Cornwall? * Our assistant surgeon, a veteran of the
Seminole War, tells me that he never saw but one other case of
so virulent a fever.†

Camp Parapet, June 29, 1862.

We have been paid at last, and so has the Eighth New Hampshire, its first money in eight months. According to the regulations troops must be paid once in eight weeks, but the regulations cannot be enforced against the government.

There was a little fight up the river a few days ago. A party of
guerrillas ambuscaded a company of Vermonters, killed or

---

* Second Lieutenant Stephen Ball was promoted to fill the vacancy. (Ed.)

† The surgeon died not long after. The swamp fever made fearful ravages among
the troops, though I rarely mentioned it in letters home. In one regiment at Camp
Parapet seven coffins were issued in one day. When the Twelfth finally took the field
to fight, it had fallen from over one thousand men to about six hundred present for
duty.

wounded thirteen men, and scampered off. This is the only
skirmish which has occurred within forty miles of here since
New Orleans surrendered. I had no idea until lately what a
Quakerly business war could be. You need not fear but what
the Twelfth will have a peaceful and inglorious campaign.
Beauregard would be an idiot to venture into this narrow belt
between the river and the swamps to attack our strong line of
fieldworks under a flanking fire from gunboats and frigates.
This is the only country I ever saw except Holland where the
water commands the land. A ship in the river looks to us in
camp as if it were on a hill.

We continue to drill every day in the broiling sun. Both the
general and our veteran assistant surgeon say that if we don't
exercise and perspire abundantly we shall get poisoned with
malaria and die. Their story seems probable, for the Eighth
New Hampshire and Fifteenth Maine, which shirk drill much
more than our lieutenant colonel allows us to, are both quite
sickly compared with us. The general, who has an old soldier's
love of smartness and liveliness, is very bitter against these unhappy regiments. He scolds the Fifteenth incessantly on brigade
drill and hardly ever speaks of it without some funny sneer.

"Oh, they are a forgetful regiment," he drawls. "They mean
to drill. But they forget it. It's dreadful when a whole regiment
has a defective memory."

Meantime the colonel of the Fifteenth, who is a rough, funny
old humorist, retaliates by speaking of the general as "Anti-
christ."

The other day, while I was at brigade headquarters to obtain
instructions concerning a court-martial record, a soldier of the
Eighth presented himself at the door of the tent, took off his hat
and asked for a pass to the city. The general glared at him, at
his slovenly uniform, at his loutish position.

"Put on your hat!" he yelled; for you must know that a soldier salutes an officer with his right hand; his hat stays on his
head. "Stand in the position of a soldier," was the next order.

The man knew enough to straighten up, bring his heels together, turn his toes out and drop his hands by his side.

"There! that's *something* like it," continued the general. "But
you are a pretty soldier! Look at your dirty clothes. Look at

your buttons; they haven't been rubbed since you got 'em. Look at your hat, all smashed and tattered, treated like a mop. You are a disgrace to your regiment; and a damn pretty regiment it is! Now go and clean yourself, and then come and let me see you." All this with an air of intense disgust and entire desperation, as if the spectacle of an unclean soldier were more than humanity could bear.

Meanwhile nobody could be more patient with ignorance which desires to be knowledge. He will instruct an officer by the half hour in the mysteries of army accounts, and invite him to call again if he needs further advice. As I mentioned above, I have been put on court-martial duty, and indeed am president of the court. Immediately on the appointment I went to the general and said, "Are you not afraid that an officer who knows nothing of this business will make sad blunders?"

"Yes, I *am,*" he replied. "I am awfully afraid of it. But I suppose the head of your regiment has looked about him and concluded that you would make the fewest blunders of anybody."

So for three days past I have been engaged in condemning poor devils to forfeiture of pay, to ball and chain, etc. As the recorder is as inexperienced as myself and much more timid, and as the third member is more ignorant than both of us together, I am pretty much everything in the court but the prisoner. I can't avoid condemning and punishing, for everybody is guilty, and nearly everybody pleads guilty. Such being the case, I must chastise according to the articles of war, or I may catch it myself.

I don't know when we shall finish our legal work. We dispose of five cases a day and get ten new ones next morning. Since payday there has been a bacchanalia of whiskey drinking. One-fifth part of the regiment keeps drunk all the time. I wish I could get rid of some thirty sots, shirks, rowdies and invalids, and replace them with as many good soldiers. Meanwhile the general takes things calmly; he says the men must have whiskey or die of country fever; even quinine won't save them without whiskey.

Among the victims of my court-martial was my once glorious Sergeant Weber. Ten days ago he was brought to camp a prisoner, stained with the mud of all the gutters of New Orleans, a pallid, shaking sufferer from his "one good drunk," just on the edge of delirium tremens. Naturally he has lost his position, and is now a private soldier under sentence of ball and chain with forfeiture of pay, unless the brigade commander should be moved to clemency.

Camp Parapet, July 13, 1862.

I HAVE closed my court and can return to my drilling, which is mere sport in comparison. We tried fifty men, found forty-five of them guilty, gave two dozen ball and chain, and docked the pay of everybody. It is worth noting that every solitary case of misbehavior originated in whiskey. Not a single man had insulted his officer, or refused to obey orders, or absented himself without leave, but he first got drunk. It seems clear that an army of teetotalers would be one-fourth more reliable and effective than an army containing the usual proportion of hard drinkers.*

From Richmond we are getting horrible news, which we naturally refuse to credit. According to the Mobile papers McClellan has been badly beaten and is now in great jeopardy. The secessionists here are exultant. In New Orleans they swarm around the newspaper offices, congratulating each other with insolent laughter, and glaring at our officers with an air which says, "Why don't you sink into the ground with fear and shame?"

A bad-looking set they are to my patriotic eyes. The whole remaining male population of the city seems to me to consist of roughs and gamblers. Scarcely a comfortably dressed man among them but has the air and expression of a "sporting character." The women meanwhile are getting themselves into trouble by wearing secession flags in the street.

General Butler does not trifle with the situation. He has issued an order that no group of more than three persons shall be

* The men became much more sober after we took the field, partly of course because whiskey was harder to get.

permitted in the streets.* The regiments are all supplied with ball cartridge, and held in constant readiness for action. But there will be no insurrection, for New Orleans is too helpless to do more than glare and mutter, and many of the Irish and Germans are our friends. Three regiments of white troops are to be recruited here, and no one expects any difficulty in finding the men. Probably half the fellows who defended the forts against us are already wearing our uniform; some of them, I know, are in the Twelfth Connecticut, and many more in the Ninth.

As to the Negroes, they are all on our side, although thus far they are mainly a burden. In spite of indirect discouragements they are continually quitting the plantations and swarming to us for protection and support. Lieutenant Potter, our brigade provost marshal, has on his roll seven hundred of them, all living in or about the camp and drawing rations. Potter wishes they were on the coast of Guinea, and sulkily asks General Phelps what he shall do with them.

"*I* don't know," squalls the brigadier, as much bothered by the "inevitable nigger" as if he were not an abolitionist. If he had his own way, doubtless, he would raise black battalions; indeed, he has already asked one of our captains if he would be willing to command a colored regiment; whereupon the captain replied that he wouldn't.

We have had a night alarm lately. Some booby on picket fired his gun by accident, obliging three regiments to seize arms in the darkness and man the ramparts. We knew all the while that there was not the slightest real need of quitting our beds; for there is not an organized enemy within fifty miles, and apparently there never will be. Our life is roundly dull and would be insupportable but for drilling, making returns and other such small chores which fritter time into digestible fragments. We wish we were on the Potomac or the Rappahannock. Why does not the president send out some of the new regiments to guard subjugated Louisiana, and so set us drilled fellows free for active service? One does not want to go into the army merely to return home without seeing a battle. Besides, there are no promotions; nobody is killed and nobody gets scared into re-

* This was camp hearsay, perhaps erroneous.

signing; there is not a chance for a captain to become a field officer.

We hear that General Phelps will be ordered north in consequence of differences with General Butler concerning the "peculiar institution." I hope that this is not true, for we could not easily find a better commander. He is a thoroughly educated soldier, patient with those who try to learn their duties, severe to the lazy and negligent. He knows French and German, I hear, and is generally a well-read man.

Gunboat *Greycloud*, July 31, 1862.

I HAVE stumbled upon a chance of service in the way of a scouting expedition commissioned to trouble the coasts of Rebeldom hereabouts.

It consists of the armed ferryboat *Greycloud* carrying five companies of our regiment and five cannon. When it started I was on the sick list with a chance of having country fever, and so was sent for a week's absence to the Lake House on Lake Pontchartrain, where there is a little air which answers feebly for a seabreeze. I was picking up strength a bit when the *Greycloud* dropped in there. The officers had fairyland stories to tell. They were exploring a narrow, shadowy stream near Madisonville when they were suddenly fired on by militia hidden in the thickets on the banks. The infantry promptly returned a musket volley, and the artillery banged away with shell and grape. The enemy fled, and the uproar ended in five minutes, two of our men being slightly buckshotted, and two others dying later of sunstroke.

The officers promised me more fun of the sort, and the temptation was irresistible. So here I am, a volunteer raider, a captain without a company, and indeed without arms. But hitherto I have needed none, for not another squabble have we been able to kick up, though we have prowled the whole lake in search of an enemy. It is quite natural that mere guerrillas should not want a misunderstanding with us. We have three hundred infantry, two long thirty-two pounders belonging to the boat, a twenty-pound Parrott and six-pound sawyer from Holcomb's battery, and a brass howitzer from Duncan's.

Quitting the lake, we ran through Mississippi Sound to Pass Christian, where we were told a fight was waiting for us. Rebels were encamped there who had planned to capture the next boat which should arrive, by lodging an ambuscade in a large storehouse on the wharf and making therefrom a rush to board. Consequently we devised a stratagem to take the alleged camp between two fires. At daybreak the infantry and fieldpieces landed two miles from the village to reach it in rear while the boat should steam boldly up to it in front.

We had a lovely sail down a winding coast fringed with forests. At last we espied a charming village, embowered among shade trees and flowering thickets, stretching upwards of half a mile along the shore. All was quiet; no musketry was to be heard; but we could see a dark mass of troops in the main street. Alas! they were our own fellows who had got there before us, as safe from Rebels as though they had marched through the garden of Eden.

I strolled for some time about the place. The only discoverable inhabitants were half a dozen men and some scores of women and children. The women seemed rejoiced to see us, blessed God we had come, and begged us to hold the place. A few guerrillas, they said, had been there the day before, and five hundred the week previous. There was really a camp, they declared, but quite a distance from the seashore. The regular inhabitants of the village, especially the wealthier families, had long since fled to the interior.

These poor people were on the verge of starvation; flour thirty-five dollars a barrel, and no money wherewith to buy it; everything else in proportion. They looked famished and every way miserable; the women in shabby calico skirts clinging around their lean frames; the men without coats, and all as dirty as they were ragged. The large hotel was closed, and nearly all the private houses. We could find no food for sale but a few watermelons, a few stale gingercakes and a dozen loaves of bread. As we bought these, I can't imagine what the people ate next day, unless it might be each other. If the war does not end soon, the South will starve to death.

These paupers expressed no hostility; on the contrary they urged us to remain and protect them; they feared that the guerrillas would hang them for speaking to us. When we re-embarked, after two hours in this deserted village, a few ill-looking men crept out of the houses to watch our departure, but avoided intercourse. To get at the camp which had been reported to us, we steamed some distance up a narrow river, but ran into a jungle of thicket and vines, and had to back out.

During the afternoon we reached Shieldsborough, another charming village on the shore of the Sound. It is a bathing resort, frequented in peaceful summers by four or five thousand people, but reduced now to about thirty-five families in a state of semi-starvation. We had a long palaver with an Englishman of bitter secessionist opinions. He told us that many of the residents, persons who had once been well off, habitually ate but one meal a day and were not sure of that. He and his Southern friends thought it very inhuman of Butler to cut off their trade with New Orleans.

We explained that this had been done because they harbored and aided the guerrillas. For instance, a fortnight ago this very boat had touched at Pascagoula, making no preparations for fight because the front of the wharf was lined with women and children; but presently these noncombatants opened to right and left, and a swarm of men who had been concealed behind them fired a volley which hit fourteen of the crew. Then they fled, and nothing could be done in reprisal, because the captain was too humane to shell unarmed people and destroy the village. To this story our listeners made no reply except by a quiet smile of satisfaction.

The Englishman boasted that McClellan had got a severe whipping; declared that the Southerners, starving as they were, would fight to the last breath; and exulted in the belief that foreign intervention was highly probable. The natives assented by their looks, but kept a discreet silence. In regard to the *Greycloud's* skirmish at Madisonville they asserted that our artillery had killed a woman and child, as well as four guerrillas.

I made an effort to buy matches, but was told that they used
flint and steel. I enquired for tobacco, but that was as scarce as
matches. Nearly all these people looked hungry, gaunt, ghastly
and yellow. I noted one girl with very handsome features, but
so pale and thin that she was pitiful to see. Some of the women
begged us to take them to New Orleans, but of course that could
not be done.

From Shieldsborough we returned to the Lake and touched
anew at Madisonville, but without finding any guerrillas to
skirmish with. I am now at Camp Parapet, much the better for
my trip.

Camp Parapet, August 6, 1862.

IT is useless to urge me to get a furlough; I am quite sure that
General Butler would not grant it; indeed, I am sure that he
ought not. He has been disgusted and angered by the number of
applications from officers for leaves of absence. They have set a
bad example to the soldiers, and he will allow no more of them
to go home, at least for the present. Even the enlisted men, even
confirmed invalids and worthless shirks now find difficulty in
getting furloughs or discharges. I have sick fellows on hand
whom I would like to be rid of, because they are too broken ever
to do duty again, and will probably die if they stay here. But I
have little hope of inducing the general to let them go.

The truth is (although you must not publish it) that the division has run down terribly in numbers. There is a constant
drain on troops in the field, much heavier than a civilian would
suppose. Something like one fifth of the men who enlist are not
tough enough nor brave enough to be soldiers. A regiment
reaches its station a thousand strong; but in six months it can
only muster six or seven hundred men for marching and fighting
duty; the rest have vanished in various ways. Some have died
of hardship, or disease, or nostalgia; as many more have been
discharged for physical disability; others are absent sick, or
have got furloughs by shamming sickness; others are on special

duty as bakers, hospital nurses, wagoners, quartermasters' drudges, etc.; a few are working out sentences of court-martial. Thus your division of fifteen thousand men has dropped to ten thousand or perhaps eight thousand effectives. The companies have each lost one if not two of their original three officers. There you have our history.

Meantime the government is raising new organizations, instead of filling up the old ones; and to make matters as bad as possible it is putting its green regiments into the hands of green officers. To be effective, troops must have drill and discipline; and the only way to give them these qualities is to give them commanders who know their business; why shouldn't even a politician understand that?

Our whole system of raising an army is wrong; we ought to raise it by draft, by conscription. Then our governors, instead of appointing officers who can merely electioneer, could appoint such as have learned how to command. The South has resorted to conscription, and it will beat us if we don't follow suit. With a far inferior population it can levy soldiers faster than we can, and it can put them under experienced colonels and captains.

What is it but drafting which has enabled it of late to resume the offensive? Here is Breckinridge invading Louisiana; losing the battlefield, to be sure, but still awing us out of Baton Rouge; and only a little while ago we held the river up to Vicksburg. Where did Jefferson Davis get the materials for these new armies? The whole secret of their numbers, and of their energy and effectiveness too, is conscription.

But if I keep on you will know as much of war as I do, which would be very improper in a woman and might lead to more rebellion.

CHAPTER III

DURING the summer of 1862 McClellan failed to capture Richmond in the Peninsular Campaign; and Pope likewise, when he had been put in command of the Army of Virginia, proved no match for Lee at the second battle of Bull Run. Union troops in the Department of the Gulf, on the other hand, had suffered no such defeats but had won their initial objective. Consequently they had confidence in their military organization and did not share the pessimism which was current in the North.

The problem of Negro camp followers around the barracks of the Twelfth Connecticut became so perplexing that Major Frank H. Peck wrote to his commanding general for regulations to guide the officer of the day in dealing with these "unfortunate persons." Under the urgent need to bring order to the growing crowd, General Butler finally appealed on August 22, 1862, to the free Negroes of New Orleans to enlist as volunteers in the Union armies. From September to November, 1862, four regiments were formed of the troops thus recruited: the First, Second, and Third Regiments Louisiana Native Guards, and the First Regiment Louisiana Heavy Artillery. De Forest later gave serious consideration to the possibility of applying for a colonelcy in one of the Freedmen's regiments. (Ed.)

MORE CAMP LIFE IN LOUISIANA

Camp Parapet, August 13, 1862.

THIS is the rainy season here, but by no means a cool season. I cannot give you the temperature, for there is not a thermometer in the brigade; but in scorching and sweating a man's strength away it beats anything that I ever before experienced. Sitting in my tent, with the sides looped up all around, I am drenched with perspiration. I come in from inspection (which means standing half an hour in the sun) with coat and trousers almost dripping wet, and my soaked sash stained with the blue of my uniform. There is no letup, no relenting, to the heat. Morning after morning the same brazen sun inflames the air till we go about with mouths open like suffering dogs. Toward noon clouds appear, gusts of wind struggle to overset our tents, and sheets of rain turn the camp into a marsh, but bring no permanent coolness.

The night air is as heavy and dank as that of a swamp, and at daybreak the rotten odor of the earth is sickening. It is a land moreover of vermin, at least in this season. The evening resounds with mosquitoes; a tent hums with them like a beehive, audible rods away; as Lieutenant Potter says, they sing like canary birds. When I slip under my mosquito bar they prowl and yell around me with the ferocity of panthers.

Tiny millers and soft green insects get in my eyes, stick to my perspiring face, and perish by scores in the flame of my candle. Various kinds of brilliant bugs drop on my paper, where they are slain and devoured by gangs of large red ants. These ants rummage my whole habitation for rations, crawl inside my clothing and under my blanket at night, and try to eat me alive. I have seen many large "lightning bugs," such as the Cuban ladies sometimes wear in their hair. Also there are black grasshoppers two or three inches in length, with red and yellow trimmings to their jackets, the most dandified fellows of their species that I know of.

Amid these discomforts we remain in better condition than one could fairly expect. The brigade surgeon says that the Twelfth is the healthiest regiment in the division. The general praises us for our vitality, and sometimes for other points of behavior. Talking lately with Surgeon Brownell about the men who have been assigned to the heavy guns, he said, "Why, Doctor, it's wonderful how intelligently those fellows go at their work. It is too bad that such fine material should be exposed to this climate."

Then, fearing lest we should get conceited, he added, "But you have some great rascals, Doctor. I'm afraid the sweet potatoes your men eat don't always belong to them."

Just now a perfectly naked mulatto boy, perhaps three years

old, toddled past my tent, stopping a moment to kiss a black baby which was being nursed by its mammy, and then hastening after an elder brother who had him in charge. This pickaninny has been about the camp all day in a state of nature.

Today two hundred Negroes have been shipped down the river to work on the fortifications of Fort Jackson. General Phelps has read me with exultation a letter from General Neal Dow stating that he is teaching his contrabands heavy artillery service.

Camp Parapet, August 27, 1862.

THE garrison of Baton Rouge has all come down the river, and we now have ten regiments here with five batteries. Breckinridge will not dare to attack; twenty thousand men could not dislodge us. Complaints having reached us that the troops broke loose at Baton Rouge and plundered the dwellings, General Phelps appointed six officers from his own brigade to inspect the knapsacks of the new comers. But we found nothing queer, barring a couple of powder horns, half a dozen rusty pistols, a shaving glass and other such trifles, all of which might have been picked up on the battlefield.

Five hundred Negroes arrived with the Baton Rouge column; and they drift hither in gangs every day from the plantations. They dot the fields in front of the rampart, women and children squatting in the wet grass under pouring rain, all waiting for liberty to remain here. The earlier comers have already built themselves huts of cane or of rails, leaky and wretched shelters enough, far inferior to the cabins they left. Fifty or sixty good tents have been furnished to a large squad which General Phelps has commenced drilling. Rations are issued to all, and a roll of names is kept by our provost marshal, who is amusingly "sick of niggers."

What would happen to the creatures if we should leave? I begin to think that the government will be driven to enlist them as soldiers. They take to drilling kindly; they learn to keep rank and step in a very short time; and those who have been tried at the heavy guns work them as well as our fellows. At Baton Rouge the officers' waiters and other black camp followers picked up the rifles of the wounded and fought gallantly.

Everybody here is coming over to the notion of enlisting the darkeys. Even old Democrats, even the Hibernian rank and file of the Ninth Connecticut are talking in favor of it. Even General Butler, who has been quarreling over the matter with General Phelps, is about to raise two regiments of free colored people and add them to the state militia.

Camp Parapet, September 2, 1862.

LAST evening I thought that Breckinridge had come, and that the Twelfth was about to fight its first battle. About nine o'clock scattering musket shots broke out on the picket line, running along the front from the river to the cypress swamp. Then, before I could buckle on sword and revolver, there was a yell from the sergeants of "Fall in!" followed by the long roll of all the regiments roaring sullenly through the damp night.

The rain had poured nearly all day, and the camp was a slop of mud and puddles. My men splashed through the sludge and halted on the little company parade, jabbering, reeling and scuffling. I saw at once what was the matter: payday had worked its usual mischief: one third of them were as drunk as pipers. In my rage at their condition I forgot all about the enemy. I pushed and flung them into their places, and called them sots, and used other bad language.

"If I was the angel Gabriel," said my second lieutenant, "I should take my trumpet out of my mouth to swear."

The company had scarcely counted off when there came a yell from the piercing voice of the lieutenant colonel: "Battalion! load at will; load!"—When the rattle and thud of the ramrods ceased he added, "To the parapet!—double quick; mar—ch!"

Through the mud we trotted, jumping the ditches which pretend to drain the camp, and forming battalion-line along the base of our earthwork. Ten minutes of silence followed, and then came an order from the general to return to quarters, the alarm having been a false one, perhaps for practice. Now ensued a real fight among my bacchanals, which I quieted by sending one man to the guardhouse, pushing others into their tents, and ordering lights out.

To comprehend this drunkenness you must understand that many of my men are city toughs, in part Irish; also that they are desperate with malaria, with the monotony of their life, and with incessant discomforts; finally, that intoxication in itself is not a military offence and not punishable. If you could look into our tents you would not wonder that consolation is sought for in whiskey. The never-ceasing rain streams at will through numerous rents and holes in the mouldy, rotten canvas. Nearly every night half the men are wet through while asleep unless they wake up, stack their clothing in the darkness, and sit on it with their rubber blankets over their heads, something not easy to do when they are so crowded that they can hardly move.

It must be added in fairness that intoxication is not confined to the soldiers. The officers are nearly as miserable, and are tempted to seek the same consolation. Lately a lieutenant reeled into my tent, dropped heavily on a bed, stared at me for a minute as if to locate me, and said in a thick voice, "Capm, everybody's drunk today. Capm, the brigade's drunk."

One toper has lately got a stinging lesson. Charley Counsel, a huge, rawboned Irishman, is one of the regimental nuisances and spends half his time in the guardhouse. He has been in three different companies, captain after captain getting wearied of his rampagings and transferring him to whomsoever will take him. Yesterday morning, being in the guardhouse as usual, he swore he would break out of it, whereupon the officer of the day ordered the sentry to shoot him if he tried it. Counsel rushed at the sentry with a yell and wrested the bayonet off his rifle.

"Try that again, and I'll drop you," said the man.

Counsel made another plunge, and fell with a hole through his thigh an inch or so in diameter. Braley, who is Counsel's present captain, came up and gave the sentry five dollars. The lieutenant colonel followed shortly and asked, "Did you shoot that man? All right; I'll make a sergeant of you."

Counsel was borne off to the hospital, where he got up an outrageous rumpus, throwing a spittoon at his nurse with such force as to smash it against the wall, and yelling loud enough to be heard across the Mississippi.

Yet with all this disorderliness we get not a little praise. Our brigade chief declared lately that we marched better than any other regiment in his brigade; and he urges us to apply for transformation into heavy artillery because we are too highly gifted for infantry.

"Your men are the most intelligent men that I ever commanded," he says. "Never saw such good material in a regiment before. Fine young fellows! so quick and lively in drilling!— almost too quick."

This is an advance upon our status at Ship Island, where he told me that he had never had but three regiments which he would trust in fighting, the First Vermont for defending fortifications, and the Twenty-sixth Massachusetts and Ninth Connecticut for field engagements.

Camp Parapet, September 8, 1862.

LITTLE expeditions are now and then sent from here to feel for the enemy; but the Twelfth takes no part in them, perhaps because it is training in heavy gunnery.

A detachment of the Seventh Vermont was lately ambuscaded some miles up the river and badly cut up, losing forty-eight men out of sixty. Yesterday another detachment of the same regiment was reported as all killed or captured; so three regiments and a battery have been dispatched by gunboat to exact vengeance. This afternoon a native drops into camp and informs us that when he left home, twenty miles above us, a severe battle was going on if one could judge by the cannonading.

It is curious how indifferent we have become to incidents of this sort. If the aforesaid fight were transacting within sight of us, I believe the men would still play bluff and poker, and growl at their rations, and drink whatever whiskey could be got at.

Although our annihilation at the hands of Breckinridge is daily predicted by our secessionist neighbors, I have fifteen fresh court-martial cases in my company as a result of the last payday. Nobody believes in a fight, and nobody cares about it, and many wish for it. "By—! I wish they *would* come," is the habitual comment.

It is wonderful how profane an army is. Officers who are members of the church, officers who once would not even play a game of cards, have learned to rip out oaths when the drill goes badly, or when the discipline "gets out of kilter." You perhaps remember that Corporal Trim's comrades "swore terribly in Flanders." The habit results partly from ennui and vacuity of mind. "He knew not what to say, and so he swore," is Byron's explanation. Furthermore, we are all irritable through hardship, and passionate through habits of domination coupled with imperfect obedience.

New Orleans, September 17, 1862.

I WROTE you on the 12th * describing our farewell ovation to our fine old commander, General Phelps, who has been at last bullied out of the service.

Since then I have been detailed on a general court-martial which brings me daily to New Orleans and sometimes keeps me over night. Last night was the first that I have passed in the city since we marched out in early May. An officer of the Thirteenth invited me to dine and lodge with him, and the temptation of having a roof over my head was too novel to be resisted.

I found it very odd to be once more in a fine house furnished with elegant bedsteads, sofas, pier glasses and other such luxuries. Observe that it was my first night inside of walls in over six months. I could not sleep; the broad mattress and clean sheets were torments; the indoor air was an oppression. I tossed about till near morning, when I dressed in desperation, stole down to the parlor, and there caught a nap on a sofa.

* Letter lost.

The house belongs to one of the wealthy men of New Orleans, now serving as captain in the Confederate army. He left his family in it, but my entertainer made a requisition for it and got it. That is the way they do in these garrison regiments which are favored by General Butler. Even lieutenants secure quarters in fine dwellings, where they use the plate, drink the wine cellars dry, and in various ways spoil the Egyptians. Meanwhile we field regiments sleep in tents as hot as ovens and as leaky as sieves.

Colonel Deming returned, day before yesterday, from Washington, quite gloomy about affairs in that quarter and declaring that he is glad to get to a place of safety. General Butler says he thinks of offering President Lincoln an asylum in New Orleans and advising him to bring along the public archives and treasures.

The *Marion* has arrived; also news through Confederate channels; and through both we learn that Jackson is in Maryland. So the Rebels in their turn propose to try the risky experiment of dividing an army. Pope has been beaten; I am not surprised. We have reappointed McClellan; I am frightened. Of only one thing am I confident; that is the final triumph of the Union.

While I was writing the above the president of our court-martial appeared, and we were able to commence business. He is lieutenant colonel of a New York regiment, a pretty little fellow of not above two and twenty, with a boyish face and grave black eyes. The fact that he is a West Pointer explains his early advancement. He comes in blushing, with his handkerchief held to his mouth, like a bashful girl at her first party. But he has been the disciplinarian and drillmaster of his regiment, and he is familiar with the articles of war and the procedure of courts-martial. It would be a prodigious advantage to us if we could head all our volunteer regiments with West Pointers.

The decorum and ceremoniousness of our court observances are rather solemnizing. We are in full uniform, except that we may lay our swords and sashes on the table before us. The witnesses are accoutred in like fashion; the accused is in uniform but without arms. In reaching a sentence, each member writes out one and hands it to the judge advocate, who, beginning with the mildest, puts them successively to a vote, the first that is carried being of course the final one.

Owing in great measure, I think, to the influence of our West Point president, the punishments are terribly severe. One poor blockhead, who had merely been absent without leave for five days, was allotted three years at hard labor on fortifications with loss of all pay and allowances except enough to cover his washing bill. As for the man now before us, a brutal Irishman who killed a comrade in a fight, I don't see how he can escape shooting.

New Orleans, September 22, 1862.

As matters go on now this court-martial will occupy us for months. We commenced with sixty cases and get an average of four new ones a day, while we dispose of perhaps two.

But, aside from the cruel sentences, I find the job an agreeable one. It is a pleasant, breezy trip down the river, and a pretty ride back to Carrollton by the cars, and a fine walk thence along the levee to Camp Parapet. Moreover, I am glad to escape our monotonous drilling and to catch glimpses of even such a desolate city as New Orleans.

There are a few fine shop windows here and a few pretty ladies; fewer of the pretty ladies, by the way, than of the fine windows. Many of the women are still pertly or sullenly hostile in their behavior. Lately one of our officers (sadly in drink at the time) retorted scorn for scorn. The lieutenant climbs into an omnibus, and a lady immediately flounces out, grimacing and switching her skirts.

"Sit still, old girl," maunders the lieutenant. "You needn't rise on my account."

This, so far as my knowledge goes, is the sauciest assault yet made upon New Orleans femininity by man or officer. The howling of the London *Times* over Butler's famous woman-order has not been justified by facts.

You want to come on here, but you would be glad to get back, or at least you should be. Camp Parapet is no decent place of residence for a lady, and you might reach there just in time to see me leave for the field. Let me console you for your disappointment by showing you a woman far unhappier than yourself.

Yesterday's mail brought me a letter from the wife of one of my private soldiers. She had not heard from her husband for a month, and she wanted to know if he was in trouble or was dead. She had received nothing from him since he enlisted but one remittance of nine dollars. A mortgage on her house had been foreclosed; and as her husband is not a Connecticut man, the authorities of her township will not allow her the "family bounty"; hence she and her children are likely to be homeless as well as penniless.

I fear that she will get little aid from her husband. He is a mild, weak young fellow, easily led away by comrades, low-spirited under the slightest illness, given to cosseting himself with sutler's trash, and given also to seeking courage in whiskey. Thirteen dollars a month can easily be spent in these follies.

The letter is nicely written and correctly spelled; moreover, it is well phrased and loving and touching. It is full of her husband; full of adoration for the poor creature and of prayers for his unimportant safety; pious terrors lest he may have been drawn into evil ways; prayers to me that I will not conceal from her the possible worst; then declarations that the feeble lout is the best of husbands; it is no fault of his—no fault of Henry's —that his family suffers.

In short, here are four pages of pathos which make me want to call in Henry and kick him for not deserving them. Apparently a fairly educated and quite worthy girl has married a good-looking youth of inferior nature and breeding who has not the energy to toil effectively for her, nor the affection to endure privations for her sake. I shall give the letter to him with a few words of earnest, epauletted counsel. It may stop him from drinking himself into the gutter twice after every payday, and from sickening himself with bushels of abominable gingerbread and shameless pie.

New Orleans, September 29, 1862.

I SAW last evening something very curious and interesting to me. I saw a new race; a race which is seeking to win a respectable footing in human society; a race which holds such a footing in Europe though scorned by us. One of our lieutenants, a dandified, pleasant youngster, fell ill a few weeks since and was sent to a city hospital, not far from the barracks of one of Butler's newly raised colored regiments. When he got strong enough for duty he volunteered to act as adjutant of this corps and held the position for about a fortnight. There was not an officer in it who was not a whiter man than himself; hence he treated them like white men, and so won their exceeding good will. The consequence is that, since he returned to our camp, they invite him to dinners and suppers.

Yesterday he asked me to join him at an entertainment given by a wealthy business man named Dumas, whose brother is captain in the First Colored and will be major of the Second. The ladies were very pretty, he said, and had not a trace of the African in their faces. So down to the city I went with the lieutenant and our regimental adjutant. At Dumas' house we found six other officers, three of them from white regiments and three from colored. Our entertainer is a man of about thirty who looks like a West Indian; his brother has the complexion of an Italian and features which remind one of the first Napoleon. Both of them, although natives of New Orleans, have spent a great part of their lives in Paris, and speak good French, but nothing else. They did not differ in air and manners from the young Frenchmen whom I used to know abroad. One of the three officers present, of this mixed blood, was an extremely blond youth with curly yellow locks.

Madame Dumas, about twenty years old, with regular features, handsome dark eyes, wavy black hair and a pale but healthy color, looks like a Jewess of southern Europe. Her sister, a few years older, resembles a Jewess of the swarthy, heavy type. Then there were two girl-cousins of sixteen, lately from convent schools in Paris, two jolly little brunettes with slim figures and lively French manners. What a happy evening they passed with our dandy lieutenant and adjutant! It was giggle and jabber for two hours in their end of the room, all the funnier because the two boys spoke no French and only one of the girls knew a little English. Being the only linguist in the party, I had to do not a little interpreting. The supper was a collation of cakes, confectionery, creams, ices and champagne, followed by *café noir,* cognac and delicious cigars.

Then came the piano, with French songs and American patriotic songs, followed by dancing. How enchanted the girls were to waltz and polk with our two youngsters! It was really delightful to gaze once more upon coquetry and courting; it was pleasant also to speak to an intelligent woman without being repelled by an angry stare. Since my arrival here until last evening I had not uttered a word to one of your sex, barring my charcoal-tinted washerwoman and the cocoanut-brown damsel who waits at our mess-table.

New Orleans, October 1, 1862.

I HAVE been looking into the way of life of our garrison in this city. It seems outrageous that, while we of the field regiments have been stick-in-the-muds for months, badly fed and so vilely lodged that I would have been grateful for a stable to sleep in, these fellows should have elegant houses, cellars full of choice wines, encouragement to plunder, and generous promotions. I dined with one of the colonels and passed the night with his adjutant. Of course I was not indignantly surprised to find the field officer grandly lodged and abounding in foraged claret. But I really was disgusted at receiving an even more luxurious hospitality from a mere lieutenant.

The adjutant's house is small, but it is a treasure box. Bills found in a secretary prove that the furniture, all of Parisian make, cost fifteen thousand dollars. The bedsteads are lofty four-posters, elaborately carved and of solid mahogany. The washing set of my bedroom is a cream-colored ground glass, very pretty and curious if not expensive. One of the most valuable articles is a small bureau encrusted with patterns of gilt enamel set in tortoise shell.

Knicknacks lie about in profusion, such as Swiss boxes, delicate wood carvings, amber-mouthed Turkish pipes, volumes of engravings, dress swords, old Toledo blades and inlaid pistols. Embroidered handkerchiefs, worth from twenty to fifty dollars apiece, lie tumbled in an armoire. Trunks and sandalwood chests contain embroidered jackets, silk shirts and undershirts, fine linen underclothing and other articles of raiment by the dozen. A superb crimson scarf, such as is worn by officers, lies on a pile of soiled linen.

The adjutant told me the story of the vanished proprietor. He was a rich swell, of the old French colonial stock, who journeyed with his wife to Paris, and there fell in with an actress; the result being that the wife returned alone, while the husband and the *parisienne* followed in company. The wife got a separation in due time, and this pretty box was built for her successful rival. Now the man is a captain in the Rebel army, and the actress is petitioning our military governor for recovery of her wardrobe and other property.

I must not forget the smoking room and the wine cellar. The former is an isolated kiosk in the court, eight-sided and with a pointed roof of Morisco type, the inner walls and ceiling lined with a figured matting. Leather-covered lounges surround a large table strewn with such articles as smokers delight in, including an amber-mouthed German pipe, two amber-mouthed Turkish chibouks, a Damascene cocoanut-shell nargile, and a very rich Constantinopolitan nargile. Other toys of the sort, I understood, had been carried off.

The adjutant and the lieutenant who lodges with him are making themselves at home; for instance, I heard the latter say, "I think I shall send this thing to my wife." He held in his hand a large tortoise-shell fan which I judged must have cost fully one hundred dollars. I suspect that he had no idea of its value and had never heard of fans worth more than a dollar or two.

The cellar is well stocked with madeira and burgundy, some of the vintages being twenty years old, if one may credit the invoices. As there was no champagne in it, the adjutant plundered two other private wine cellars, one of them belonging to Soulé.* He told me that in one day he and his friends drank forty-six bottles. I found the burgundy soured and corky, although he did not know it, the barbarian; but the sauterne, which he served iced for breakfast, was in good condition and of superior quality. The breakfast was exquisite, and no wonder, for the cook is a noted *artiste,* a handsome quadroon named Alick, formerly chief in one of the best restaurants here.

Now all this looting and foraging is a disorder and a shame. Of course it is General Butler who is chiefly in fault for it. He could stop it at once, but he leaves the doors open for it, and the officers understand that he likes to see it. So they use what they want, and pack up the residue to carry away, and believe that they are doing right.

It is a very different regime from that of our old general, Phelps, who would not take a private house for himself and fretted over the theft of a sweet potato.

Camp Kearney, October 10, 1862.†

THE court-martial has closed, and I am again on company duty. We have settled down into a new station and are brigaded under Weitzel, a young regular officer who has lately been made general.

Do you fancy the idea of my applying for the colonelcy of a colored regiment? Important people here advise it and promise to help me with recommendations. It would be a comfortable position, I suppose; but there are some obvious serious disadvantages. The colored troops will probably be kept near here and used to garrison unhealthy positions; they will be called on

* Pierre Soulé, a jurist of great influence in New Orleans who had helped to shape the Ostend Manifesto. (Ed.)

† Camp Kearney was near Carrollton, nearer to New Orleans than Camp Parapet.

for fatigue duty, such as making roads, building bridges and draining marshes; they will be seldom put into battle, and will afford small chance of distinction.

Since writing the above I have talked on the subject with Colonel Deming, who is acting mayor of New Orleans and well informed concerning affairs at headquarters. I had decided to apply for a black regiment, and I wrote to him for an introduction to General Butler. Thereupon he sent for me, treated me to a fine dinner and gave me his views.

"I advise you," said he, "not to make your proposed application, for fear it might be successful."

Then he went into details concerning the character of the officers who would be associated with me, and the nature of the service that will be assigned to the Negro troops, which details I do not feel free to repeat. In short, he counselled me so urgently against the step that I have given it up and decided to fight my way on in the Twelfth, if it is ever to have any fighting.

I must tell you of an adventure of mine with one of the heroines of secession. On my way down to the city in the crowded, dirty cars, I saw behind me, standing, a lady in half-mourning, a pallid and meagre young woman, with compressed thin lips, sharp grey eyes and a waspish expression. Much doubting whether my civility would be well received, I rose and offered her my seat. She would not look at me; she just conceded me a quick shake of the head and a petulant shrug of the shoulders; then, pinching her pale lips, she stood glaring straight before her.

After waiting her pleasure a moment I resumed my seat. Presently a rather pretty lady opposite me (a young mother with kindly eyes and a cultured expression) took her little girl into her lap and beckoned the scowling heroine to the vacant place. She accepted it with lavish thanks, adding in a loud, ostentatious tone, "*I* wasn't going to take a seat from a Yankee. These cars used to be a fit place for ladies. Now niggers and Yankees crowd decent people out."

The lady with the kindly eyes threw me an apologetic glance which seemed to say, "I hope you did not hear." There ended the comedy; or was it a tragedy?

We hear of a raid which our brigade will shortly undertake;

and Weitzel himself tells people that we shall move before long. But these confidences to the public, so unusual in advance of military operations, seem to me a stratagem and a blind. I cannot yet believe that the becalmed Twelfth Connecticut is going to get a breeze of luck and see active service.

CHAPTER IV

AT the end of the summer of 1862 De Forest's regiment, which had been part of the First Brigade under General Phelps, was transferred to the Reserve Brigade commanded by Brigadier General Godfrey Weitzel. In October it was chosen as one of the five regiments of infantry to move through western Louisiana in an attempt to disperse the enemy forces which General Alfred Mouton was assembling on the west bank of the Mississippi. De Forest's account of the ensuing engagement at Georgia Landing, two miles above Labadieville, is complete, as far as the action of the Twelfth Connecticut is concerned, and agrees (except for a misstatement about the east and west and right and left banks of the Bayou Lafourche) with General Weitzel's reports later published in *The War of the Rebellion . . . Official Records*, Ser. I, Vol. XV, 166 ff. (Ed.)

THE FIRST TIME UNDER FIRE *

T HE Weitzel Brigade, when it first set forth on the war path, must have numbered about four thousand men.

It consisted of the Seventy-fifth New York, Eighth New Hampshire, Twelfth and Thirteenth Connecticut and First Louisiana infantry; also Troop C of Massachusetts cavalry with Williamson's, Barret's and Godrey's troops of Louisiana cavalry; also Carruth's and Thompson's batteries. The commander, Godfrey Weitzel, a West Pointer and lieutenant of engineers, had been for some time Butler's chief military adviser, and had lately been made brigadier general of volunteers. About twenty-six years old, with a stature of six feet four inches, he was a man of attractive and imposing presence.

It was reported that he did not want the Twelfth Connecticut

* This narrative is mainly drawn from an article with the same title published in *Harper's Monthly* [September], 1864.

in his brigade. During the long misunderstanding between Generals Butler and Phelps a belief had taken root at department headquarters that the Camp Parapet regiments were sickly, discouraged and undisciplined. Accordingly, soon after we reached Carrollton, Weitzel came upon us in one of our battalion drills and, taking command, hurried us through a long series of double-quick movements, with the supposed intention of confusing us and so finding occasion to report us unfit for field service. He sent us into doubled column, then into square, then into column again, then into line, and so on for half an hour as fast as the men could trot.

But tangling the Twelfth up in drill was a chore that nobody could do. If there was anything that our lieutenant colonel loved, if there was anything that our old general had excelled in, it was tactical evolution. We had been drilled in battalion and drilled in brigade till we went like a machine. Weitzel rode off satisfied with the regiment, and we were equally pleased with our lively young brigadier.

Butler at this time was under the necessity of securing anew the free navigation of the lower Mississippi. Mouton, a West Pointer and an officer of ability, had collected at Thibodeaux a force consisting of the Crescent regiment, the Eighteenth and Thirty-third Louisiana, the Terre Bonne militia, the Second Louisiana cavalry, and Semmes' and Ralston's batteries. The three volunteer regiments and Semmes' battery had all seen service in Tennessee and were excellent troops, but smartly reduced in numbers. The militia, the cavalry and Ralston's battery were as ignorant of serious warfare as Weitzel's brigade.

It was conjectured that Mouton proposed to march up Bayou Lafourche and establish fortifications on the Mississippi at Donaldsonville. Weitzel believed that he could bag the whole Rebel column by hunting it back to Brashear City while a gunboat fleet should sail up Berwick Bay and prevent escape across the Teche. Our secessionist friends at Carrollton and New Orleans brought us hair-raising stories about the strength of the force at Thibodeaux. It numbered fifteen thousand men, they said, and would make but one mouthful of us. These bugaboo inventions were probably set afloat by Mouton, who could not muster above twenty-five hundred soldiers including militia, and would have been glad to evade an immediate struggle.

On the 24th of October, 1862, Weitzel's brigade steamed up the Mississippi about one hundred miles and landed during the following day at the once flourishing little town of Donaldsonville, just then a desert of smoke-blackened ruins. It is on the western bank, astride of Bayou Lafourche, one of the largest of the numerous outlets of the Father of Waters. Destruction had befallen it, some months before our arrival, as a retaliation for firing upon Farragut's gunboats. Our regiment slept on the floor of a Catholic church, and I ate my supper off a tombstone in the cemetery.

At six in the morning, leaving the First Louisiana to hold Donaldsonville with the aid of three gunboats, we commenced our march in search of Mouton, following the bayou in a westerly and then in a southerly direction, one regiment of infantry and one troop of cavalry on the eastern * bank, the rest of the brigade on the western.* Communication was secured by two enormous Mississippi flatboats (easily convertible into a pontoon bridge) which were towed down the current by mules and contrabands.

We made an easy march of twelve or fifteen miles without being disturbed by an enemy. The men, weak as yet from the summer's heat and quite unaccustomed to field service, complained of the weight of their knapsacks and straggled wofully. At night the Twelfth had its first experience in bivouacking. I got a bed of cornstalks, but supposed I was roughing it and slept badly through cold and anxiety. It was the exposure to night air which worried me, and not the proximity of hostile balls and bayonets. And when I was roused at dawn to continue the march, I felt more fearful of being broken down by lack of proper rest than of being shot in the approaching engagement.

Meantime our general also found slumber difficult and uneasy. His first battle, and the first battle of every one of his regiments, would come on the morrow. Had he made all possible and needful preparation for it? About four in the morning he

* According to General Weitzel's report in *The War of the Rebellion* . . . *Official Records,* Ser. I, Vol. XV, 168, the Eighth New Hampshire and Perkins' troop of cavalry advanced on the right bank of the Bayou Lafourche. Since the river flows from north to south, this would be the western side; the rest of the brigade was on the left or eastern bank. (Ed.)

remembered that he had no corps of engineers to cut down the levee, in case it should be necessary to pass troops across the bayou. He ordered a detail of soldiers and Negroes for this labor and had them furnished with spades, picks and axes. Was that all? He thought over his preparations and found them complete; so, lying down in his cavalry overcoat, he slept till the column started.

This day (Monday, October 27, 1862) the Eighth New Hampshire and Perkins' troop of cavalry held the right bank of the bayou, parallel with the head of the main column. It was prudent to keep our principal force on the western * bank because that furnished the easiest line of retreat in case of a repulse. The troops marched like greenhorns, straggling about the road, the levee and the fields, and taking advantage of every discoverable cut-off. A few months later we would have been ashamed to exhibit such a spectacle of disorder. We passed pretty residences, flourishing plantations and endless flats of waving cane. But the owners of this comfort and wealth were not visible; not a vehicle, nor even an equestrian, appeared on the highways. The only planter discoverable was a tall, cadaverous man with lank iron-grey hair and the voice of a camp-meeting preacher, who shouted lugubrious warnings to us.

"Ah boys! boys! you don't know what awaits you. You are going to defeat and rout and slaughter. Better turn back while you can! Better turn back!"

Some of the youngsters yelled impertinences to him, and he stalked solemnly into his house, leaving our impenitent array to its fate.

While the whites evaded us, or perhaps had already quitted the region, the Negroes swarmed about us with acclamations of joy. "God bless you, massas!" they cried.—"Oh, de Lawd's name be praised!—We knowed you'd come.—Ise a gwine 'long with you."

And go with us they did by hundreds, ready to do anything for their deliverers and submitting unmurmuringly to the tricks and robberies which were practiced upon them by our jokers and scapegraces. Nowhere in the South did I ever find or hear of one Negro who was hostile to us. But meanwhile they were not

* i.e., eastern; see pages 55 n. and 71. (Ed.)

vindictive toward their masters, at least not to the extent of insurrection, or massacre, or murder.

For some hours we marched without a military incident of any consequence. Looking ahead down the sinuous bayou, we occasionally saw the parti-colored flags of the signal corps syllabling back the discoveries of the advanced scouts. Once we came upon a freshly deserted bivouac of cavalry, and learned from the Negroes that it had numbered about five hundred troopers, mostly armed as mounted infantry. Meantime I had no expectation that I should soon get into a fight, especially as the Twelfth formed the rear of the brigade, and I, as officer of the day, commanded the rear guard of the regiment.

But presently came a rumor that fighting had been going on in front for an hour, and that the Thirteenth Connecticut had already lost seventy killed and wounded. There was precious little truth in this, for the Thirteenth had not yet been engaged, and the losses thus far had been trifling. Nevertheless, the Eighth New Hampshire and Perkins' cavalry, both on the other side of the bayou from us, were really skirmishing with the enemy. I learned afterwards from a trooper that the affair commenced with a romantic adventure which befell a squad of Perkins' fellows. A sergeant and five men, scouting well in advance of the column, passed an open field some five hundred yards in length and halted at a point where the road lay between the levee and a wood thickened with underbrush. Here one of the troopers muttered, "Sergeant, there they are—to the right—lying down."

The sergeant turned his eyes without turning his head and discerned an ambuscade of men in grey or butternut uniforms lying still under the shelter of leaves and long grasses. Rising in his stirrups, he coolly surveyed the road in front of him, and then a country crossroad which fell in from the right. "Nothing here," he said aloud. "We'll ride back and report."

The party went off at a walk until they were some twenty rods away from the ambuscade, when they put spurs to their horses and made a burst for the head of the advancing Eighth New Hampshire. A Rebel whom we captured three hours later said to us, "If that sergeant hadn't been so cool, he would have caught his death. I had a bead drawn on him; but the officers wouldn't let us fire. They thought the coons didn't see us, and they allowed they was going to bag the whole column."

Perkins advanced his men as skirmishers and opened fire on the ambush. The Rebels responded vigorously, developing a strong force of sharpshooters and establishing two fieldpieces at the angle of the wood where our troopers had been so nearly entrapped. The horses of this artillery were mistaken for cavalry, and the Eighth deployed two companies in skirmish line to relieve Perkins, while the other eight companies formed square.

On the other side of the bayou Weitzel advanced the Seventy-fifth New York and Thirteenth Connecticut in battalion columns to meet a supposed force in front of his main body. There was such a force, the Thirty-third Louisiana and Ralston's battery; but it numbered little more than four hundred men and was held back out of action. The New Yorkers and the Thirteenth struggled for an hour through interminable green canefields, which broke up the columns and forced them to halt and reorganize.

"This is a false scent," decided Weitzel. "The fighting will be on the other bank."

The two regiments were hurried back, the Thirteenth to join the Eighth, the Seventy-fifth to guard the crossing place. Already an aide had instructed the Twelfth Connecticut to throw off knapsacks, leave two companies in charge of the baggage train, and hasten to the battlefield. Meantime the engineer squad which had been organized during the night hastily dug a road through the levee; the unwieldly pontoon bridge was swung into position, and two twelve-pound howitzers were stationed so as to protect it.

It will be remembered that I had commenced the day's march as commandant of the rear guard. When we received Weitzel's orders to move forward I obtained permission to drop this business and rejoin my company. With drums beating, fifes screaming and banners flying we tramped along, listening to the slow *pumming* of artillery two miles away. I was anxious, but thus far only for my men, not knowing how they would behave in this their first battle. I commenced joking with them, not because I was gay, but because I wanted them to be gay. I have forgotten what I said; it was poor, coarse fun enough probably; but it an-

swered the purpose. The cheerful yet steady countenance of the
company, and of the whole regiment as well, was all that one
could desire.

We found the bridge in place, and the two sentinel howitzers
barking at intervals, while an invisible Rebel battery responded
with similar deliberation. Here we first came under fire, and
here I first beheld a wounded man. In a country carriage, up-
held by two Negroes, was a ghastly sufferer, his knee crushed by
a shot, his torn trousers soaked with a dirty crimson, his eyes
full of the agony of death. I did not want my men to see the
dismaying spectacle and called their attention to something, I
have forgotten what, on the other side of the bayou.

As we trotted down the inner slope of the levee a surprisingly
loud, harsh scream passed over us, ending in a sharp explosion
and a splashing in the muddy water. I was not alarmed, but
rather relieved and gratified. If they can't aim better than that
they are welcome to fire all day, I innocently thought. Then
came another shell, striking close to the crowded bridge and
spattering some of the men, but without deterring the thirsty
ones from stopping to fill their canteens. It was very good practice, considering that the guns were behind the levee half a mile
downstream, where the fellows who worked them could not see
us. But I did not believe that they could hit me, and my chief
anxiety was lest I should wet my feet in the sloppy bottom of
the boat.

In general, the terror of battle is not an abiding impression,
but comes and goes like throbs of pain; and this is especially
the case with veterans who have learned to know when there is
pressing danger and when not; the moment a peril has passed
they are as tranquil as if it had never come near. On the present
occasion I was not as yet conscious of any emotion which could
be called fear. I was still ignorant of the great horrors of battle,
and buoyed up by the excitement of a rapid advance. A regiment
of well-drilled greenhorns, if neatly brought into action, can
charge as brilliantly as veterans.

The moment we were up the western bank, on the same side
of the bayou with Semmes, he lost sight of us behind a wood and
ceased firing. Looking southerly, we noted the Eighth New
Hampshire coming toward us in double column, ready to form

square against cavalry. As we pushed on into the fields, marching tranquilly by the flank, an aide rode up with orders.

"Colonel, General Weitzel's compliments. He says the Eighth
will be on your left; you will move more to the right and give it
room to deploy. Then you will front southwards, throw out
skirmishers, and follow them in line of battle. Beyond the wood
is an open field. You will cross that and drive the enemy from
his position."

Two companies successively filed to the left and deployed as
skirmishers. The remaining six companies marched about five
hundred yards from the bayou when they fronted into line of
battle. Concealed by the wood, the Twelfth and Eighth now advanced toward Mouton's centre, while the two hostile batteries
pounded away at each other, although neither could see the other's position. Emerging from a field of tall, rustling reeds, the
Twelfth came to a strong post-and-rail fence, such as one often
sees in Louisiana.

"Down with the fence!" shouted Lieutenant Colonel Colburn, our commander. "Throw it over!"

Some rushed against it and pushed it flat, while others
climbed over it. Next came a scattered array of thorny thickets
which embarrassed us wofully. We might have met bayonets in
good order, but we were thrown into confusion by this host of
briars. The lieutenant colonel yelled repeatedly, "Centre dress!
Close up those gaps! Centre dress!" The company officers
yelled also, repeating the same orders. In our inexperience we
believed that everything was lost if the men did not march shoulder to shoulder; and all through the battle we labored to keep a
straight line with a single-mindedness which greatly supported
our courage.

"By the right of companies to the front," shouted Colburn
when he saw that the thornbushes were breaking us. The regiment filed into six little parallel columns, moving by the flank,
and threaded more easily the prickly labyrinth. When we
reached clearer ground, it was, "Halt; front; right into line,
wheel; forward, guide centre." And once more we advanced in
line of battle, agreeably conscious of having drilled well under
unfavorable circumstances, and wondering how soon the enemy
would open on us.

As we reached the wood which hid us from Mouton our skir-mishing companies dropped back upon us, and Roach, the senior captain, reported his discoveries. "Colonel, the Rebs are rather more than a quarter of a mile ahead of us. They are on the other side of a long open lot, behind a fence which lines a crossroad, and protected by a ditch in which they are lying."

"Oh!" roared one of my Irish soldiers. "They've got all the advantage of us."

"Hold your tongue, you blockhead," said I, fearing he would discourage his comrades. "Do you want all the advantages yourself?"

"No, Captain, I don't; but I want some kind of fair play; and I don't see the harrum of saying so."

As we approached the edge of the wood the hostile gunners caught sight of us, and a shell screamed over our heads, passing through the lower branches and sending down a shower of leaves. Nearly the whole regiment made a bow to it, though without halting or breaking. Stepping to the front, I turned to my men and said, "Excuse me for not bowing with you; I didn't think of it till it was too late." This was a bit of bravado sug-gested by fear that my raw soldiers were getting shaky and needed encouragement. Poor as the joke was it made them laugh, so slight as yet was their worry, if any.

The shells came fast now, most of them screeching over the colors, at which they were evidently aimed. Not only were the guns in front of us booming rapidly, but a battery across the bayou, half a mile below us, was pitching its iron about us at a venture. Meantime our two howitzers at the bridge, the only ones as yet brought into action by Weitzel, had ceased firing in order not to interfere with our advance. Of course this was absolutely necessary, but it dampened my confidence just a little. Even veterans like to hear a robust clamor from their own artillery.

The Southern shots flew lower and lower. I said to myself, "They will hurt somebody soon." I did not duck or dodge, for I reflected that a missile would hit me about the time that I should hear it; and moreover I believed that all my men were watching me, whereas they were probably staring at the enemy. It cost me no great effort to keep my head up and move onward in good parade style. I had no twitching or trembling; I was not aware of any quickening of the pulse; in short, I was not scared. The Rebel gunners might hit me, but somehow I hoped not and thought not. It seemed to me perfectly natural that others should be killed and that I should escape. I have suffered more worry in subsequent engagements than I did in this first time under fire.

Presently we came to a second stout fence of cypress posts and rails. "Now then, Twelfth!" yelled the lieutenant colonel. "I told you to break that last fence down, and half of you climbed it. Down with this one! Go at it and flatten it. Forward, battalion, double-quick!"

With a rush we flung our breasts against the fence, laying many lengths of it prostrate. But the right company, floundering ankle-deep in bog, was obliged to climb it while the two left companies were balked by a thicket of thornbushes.

"By the right flank!" ordered the captains, and they filed around the obstacle; then, "By company into line!" and they came up into position on the run. These various manoeuvres caused a disorganizing crush towards the centre; and our commander feared that his regiment was going to pieces. "Halt!" he shouted; "guides on the line; centre dress."

The company guides sprang forward, faced toward the centre with rifle-butts aloft, and coolly aligned themselves as is usual in correcting the front of a regiment. But circumstances pressed, and very hurriedly came the next order, "Guides, posts; forward, battalion; guide centre."

We were just entering a large open field, dotted by a few trees and thornbushes, with a swampy forest on the right and the levee of the bayou on the left, when the Rebels gave us their musketry. It was not a volley but a file fire; it was a continuous rattle like that which a boy makes in running a stick along a picket fence, only vastly louder; and meantime the sharp *whit whit* of bullets chippered close to our ears. In the field before us puffs of dust jumped up here and there; on the other side of it a long roll of blue smoke curled upward; to the right of that the grey smoke of artillery rose in a thin cloud; but no other sign of an enemy was visible.

Now occurred a curious incident which might have brought disaster, had I not happened to be at the right of my company, near the color guard. We had two flags, the United States flag borne by a sergeant named Edwards and the Connecticut flag borne by a sergeant whom I forbear to name. This last man, on hearing the Rebel bullets, faced about and started rearward. I never saw anything done more naturally and promptly. He did not look wild with fright; he simply looked alarmed and re-solved to get out of danger; it was the simplest and most per-suaded expression of countenance imaginable. He was not a thorough coward, and never afterward turned tail that I know of; but he was confounded by the peril of the moment and thought of nothing but getting away from it.

It would have been lawful and right to pistol him, for he ran a risk of guiding the regiment rearward and bringing about de-feat. In a great rage and with sabre uplifted, I pounced upon him as he was struggling through the color corporals, all of whom were pushing forward eagerly and gallantly. "Forward, or I'll split your head open," I shouted, catching him by the shoulder and facing him about. He obeyed in silence, with a curious dazed expression, and I pushed him into his place in the front rank of the color guard. We got two volleys after that; and at each one this man fell back a pace with a nervous start; but each time I howled "Forward!" in his ear and sent him on again.

There were plenty of other incidents, very interesting to raw soldiers. The first lieutenant of Company D saw with astonish-ment two of his men fall and roll over each other. To his mind they each seemed to be struggling to squirm undermost in order to escape the bullets. "Get into the ranks!" he ordered, hitting the uppermost with the flat of his sabre. One of them pointed to a bloody hole in his trousers and lay still; the other rose with a mazed air, picked up his rifle and ran after the company. A bullet had struck this man's gun barrel with such force as to knock him down, and then had glanced through the thigh of his rear-rank comrade, both falling in a heap.

The first lieutenant of Company G was pushing forward a laggard when the latter was struck in the breast by a fragment of shell and killed instantly. Private Judson of Company C flung up both hands with a scream and dropped dead with a ball through his heart. Private Atkins of my company had his rifle knocked off his shoulder by a bullet and hurled end over end behind him. Picking it up, he showed me the broken lock and asked what he should do.

"Fetch it along," I said. "We may have a chance to use the bayonet. We shall be up with them presently."

Bringing the gun to a right-shoulder-shift, he fell into his place and made the charge in that fashion.

At the second volley, hearing on my right a sharp crash of broken bone, followed by a loud "Oh" of pain and horror, I glanced that way and saw Color Sergeant Edwards fall slowly backward, with blood spirting from his mouth and a stare of woful amazement in his eyes. A bullet had shattered his front teeth and come out behind his left jaw. He clung to the colors as he dropped, but Corporals Dutton and Kelly dragged them out of his hands; and after a brief pully-hauly between the two they remained with Kelly, a veteran of the British army. He jumped to the front and strode onward, tranquilly chewing his tobacco and guiding his march by a tall tree in the centre of the Rebel position. I quickly saw that he was a thorough soldier, and turned to look after my own company.

All this time we were exposed to both cannon and musketry without being allowed to reply. "Oh dear! when shall *we* fire?" I heard one of the color corporals exclaim. I looked at the youngster; he was not a coward; his color was good. But to be boomed at and volleyed at without answering is one of the most serious trials of battle. There was a general feeling of relief, near akin to delight, when the lieutenant colonel's clear, metallic voice pealed out, "Halt! Fire by file! Commence firing!"

The men could not wait to fire by file, which is a graduated discharge running from right to left of each company; they leveled those five hundred rifles together and sent a grand, crashing volley into the hostile line of smoke which confronted them; for as yet we could see no other sign of an enemy. In the next second every one was loading his piece as if his life depended on the speed of the operation. Then of a sudden, to my utter amazement, the two centre companies fell on their faces. Turning upon the man nearest me, I threatened to kill him if he did not get up. "We were ordered to lie down," he explained, and my second lieutenant added, "That is so, Captain."

"It can't be," I replied. "The right of the regiment is advancing, and the colonel with it."

The men promptly rose, and firing had already recommenced, when I and others near me distinctly heard an order to lie down. Of course we obeyed, all the more smartly because just then a shell flew between the colors, screeching like a mad panther. I laughed at the haste of my plunge, and saw one of my soldiers laughing also, probably at his own undignified hurry. I never could learn positively who uttered that stentorian cry of "Lie down." One story was that it came from the Thirteenth Connecticut which was just then close in rear of us as a support. Afterwards, when I could think of it at leisure, it reminded me of those godlike voices which resounded in ancient battles, giving encouragement or spreading panic. It certainly was not uttered by our commander, for we presently heard him yelling, "Forward, Twelfth!"

In great haste we of the centre sprang up and recovered our place in line. It was the last stop or pause in our advance. We had been drilled long enough under fire, and we broke away from the lieutenant colonel. Once he tried his utmost to make us halt, dress the line and give a volley, as regulars are said to do in battle. But he might as well have ordered a regiment of screeching devils to halt. On we swept in the teeth of canister and musketry, every man loading and firing as fast as possible. There was such a pressure inward toward the colors that some of my lightweights were crowded out of their places, and we were three ranks deep instead of two. Little Sweeny, who belonged on the left of the company, fidgeted along the rear in search of a crack to poke his gun through until my second lieutenant dragged him back to his post and roared at him, "What in h—ll are you doing on the right?"

"Liftenant, I'm purtectin' thim colors," yelped Sweeny, and then sent a bullet over Mouton's rear guard.

The swearing mania was irrepressible. In the excitement of the charge it seemed as if every extremity of language was excusable, providing it would help towards victory. Did I think of the other world, which was so near? Not once. I was anxious for nothing but to keep a steady line, and to reach the enemy quickly. I did not exhort my soldiers to fight gallantly and fire coolly. They were fighting the best they knew how, and aiming as well as the quick-step would permit. Nearly all that I said might be summed up as repetitions of the two orders, "Close up" and "Guide right."

It was contrary to rules for me to remain in the front rank after the firing had commenced; but I had two lieutenants behind the line, and I thought it best to let my men see one of their officers. Marching where I did in the centre of the regiment, I noticed that it had forged slightly ahead of the flank companies, so that I could look easily in both directions. On our left the Eighth New Hampshire had been tangled up by a colonel who knew so little of drill that he tried to deploy from column into line by inversion, and kept bawling helplessly, "Deploy!" until scores of his men lost patience and hurried forward in squads, or singly, to skirmish with the enemy.

Weitzel, who was riding close at our heels, noted the disaster and hurried up the Thirteenth to replace the Eighth, which was sent back to meet a reported force of Rebel cavalry in our rear. Meantime we of the Twelfth tramped onward, keeping up our tumultuous fire and gradually straightening our line. Several times I thought impatiently, "Shall we ever get there?" I was angry because those Butternuts shot at us; and I wanted to make them quit it; wanted to whale them for it. I had sabre and revolver all ready, for of course I expected a severe hand-to-hand struggle; not having yet learned that bayonet fighting occurs mainly in newspapers and other works of fiction.

The field, as I have said, was some five hundred yards long. We had traversed more than half of it before I saw any Confederates; and their cannon I did not see at all, so well were they masked by shrubbery; I could only distinguish their position by the puffs of smoke which they shot forth. The first troops that we caught sight of came running down the crossroad from the forest on the west, as if they had been hastily summoned to re-enforce the line in front of us. I suppose that they were the Terre Bonne militiamen, about five hundred strong, mostly of French stock and not very zealous Rebels. Without forming or halting they opened a hasty sidelong fire, and then broke for the neighboring thickets, disappearing like young partridges.

Mouton's centre, the Crescents and the Eighteenth Louisiana, old soldiers and good ones, still remained firm. But ere we had got within a hundred yards of them, the guns on their right ceased firing; and a moment later swarms of men in grey uniforms sprang out of the ditch which had sheltered them, and fled at full speed; to my eyes they seemed to be jumping over each other like panic-stricken sheep. At this sight the Twelfth raised a scream of exultation and redoubled its uproar of musketry.

Just then a stunning volley, the voice of the Thirteenth coming into action, rang out on our left. It was given without orders from Colonel Birge, but the sight of the escaping enemy was an irresistible temptation. Forward trampled both regiments, smack up to the cypress fence, yelling with delight and blazing away at the woods, although the enemy had vanished like a dream. It was all that the officers could do to halt the excited men and put an end to their riotous shouting. I was amazed at the feebleness of the Southern resistance and could not imagine that we had already won the battle.

"Can't this firing be stopped?" I said to the lieutenant colonel. "Are we not wasting ammunition on a mere party of skirmishers?"

"Cease firing!" he ordered, riding down the line; and with no little difficulty quiet was restored.

"Can't the regiment push into the woods?" I now queried. "The enemy may reform there and drive us back."

The lieutenant colonel improved on my suggestion; he ordered out two companies to search the wood. Meantime the captains of the remaining companies reformed ranks, counted off their men and had the roll called. We had scarcely got into shape when we heard a cheer on our left and saw that Weitzel was making a speech to the Thirteenth. What he said to our comrades in victory I could not hear, but his address to us was an admirable bit of practical instruction.

"Twelfth Connecticut, you have done well. That is the way to do it. Never stop, and the enemy won't stay."

"That is the best speech I ever heard," commented one of my men.

Of course the regiment hurrahed vaingloriously for the general and for itself. Our lieutenant colonel now had a dialogue with us.

"Twelfth, you have done well," he declared. "But not so well as I had hoped."

A Voice. "What did you want, Colonel? We made them skedaddle."

Lieutenant Colonel. "Yes, I know that. That was all right. But I wanted you to do it more coolly. After the drilling that you have had I thought you would go through it like a parade. I tried to halt you in the middle of the field to dress the line and fire a volley. I shouted at you with all my might; but I couldn't get you to stop."

Voices. "We didn't hear a word of it, Colonel."

Lieutenant Colonel. "I suppose not. I don't see how you could hear when you were yelling so and keeping up such a fire. I never heard such a racket before. And now, color guard, why didn't you shake out those colors?"

Color Sergeant. "We rolled them up to go through the woods, Colonel."

Lieutenant Colonel. "That was all right. But next time, whenever you come to a clear spot, let them fly. Never mind the battle rents. They only make the old flag more glorious."

There was some grumbling at the unthankful tone of our commander's remarks. We thought that we had done our duty as well as could be expected, considering the difficulties of the ground and the fact that it was our first fight. Even now, after a respectable experience under fire, I declare that I never saw a more dexterous, vigorous and effective advance, and that it reflected great credit on the training which we had received from our critical commander.

We had scarcely routed Mouton's main force before his left wing, presumably the Second Louisiana cavalry, appeared in our rear and began skirmishing with our baggage guard. But when it stumbled upon the Eighth New Hampshire, and divined therefrom how the main battle had gone, it lost heart and hurried off by a circuitous route to Thibodeaux.

Meantime Perkins' cavalry, a section of artillery and the Thirteenth Connecticut followed up the Crescents and the

Eighteenth Louisiana. For half an hour longer we could hear the guns booming farther and farther southward. On the ground and in the boggy woods a fieldpiece was captured and about two hundred prisoners. The Twelfth caught the color sergeant of the Crescents up to his waist in mire, but he had torn off and hidden the cloth of his flag, and we merely secured the stick.

The night was chilly, but my servant brought up my overcoat from the rear, and I suffered little. The prisoners, being uniformed for the most part in coarse cottonade, and some of them soaked with swamp water, were piteously uncomfortable and gladly appropriated the ragged blankets of their dead comrades. Our fellows would have been as badly off, but that their clothing was all woolen. Their knapsacks and overcoats were across the bayou, three miles or more to the rear, and did not reach us till morning. But after pickets had been thrown out, the rest of the men collected rails and built huge campfires, around which they passed the night, chewing hardtack, smoking, and bragging of their victory. The Thirteenth, by the way, had returned from its pursuit, and shared our comfortless but contented bivouac.

From the prisoners we learned the cause of their precipitate flight from the battlefield. There was a swamp in their rear, and only one narrow road through it in the direction of Thibodeaux, so that retreat was difficult in case of disaster. Their immediate commander, Colonel McPheeters of the Crescent regiment, had to take this matter into consideration. He watched the fight with the Eighth composedly, until the Twelfth and Thirteenth appeared on the field. Then he said, "We could have fought that first regiment all day; but those other fellows are coming sure."

Thereupon he ordered the Crescents and the Eighteenth to jump up and run. He himself stood gazing at us, while his men thronged by him, and so standing received a bullet through the head. When our men reached him he was lying on his back and facing us, his head supported by a thornbush, his handsome face grey with death, and one eye lying on his cheek. He seemed to be about thirty years old, a man of noble height and presence, with Grecian features.

The prisoners spoke of him regretfully and tenderly as a brave officer and a thorough gentleman. It was the first retreat, they said, that he had ever ordered, although he had been in eight engagements. A captain added that our advance was a startling thing to look at from his side of the field. "We expected," he explained, "to see you come on in the usual style,— halt to fire and then advance again—not fire and come on all together."

"Your firing didn't hurt us," said a soldier. "But your coming on and yelling scared us."

One of the first men whom I beheld in the morning was Color Sergeant Edwards whom I had seen fall with what I supposed to be a mortal wound. He complained that his mouth was very sore and that he could swallow nothing but soup. All the same, having heard that we were to have another battle, he had dodged the surgeon and come to demand the colors. Of course a man with a bullet hole through his head could not fight, and he was ordered back to hospital where he had a long illness in the way of fever. One of the most noticeable things in warfare is the heroism frequently shown by the wounded.

Although I have described the combat of Labadieville at great length, it cost our regiment but three killed and sixteen wounded,* while the whole brigade lost but ninety-seven men. The fight had been short; from the passage of the first shell over the Twelfth to our victorious halt at the final fence only eighty minutes had elapsed; and during our charge across the open lot we had spoiled the enemy's aim by blazing away as we advanced. Some of the prisoners told us that, what with the whistling of our bullets and the flying of cypress splinters, their ditch was a most disagreeable hole to be in.

It was obvious that our musketry had killed the enemy's, for out of our nineteen hurt only six were hit by bullets. Notwithstanding our lieutenant colonel's criticism, I think we did wisely to blaze away while advancing, for, besides deranging the aim of the Southerners, it kept up the spirits of our own fellows, who thought they were doing as much harm as they received, and so felt that they had a fair chance. Of course there was some danger to the front rank from the rifles of the rear rank; for instance, I had my neck slightly scorched by the fire of one of my own soldiers.

* Also one officer captured or missing. (Ed.)

The battle was a scientific one, and its science is perfectly comprehensible. It was won by an unexpected concentration on Mouton's centre, and this was possible through the forethought which provided the rude but serviceable pontoon bridge. It was also a scientifically interesting battle as showing the value of minutes. If we had been slow in our advance and hesitating in our charge, we might have been attacked in the rear, thrown into confusion, and beaten.

Mouton's plan was an excellent one, so far as he knew the facts of the situation. He proposed to "amuse" our main column on the eastern side of the bayou, and to concentrate his own main force on the front and rear of the Eighth New Hampshire, which seemed to him completely isolated. There was but one flaw in his tactics; he knew nothing of our bridge until the fight began. Weitzel hurried two regiments across the bayou, and their swift charge won a swift victory with little loss.

Chapter V

THOUGH the doubtful success of the Union army at Antietam gave President Lincoln an opportunity to issue his Emancipation Proclamation, McClellan's failure to pursue Lee energetically after the battle and Burnside's defeat at Fredericksburg increased the gloom which was settling over the North in the winter of 1862–63. There was only one glimmer of hope during that season: Rosecrans' dearly bought victory over Bragg at Stone's River near Murfreesborough, Tennessee. The campaign in the West, however, had more important consequences than to raise Northern morale. It served to instruct capable generals. Thomas, then second in command to Rosecrans, was getting the experience which later helped him, as commander of the Army of the Cumberland, to win the battles of Chattanooga and Nashville. Sheridan, having distinguished himself both at Perryville and at Stone's River, was developing those qualities of leadership which were responsible in September, 1864, for the victories at Winchester and Fisher's Hill in the Shenandoah Valley. And finally, Grant and his lieutenant, Sherman, after a bitter lesson at Shiloh, were rapidly becoming the proficient military strategists responsible for the capture of Vicksburg and the March to the Sea.

As early letters in the chapter indicate, De Forest and his men remained near Thibodeaux from November, 1862, until January, 1863. During the second week in January, the Twelfth Connecticut became part of the expedition to forestall an attack by the Confederates on outlying Union forces at the head of Berwick Bay. General Weitzel's plan was to reduce the striking power of the enemy by destroying the heavily armored gunboat *J. A. Cotton,* then patrolling the Bayou Teche northwest of the bay. Though De Forest's regiment had very little fighting to do in the operation on January 14, it had a position of importance on the left flank of the attack where it would have been compelled to hold at bay the Confederate land forces if they had chosen to defend the *Cotton.* It was no empty boast when De Forest said that the Twelfth Connecticut was establishing a reputation for itself as a combat force. After the raid the unit was stationed at Brashear City until the third week in March. Though the major portion of the troops maintained their advanced position, De Forest's company and one other fell back to Bayou Boeuf to help guard General Weitzel's communications with New Orleans. (Ed.)

FURTHER CAMP LIFE IN LOUISIANA

Near Thibodeaux, November 9, 1862.

THREE days ago I sent you twelve pages telling of our first battle and victory. We are just now very much disappointed with the results, for the Confederates have escaped with the greater part of their force.

It had been arranged that, while we came upon them by the way of Donaldsonville and Thibodeaux, some gunboats and the Twenty-first Indiana should sail to Berwick Bay and cut off their retreat. They would have had to fight again and surrender, or to surrender without fighting. But the same norther which nearly froze us at Labadieville made it impossible for the gunboats to pass the bar off the Bay, and so gave Mouton the twenty-four hours which he needed to get across the Atchafalaya. Thus, through an ill wind which blew good to the enemy, we have missed taking a dozen pieces and two thousand prisoners.

It is said that Mouton is now at New Iberia, gathering reenforcements and raising entrenchments. Weitzel wanted to follow him up, but Butler paid us a visit yesterday and vetoed the project as too hazardous. Our present orders, according to camp rumor, are to stay here until every hogshead of sugar in the Lafourche country has been sent to New Orleans. How long that will take I cannot guess; but the quantity of sugar just about us is surprising; one plantation has fifteen hundred hogsheads, another one thousand, and so on.

It is woful to see how this lately prosperous region is being laid waste. Negroes and runaway soldiers roam everywhere, foraging for provisions, breaking into and plundering the deserted houses, and destroying furniture, books and pictures in mere wantonness. If the planters had remained, they would have been furnished with military guards and would have fared much better. The blacks have the credit of doing most of the looting, and they in turn are looted by the *mauvais sujets* of the rank and file. Yesterday my colored servant George brought in ten pounds or so of solid old table silver. I had no means of restoring it to the owner, who had followed Mouton with all his family; so I simplified the situation by telling George to clear out with it and never let me see it again.

We have no tents and are still sleeping on the ground in the open air, except so far as we have been able to make shanties out of rails, boards and rubber blankets. My residence is a lean-to of three stable doors, side by side, one end on the ground and the other supported by posts. It keeps off the sun, and the wind also, when they are in the right quarter; but when I lie down it has not depth enough to shelter my feet from the rain.

All the same, I am delighted with it, and sit cross-legged by the hour under its shade, and sleep comfortably in it at night. When mealtime comes I seize my tin cup, tin plate, knife and fork; I walk down to the cooking fire at the bottom of the company street; I seat myself on a log, or a pumpkin, and devour the richness of the land. For we forage here; we go without hardtack and salt horse for the present; we live on roast pig, turkey, geese, chickens, beef and mutton; as for hoecake and sweet potatoes, they are nothing accounted of.

Near Thibodeaux, November 20, 1862.

BRIGADE officer of the day yesterday; rode something like thirty miles visiting pickets; ten miles in the morning, ten in the afternoon and ten at midnight. Miserable horses; saddle went to smash miles from camp; had to draw my sword on plantation dogs. I would rather have marched thirty miles on foot. One result of this wearing job will be a short letter.

I have lately been on a "military commission," trying various kinds of bad subjects, wandering soldiers, ornary Southerners and loose Negroes. It is necessary to do something to put down the multifarious anarchy which we and the rebellion have brought upon this region. A stolid plantation hand (with less intellect than a learned pig) who had criminally assaulted a white girl was condemned and hung. Being recorder of the court, I have had much writing to do, and also some translating from the French, for several of the witnesses were Cajuns and knew not a word of English. You must understand that the Cajuns are descendants of the exiled Acadians celebrated in Longfellow's *Evangeline.* Judging by the specimens thus far known to me, they are ignorant, stupid and unpoetic.

Near Thibodeaux, December 7, 1862.

I HAVE received your comments on our Lilliputian battle at Labadieville. You must understand that I took post in the front rank during the charge for a good reason. As my men had never been under fire before, I was afraid they might get startled and disordered, and I wanted to set them an example in facing danger. I can trust them now and shall hereafter march in rear of the company, where a captain should be according to the drill book.

I have discovered why officers are in general braver than soldiers. The soldier is responsible for himself alone, and so is apt to think of himself alone. The officer is responsible for his company, and so partially forgets his own peril. His whole soul is occupied with the task of keeping his ranks in order, and it is only now and then that he takes serious note of the bullets and shells. It would demand a good deal of courage, I think, to be a mere looker-on in a battle.

An officer of the ——th gave me an amusing account of the chaplain of his regiment; sitting his horse calmly in rear of the charging, yelling line and peering after it through his specs with an expression of enlightened curiosity; now glancing at the rolls of smoke which marked the Rebels' position and now at the tufts of dust thrown up by their shot; the whole man as bland and content as if he were in a prayer meeting. He is a terrible forager, this valiant young son of the prophets. He makes frequent pilgrimages after provisions for his flock and helps personally towards devouring the substance of the enemy. Some days ago he presented himself at regimental headquarters and said, "Colonel, the health of this battalion requires sweet potatoes, and I should like permission to take up a contribution. By the way, it is Sunday, I believe. If I get back early enough, I shall preach this afternoon."

Off he went with a couple of soldiers, impressed a plough and a pair of mules at a plantation, and returned with a load of vegetables.

But we have nearly worn out the foraging business. The land for miles around is as bare of pigs as if a legion of devils had run away with them all. Meantime I am nourished at a moderate cost in an honest fashion. One of my men has been detailed as guard over two large plantations, his duty being to drive off plunderers and to make the Negroes get in the sugar crop. The owners are humbly thankful for his protection; they have given him a pony, a hogshead of sugar and a barrel of syrup; and they allow him to bring me poultry at fair prices and vegetables for nothing.

Having been paid off lately, I am able to purchase, and we live well. Occasionally there is a hiatus; for instance, our sweet potatoes and turnips and cabbages arrived late this morning; consequently we had nothing for dinner but bread and roast turkey. But "accidents will happen in the best regulated families."

I am pleased to tell you that Weber and my other "court-martial ducks" all behaved so well in the late battle that I was able to induce General Butler to remit their sentences.

Near Thibodeaux, January 6, 1863.

OUR heavy baggage has arrived, and we are in regular camp. I send you a ground plan of my tent, by which you can see that it is well crowded, though I have not marked down the three chairs and the boxes of company clothing. Beneath the table are cabbages, a sack of turnips, a sack of sweet potatoes, and two knapsacks of deceased soldiers which I as captain must administer upon.

Lieutenant Ball's bunk and mine are alike, each being made of a stable door supported by four posts driven into the earth, all without carving or varnish. My overcoat, folded in soldierly fashion, serves me for a pillow, while I lie on my blanket and one half of a thin coverlet, the other half being thrown over me. Ball is inclined to be rheumatic and has a bedsack stuffed with corn husks, which looks effeminate. The mess-chest contains our tin plates, iron cups, knives and forks, a tin pail of brown sugar, two canisters of coffee, a plate of butter, a loaf of bread and some cold meat. Near it is a box half full of Indian corn meal, also a wooden pail half full of molasses.

Ball's servant, a fat and dirty nigger named George Morris, does the cooking passably well, and robs us to feed his friends and wives. Lieutenant Berry's man, a blubber-lipped loafer called John Bull, ran away several days ago for reasons unknown to me and probably not worth mentioning. My mulatto, Charley Weeks, had deserted some time before. I then got a little yellow vagrant named Harry, and promptly dismissed him for never being on hand when wanted. My present waiter is a good-looking and decently behaved full-blood who answers to a yell of George! These fellows work well and are fairly faithful till they are paid, when they seem to be taken with an irresistible desire to see the world. I suppose that I should have the same nomadic longing if I had always been shut up on one plantation.

All sorts of stories are afloat here as to future movements and as to the reasons of our present inaction. We are going to Texas; we are going to Mobile; we are going to Port Hudson; we are not going anywhere. We remain in Louisiana to keep the French from adding it to their Mexican conquest. There are guesses to please everybody except the few homesick chaps who want peace.

It is a pity that we cannot be making military use of this healthy season and of our present superiority in numbers. It is also a pity that our new levies cannot be clapped into the old organizations, and so get converted at once into soldiers. I have seen one of the nine-months' regiments from Connecticut. It is composed of noble-looking fellows, the finest material that I ever beheld in any service, but as green as grass from the colonel to the fifer, grumbling at their small hardships and anxious to get home. I need twenty men to fill up my company; and if I could draft them out of this regiment, they would be something like veterans in a fortnight; whereas it will take six months to bring them to the same point under their own raw officers and sergeants.

Brashear City, Louisiana, February 25, 1863.

IT was supposed that the arrival of Banks with his fleet and army would set us all agoing in the way of active operations; but so far as our brigade is concerned nothing more remarkable has happened than a change of station.

Brashear City is at the head of Berwick Bay, forty or fifty miles west of New Orleans. As it is the terminus of a railroad, it has a depot and storehouses; and as it is a port of entry with a respectable harbor, it has wharves and a few small craft; but all the same it is what we at the North would call a village. Two or three of our gunboats are anchored off the landing; on shore are the tents of four regiments of infantry, two batteries of artillery, and a troop of cavalry; and there you have about the whole population.

Whether we are to stay here in garrison, or to cross the Teche and fight again, I cannot say.* But meanwhile we are looking after our comfort, which we have at last learned to do promptly, even when we are not sure of stopping overnight. I have a bunk made of four flat rails stretched between two logs. A sawmill has been set running to get out flooring stuff, and the men are diligently hunting up scraps of lumber for their own use. Wherever

---

* On the 13th and 14th of January the Twelfth had taken part in Weitzel's expedition which destroyed the Confederate gunboat *Cotton*. The letter describing this affair has been lost.

we go now the rail fences and board fences vanish as if by magic, for the cooks must have firing wood, and everybody must have tent pins. Lucky is the man who has been able to steal a hatchet; he is much courted and truckled to by his comrades.

Our campground is the finest that we have had in Louisiana. It is an old canefield seamed and humped with furrows and hillocks; but there is green grass on it, which is a delightful sight to Northern eyes; and, wonderful to relate, it is fairly dry. At Camp Parapet we slopped about in mud nearly all summer. At Thibodeaux the bayou was six feet higher than the adjoining land, the levees were aleak in many places, the roads were quagmires. The Teche, as I understand, rarely overflows its banks; nevertheless, the scenery is altogether Southern. To our right is the usual swampy forest of cypress, with its tall, grey, moss-hung trees; and in front of us is a deserted plantation, its wooden mansion and brick sugar-house shaded by evergreen oaks. The straggling, unprosperous, mouldy village is nearly deserted, and most of its dwellings are closed. A wild March-like wind is rattling the shutters, shaking the trees and door-yard thickets, and struggling to overturn our tents.

The Twelfth is winning a terrible name for discipline. Within a few weeks past its sentries have shot three men dead for trying to run guard. One victim I heartily pitied, for he belonged to a new regiment and probably knew no better than to scuttle when challenged. Another unfortunate was even more pitiable, he being an old Negro quite ignorant of martial ways. The third man deserved his fate, inasmuch as he belonged to the Seventy-fifth New York, a veteran and well-trained regiment. With this punctilious execution of orders our general is much pleased. When he learned that some of our officers blamed the sentry who killed the Negro he threatened to have them court-martialed for language subversive of good discipline. You must understand that guard duty is the very last duty that soldiers learn to perform accurately and thoroughly.

The change which has come over our men since their two little battles is very curious. Not so very long since they were like the nine-months' fellows; they nearly all wanted to go home. Now it is difficult to get even a broken-down man to accept his discharge. They rarely grumble about the restraint in which they are kept; they stay contentedly within the narrow limits of the regimental camp; one would think that they were afraid to leave it. This is an odd state of mind for six hundred healthy fellows, some of them wild heretofore in life and reckless in character.

You would stare to see how little interest is aroused by the fact of a man being shot dead. Half a dozen gather to look at the body and promptly disperse to tell the tale to their comrades, who meanwhile have not left their bunks or their suppers. For a day or so the tragedy is discussed carelessly; there is a little blame and more praise for the sentry; then the regiment talks of other things.

But the men are not so *good* as they were once; they drink harder and swear more and gamble deeper. De Quincey is right in his statement that if homicide is habitually indulged in, it leads to immorality.

Brashear City, March 15, 1863.

Two days ago a foraging party, protected by a gunboat and a company of infantry, crossed the Atchafalaya and was attacked by cavalry. I heard some lively skirmish firing; then came half a dozen shells from the gunboat; then the uproar suddenly ended; the enemy had fled. I have not heard whether anyone was hurt, and indeed have not asked. We have come to be monstrous hardhearted.

Some of the new regiments are very sickly, as is apt to be the case with new regiments. But our seasoned and disciplined fellows of the Twelfth are surprisingly healthy. Only about a dozen men a day are excused from duty by the surgeon, which is not more than two per cent of the regiment here in camp, while the regulations of the medical department are based upon an estimate of ten per cent. So you perceive that we are five times as healthy as we are required to be.

March 22. We are now on Bayou Boeuf, eight or ten miles east of our late position. The story goes that Mouton had planned to send a column down this bayou and cut us off from

New Orleans, while his armored gunboats, the *Webb* and *Queen of the West,* should beat our mosquito fleet and shell us out of Brashear City. As Banks is now threatening Port Hudson with the mass of his troops, it was important to evade every chance of disaster in his rear, and so we retired upon this line of defence.

Before the brigade moved there was a wing of a newly raised regiment of New Yorkers here. Then Weitzel got anxious about the post and sent up my company and Captain Clark's, with a fieldpiece, "to make sicker." We arrived three days ago, and reported to the New York lieutenant colonel for orders. It was rather funny to receive instructions from an officer who had never been in action and only a few months in service, and who evidently did not know what ought to be done.

For instance, he ordered the artillery sergeant to plant his gun on a wooden platform near the station. As this platform was only twelve feet square, and the gun would have kicked itself off at the first shot, Captain Clark suggested that the sergeant should be allowed to pick out an emplacement. Thereupon the gun was established on solid earth and twenty of Clark's men were detailed in support. "And now, sir," said the colonel to the captain, "you must defend that piece to the last."

Then he sent me across the bayou on a railroad bridge to occupy an isolated house and hold it against the alligators, who bellowed around us all night like bulls of Bashan. The position was perfectly ridiculous, and, if the enemy had appeared, it would have been disastrous. My company was completely separated from the rest of the troops, and right in the way of their fire if they aimed up the bayou. Apparently the colonel had not the least idea how far a cannon or a rifle would carry.

A little before dusk the major, a handsome fellow of about twenty-five, came over to my post. "That's a fine looking sergeant in charge of that gun," he said. "Is he your sergeant major?"

This question astonished me, for we were unmistakably infantry, while the sergeant wore the red chevrons of artillery. But there was more of the same sort to come. "I want to reconnoitre this plain," he continued. "We may have to fight over it. Are your men accustomed to act in battalion?"

As my company was not a battalion, and as there was no possibility of getting his regiment across a skeleton bridge by night, he might as well have asked if we were accustomed to act in brigade. He had brought along Adjutant Smith of the Twelfth to help him reconnoitre. "I shall want you too, Captain," he said. "You can leave your company to your sergeant."

I thought of suggesting that one officer would suffice for the expedition, and that there should be an escort to guard against possible ambuscades. But it is part of a man's business in the army to obey and respect his inferiors. So we three officers set off unaccompanied and tramped over the flat until well after dark, visiting lonesome little farmhouses and learning from the Cajuns that there were no guerrillas in the region. The major was amusingly particular in enquiring whether the cypress forest was or was not a "dry swamp"; and I inferred that he was considering the chances of "acting in battalion" through it, if the enemy should appear. He became somewhat deferential when he found that I spoke French and that our regiment had been under fire.

At one farmhouse Smith was charged by a mob of howling dogs and sent them off yelping with a shot from his revolver. Then came a Gallic shout from within, "Who is there?" to which I replied in French, "Friends! Come out." Hesitatingly, and after much cautious peering, the *habitant* made his appearance, so shaky with fright that he could hardly speak. The major learned once more that the forest was a "dry swamp" and passable to troops in battalion. After an hour's fooling he brought around to my quarters, where he dispersed most of my company on picket and left us in peace with the mosquitoes and alligators. Fortunately for men so absurdly posted, no other enemies were anywhere near us.

Bayou Boeuf, March 31, 1863.

THE Twelfth Connecticut has suffered a considerable misfortune. A few days ago the gunboat *Diana* was ordered to reconnoitre Grand Lake and Bayou Teche * for Rebel encampments, taking along as a defence against guerrilla ambushes our Company A and a company of the 160th New York. The affair was looked upon as a sort of picnic, and several officers volunteered to join it. Lieutenant Francis of our regiment, who was at Brashear City on leave, borrowed equipment and jumped aboard, followed by our Sergeant Major Sherman.

The *Diana* patrolled the Lake and looked into the mouth of Bayou Teche, where it should have stopped. But the captain wanted to be wiser than his instructions; why not dive into the Teche and examine it thoroughly? He had not gone very far when bullets came singing over the boat and a line of cavalry appeared. The gunboat shelled the troopers, who promptly slipped aside and disclosed a battery, which opened with round shot and canister. Then two other batteries, one above and one below, came out of ambuscades and joined in the fight, until there were sixteen or eighteen pieces playing at short range on the entrapped *Diana*. Infantrymen were at hand, too, and soon swarmed along the banks, shooting our artillerymen at the guns and driving everybody to seek cover.

The two companies on board were sent into the hold or the iron-plated engine room; and the *Diana,* giving up the fight, tried to run the gantlet of the batteries and get back to the Lake. But the captain and his mates were killed, the rudder and steering wheel disabled, the steam pipe shot in two, and the boat reduced to a drifting wreck. Lieutenant Allen, one of the general's aides, was now in command. He had a ball through one arm, but he tied a white handkerchief to a splinter and waved it in token of surrender.

"Stop your engine!" shouted a Rebel officer. "We shall keep firing as long as your wheels keep moving."

But the engineer and the pilot, who were Louisianians and afraid of being hanged if caught, had already jumped into the bayou and made for the other shore. No one on board knew how to stop the engine, and the fire continued till the little steam in the boiler had escaped, when the boat drifted against the bank and everybody surrendered.

* Really, the Atchafalaya.

We hear that Lieutenant Francis got a bullet through the lungs. Few of Company A were hurt, for the detachment consisted of only thirty-five men and two officers, and they were stationed on the lower deck, which was fairly well sheltered. This wretched affair was all the more shameful because the commandant of the *Diana* had been warned of the batteries by Lieutenant Perkins who had pushed a brilliant reconnoissance up to the Teche some days ago.

We at Bayou Boeuf, ten or twelve miles from the fighting, heard the cannonade distinctly and set it down for a gunboat skirmish. Indeed, we hardly thought about it at all, so accustomed are we to such uproars and so indifferent to everything which does not directly concern ourselves.

Chapter VI

At the close of 1862 General Butler had been relieved of his post, and Major General Nathaniel P. Banks had assumed control of the Department of the Gulf. In the spring of 1863, before he could send troops northward to help Grant seal off the Mississippi, the new commander first had to capture or scatter the Confederate units in the Teche country west of New Orleans. His object was to safeguard his communications with that city while a large portion of his army was campaigning farther up the river.

The Union strategy was to surround the Southern forces at Camp Bisland near Pattersonville by keeping them occupied to their front until Brigadier General Cuvier Grover's command could move into position in their rear. The plan miscarried, however, and the enemy escaped. In explaining the failure to trap the Confederate troops De Forest wrote that the encircling division was sent to the wrong rendezvous. In this explanation he was perhaps more candid than was Banks, who in his official report to his superiors (*The War of the Rebellion . . . Official Records,* Ser. I, Vol. XV, 296–298) attributed Grover's delay to the fog which held up the transports on Grand Lake and to the poor roads leading inland from the point of debarkation. (Ed.)

FORCED MARCHES *

THE Teche country was to the war in Louisiana what the Shenandoah Valley was to the war in Virginia. It was a sort of back alley, parallel to the main street wherein the heavy fighting must go on; and one side or the other was always running up or down the Teche with the other side in full chase after it. There the resemblance ends, for the Teche country is a long flat, hemmed in by marshes and bayous, which,

* In place of letters I introduce here a narrative called "Forced Marches," originally published in the *Galaxy* [June, 1868].

as everybody but a blind man can see, is a very different thing from a rolling valley bordered by mountains.

In the Teche country I fought in two engagements, each time coming off conqueror, which is the next worst thing to being beaten, inasmuch as it is almost equally sure to involve you in that most terrible physical trial, a forced march. I have fought quite enough to know that human nature hates to be shot at; but I think I would rather take my chance in another battle than chase Texans again from Camp Bisland to Alexandria. Aware that the phrase "from Camp Bisland to Alexandria" means about as much to the ordinary gentile as the other phrase "from Dan to Beersheba," I will state that the distance between the two points is something like one hundred and eight miles.

My first adventure in this region was in January, 1863. Weitzel dashed up to the confluence of the Teche and Atchafalaya with five or six regiments, scared Mouton out of his position there, smashed the Confederates' new iron-clad gunboat *Cotton,* and returned next morning. Although pestered with cold and hunger, our march homeward was as hilarious as a bacchanal procession. It was delightful to have beaten the enemy, and it was delightful to be on the way back to our comfortable quarters. The expedition was thus brief because it had fulfilled its object, which was to weaken the Confederate naval power on the Teche, and thus enable Banks to take the back alley in his proposed advance on Port Hudson.

But why should he go by the back alley of the Teche instead of by the main street of the Mississippi? Because it was necessary to destroy the army of Mouton, or, at least, to drive it northward as far as possible, in order to incapacitate it from attacking New Orleans while we should be engaged with the fortress of the bluffs. The story ran in our brigade that this sensible plan originated in the head of our own commandant, Weitzel. I believed it then, and I have learned no better since, although I can affirm nothing. The reader will please to remember that there is a great deal of uncertainty in war, not only before but after.

On the thirteenth of April, 1863, I was once more at the confluence of the Teche and the Atchafalaya. This time Mouton was there in strong force, posted behind entrenchments which seemed to me half a mile in length, with an impassable swamp on his right and armored gunboats on his left. Banks's army was far superior in numbers and, supported as it was by a sufficient fleet of gunboats, could doubtless have carried the position; but the desirable thing to do was of course, not so much to beat Mouton as to bag him, and so finish the war in this part of Louisiana. Accordingly, by mysterious waterways of which I know nothing, Grover's division was transported to Irish Bend, in Mouton's rear, while Emory's and Weitzel's divisions should amuse him in front. And here I am tempted, notwithstanding the title of my chapter, to describe this same amusement. The first part of the joke was to push up Weitzel's brigade to draw the enemy's fire. In a single long line, stretching from the wood on the left well toward the river on the right, the brigade advanced directly toward the enemy's works, prostrating or climbing fences, and struggling amid horrible labyrinths of tangled sugar cane.* Rush through a mile of Indian corn, taking the furrows diagonally, then imagine yourself three times as tired and breathless as you are, and you will form some conception of what it is to move in line through a canefield. At first you valiantly push aside the tough green obstacles; then you ignominiously dodge under or around them; at last you fall down with your tongue out. The ranks are broken; the regiment tails off into strings, the strongest leading; the ground is strewn with panting soldiers; the organization disappears.

The cane once passed, stragglers began to come up and find their places; the ranks counted off anew while advancing, and we had once more a regiment. Now we obtained a full view of the field of projected amusement. Before us lay a long and comparatively narrow plain, bounded by forests rising out of swamps, and decorated by a long low earthwork, a third of a mile ahead of us, and barely visible to the naked eye. Away to our right were two half-demolished brick sugar-houses, near which there was a scurrying of dust to and fro, bespeaking a skirmishing of cavalry. Otherwise the scene was one of perfect quietness and silence and desertion.

Of a sudden *bang, bang, bang,* roared an unseen battery, and *jiz, jiz, jiz,* screeched the shells over our heads. Then our own

* This cane had been left ungathered in consequence of the war.

batteries joined in with their *bang, bang, bang, jiz, jiz, jiz,* and
for twenty minutes or more it was as disgusting as a Fourth of
July. The shelling did not hurt us a bit, and consequently did
not scare us much, for we were already accustomed to this kind
of racket, and only took it hard when it was mingled with the
cries of the wounded. I never assisted, as the French phrase it,
at a noisier or a more harmless bout of cannonading. Not a man
in my regiment was injured, although the shells hummed and
cracked and fought each other in flights over our heads, dotting
the sky with the little globes of smoke which marked their ex-
plosions, and sending buzzing fragments in all directions.

Meantime our point was gained; the enemy had defined his
position. There was a battery in the swampy wood on his right,
which would enfilade an attacking column, while on his left the
same business would be performed by his armored gunboats in
the Teche. Now came an order to take the brigade to the rear.
A greenhorn of an aide, shrieking with excitement, galloped up
to our commander and yelled: "Colonel, double-quick your
men out of range. Double-quick!"

I remember the wrath with which I heard this order. Run? Be
shot if I would run or let a man of my company run. The regiment, hearing the command, had faced about and was going to
the rear at a pace which threatened confusion and panic. I
rushed through the ranks, drew my sword, ordered, threatened,
and brought my own company from a double-quick down to the
ordinary marching step. Every other officer, from the colonel
downward, instinctively did the same; and the regiment moved
off in a style which we considered proper for the Twelfth Connecticut.

That night we bivouacked with mosquitoes, who drew more
blood than the cannonade of the afternoon. Next morning the
heavy guns of the opposing gunboats opened a game of long
bowls, in which the Parrotts of the Twenty-first Indiana took a
part, sending loud-whispering shells into the farthest retreats
of the enemy. At ten, the whole army, three lines deep and
stretching across the river—a fine martial spectacle—advanced
slowly through the canefields toward the entrenchments.
Marching in my preferred position, in the front rank of my

company and next to the regimental colors, I felt myself to be an undesirably conspicuous person, as we came out upon the open ground in view of the enemy, and received the first discharge of their artillery. It is a grand thing to take the lead in battle, but all the same it is uncomfortable. The first cannon shot which I noticed struck the ground sixty or eighty feet in front of our color guard, threw up the ploughed soil in a little cloud, leaped a hundred feet behind the regiment, and went bounding off to the rear.

"That's bad for the fellows behind us," I said to my men, with that smile which a hero puts on when he makes the best he can of battle, meantime wishing himself at home.

The next shot struck within thirty feet of the line, and also went jumping and whistling rearward. They were evidently aiming at the colors, and that was nearly equivalent to aiming at me.

"You'll fetch him next time," I thought, grimly; and so, doubtless, thought hundreds of others, each for himself.

But at this moment one of our own batteries opened with great violence and evidently shook the nerves of the enemy's gunners, for their next shot screeched over the colors and first struck the ground far in rear of the regiment, and thereafter they never recovered their at first dangerously accurate range. Now came an order to the infantry to halt and lie down, and no veteran will need to be told that we obeyed it promptly. I never knew that order to be disregarded on a field of battle, not even by the most inexperienced and insubordinate of troops, unless, indeed, they were already running.

The battle of Camp Bisland was an artillery duel of fifteen or twenty pieces on a side, lasting hotly from eleven in the morning till six in the evening, with a dash of infantry charging and heavy musketry on either flank, and a dribble of skirmishing along the whole line. Where we were, it was all artillery and skirmishing, noisy and lively enough, but by no means murderous. Bainbridge's regular battery on our right pitched into a Louisiana battery on our left front, and a little beyond it a battery of the Twenty-first Indiana pounded away at the Confederate gunboats and at an advanced earthwork. The loud metallic spang of the brass howitzers, the dull thud of the iron Parrotts, and the shrieking and cracking of the enemy's shells made up a *charivari* long to be remembered.

Meantime, companies moved out here and there from the line of infantry, deployed as skirmishers, advanced to within two or three hundred yards of the breastworks, and opened fire. This drew the Rebel musketry and made things hotter than ever. The order to lie low passed along, and we did the best we could with the cane-hills, wishing that they were bigger. As I lay on my side behind one of these six-inch fortifications, chewing the hardtack which was my only present creature comfort, several balls cut the low weeds which overhung me. Yet, notwithstanding the stunning racket and the quantity of lead and iron flying about, our loss was very small.

Nor could the enemy have suffered more severely, except on our left. There the Seventy-fifth and 114th New York, drawn up in the swampy wood which at that point separated the two armies, repulsed with a close volley of musketry a swarm of Texans who attempted to ford the morass and turn our flank. There, too, the heaviest fire of our batteries was concentrated and made havoc, as I afterward heard, of the enemy's artillery. An officer of one of our skirmishing companies, whose position enabled him to see this part of the enemy's line, assured me, with a jocose exaggeration founded on fact, that "the air was full of horses' tails and bits of harness." But, in a general way, there was very little slaughter for the amount of powder expended. We were not fighting our hardest; we were merely amusing the enemy. The only serious work done was to smash one or two of his gunboats. Meanwhile, it was hoped that Grover was gaining Mouton's rear and so posting himself as to render escape impossible.

An officer, major of a Texas regiment, as I was told by prisoners, attracted the notice of both armies by riding from left to right of the enemy's position in full view of our line. He was behind the entrenchment, it is true, but that was little more than a rifle pit and hardly concealed the legs of his horse. He was undoubtedly a staff officer engaged in carrying orders to the battery in the wood. As he came back on his perilous mission every skirmisher fired at him, and many men in the line of battle added their bullets to the deadly flight which sought his life, while all our brigade watched him with breathless interest. Directly in front of me the horse reared; the rider dismounted and seemed to examine him; then, remounting, cantered a few yards; then leaned backwards and slid to the ground. Away went the horse, wildly, leaving his gallant master dead.

About five o'clock an order arrived to move out of range of fire. The skirmishers came in; the men rose and took their places in line; and we marched slowly back to our position of the morning. During the night we fought mosquitoes, not with the idea of amusing them, but in deadly earnest. During the night, also, the colonel in charge of the pickets, a greenhorn of some nine-months' regiment, distinguished himself by an exhibition of the minimum of native military genius. Early in the morning he reported to Weitzel that the enemy had vacated their position.

"How do you know?" demanded the startled general.

"I heard their artillery going off about two o'clock."

"Good God, sir! why didn't you inform me of it immediately?"

"Why, General, I thought you wanted them to clear out; and I didn't like to disturb you after such a hard day's work."

Thus collapsed the plan by which we were to stick like a burr to the enemy and pitch into his rear whenever he should attempt to force his way through Grover. Sling blankets and shoulder arms was the order now, and we set off on our long chase to Alexandria. Mouton had gained five or six hours the start of us, and Texans on horseback can travel faster than Yankees on foot, so that, although we marched furiously that hot day, making twenty-four miles before nightfall, Grover had finished his battle long before we reached him. Unacquainted with the country and ordered to the wrong place, he had gone to the wrong place. He had posted himself on one of two parallel roads, instead of where the two met in one, affording him a chance to fight decisively. The consequence was a sidelong battle, both sides suffering, but the enemy escaping.

Forward at full speed the next day and the day after, scurrying and popping of cavalry in the front, as our van skirmished with their rear. At times a great distant dust, showing how close we were upon the Rebel flight. It is a solemn and menacing phenomenon, the dust of a marching enemy, but more particularly so, of course, when it is advancing upon you. The smoke of burning cotton streaked the day, and the flare of it luridly starred the night; for even in his haste Mouton was determined that no fraction of the financial king should fall to the Yankees. Stragglers in grey and butternut dropped back among us with pacific waving of caps and handkerchiefs; for although we could not catch the Texan horsemen, we were marching the Louisiana infantry to tatters. It seemed like meeting old friends to come across the fellows of the Crescent regiment, whom we had encountered six months before at Labadieville, or Georgia Landing. Shouts of recognition took place, gayer on our side than on theirs. They told us that their officers were driving the men on with drawn sabres, or the whole force would have gone to pieces under the exhaustion of the retreat. Mightily encouraged by these statements, we blistered our soles with renewed energy.

Oh, the horrors of marching on blistered feet! It is an incessant bastinado applied by one's own self, from morning to night. I do not mean a single blister, as big as a pea, but a series of blisters, each as large as a dollar, or, to judge by one's sensations, as large as a cartwheel. I have had them one under the other, on the heel, behind the heel, on the ball of the foot, on every toe, a network, a labyrinth, an archipelago of agony. Heat, hunger, thirst, and fatigue are nothing compared with this torment. When you stand, you seem to be on red-hot iron plates; when you walk, you make grimaces at every step. In the morning the whole regiment starts limping, and by noon the best soldiers become nearly mutinous with suffering. They snarl and swear at each other; they curse the general for ordering such marching; they curse the enemy for running away instead of fighting; they fling themselves down in the dust, refusing to move a step further. Fevered with fatigue and pain, they are actually not themselves. Meantime, the company officers, as sore-footed as anyone, must run about from straggler to straggler, coaxing, arguing, ordering, and, perhaps, using the flat of the sabre. Instead of marching in front of my company, I followed immediately in the rear, so that I could see and at once pounce upon everyone who fell out.

It was curious to note how cheerful everyone became if cannon in front told of the proximity of the enemy. We were ready to fight the bloodiest of combats rather than march a mile further. We filed into line of battle delighted, and then resumed our pursuit heartsick.

It will be asked, perhaps, whether I, an officer and claiming, of course, to be a patriot, preserved my staunchness under these trials. I must confess, and I do it without great shame, conscious of being no more than human, that in my inmost soul I was as insubordinate as the worst men were in speech and behavior. In my unspeakable heart I groaned and raved. I wished the bridges would break down—I wished the regiment would refuse to take another step—it seemed to me that I should have been silent in the face of mutiny. But nothing of all this passed my lips, and none could suspect it from my actions.

When we bivouacked at night came the severest trial. Our regiment was on the left of the brigade, and as we always slept in line of battle, this threw us half a mile from the bayou, along which we marched, and which was our only source of water. It was necessary to order a squad of the blistered and bloody-footed men to bring water for the company's coffee. The first sergeant takes out his book and reads off the fatigue detail: "Corporal Smith, Privates Brown, Jones, Robinson, and Brown second, fall in with canteens to get water."

Now ensues a piteous groaning, pleading, and showing of bloody heels or blistered soles, on the part of the most fagged or least manly of the victims of rotation in labor. The first sergeant feels that he has no discretion in the matter, and he knows, moreover, that the other men are fully as incapable of marching as these. He stands firm on his detail, and the opposition grumblingly yields. Slowly and sadly Messrs. Brown, Jones, Robinson, and Brown second take up the canteens of the company, each backing six or eight, and limp away to the river, returning, an hour later, wet, muddy, dragged out, and savage.

Somewhat similar scenes happened on the march. Aides passed down the length of the trailing column with the order,

"Water half a mile in front; details will be sent forward with canteens." Under these circumstances, roguish soldiers would sometimes use the chance to forage, falling in an hour later with a load of chickens as well as of fluid.

Having tried various alleviations for the hardships of marching, without much benefit, I conclude that man was not made to foot it at the rate of thirty miles a day. Soaping the inside of the stockings does some good, by diminishing the friction and, as a consequence, the blistering. It is also advisable to wash the feet before starting, always providing you have sufficient time and water. Beware of washing them at night; it cracks the heated skin and increases the misery. Beware, too, of trying to march on the strength of whiskey; you go better for a few minutes, and then you are worse off than ever. Opium is far superior as a temporary tonic, if I may judge by a single day's experience. I started out sick, took four grains of opium, marched better and better every hour, and at the end of twenty-two miles came in as fresh as a lark.

It must be understood by the non-military reader that company officers of infantry are not permitted to mount horses, whether by borrowing or stealing, but must foot it alongside of their men, for the double purpose of keeping them in order and of setting them an example of hardihood. On this march, General Banks impounded, at a certain point on the road, more than a dozen infantry officers who were found astride of animals, causing each to rejoin his command as it passed, placing some under arrest and summarily dismissing one from the service. They looked exceedingly crestfallen as they stood there, cooped up in a barnyard under charge of the provost guard. The passing soldiers grinned at them, hooted a little, and marched on, much cheered by the spectacle.

If it had not been for the counter irritant of blistered feet, we should have heard a mutinous deal of grumbling on account of thirst. A man strapped up as a soldier is, and weighted with forty rounds of ammunition, knapsack, three days' rations, canteen containing three pints, and rifle, perspires profusely. I have seen the sweat standing on the woolly fibres of their flannel sacks like dew. To supply this waste of moisture they pour down the warm water of their canteens, and are soon begging for leave to fall out of the ranks in search of incredibly situated springs and rivulets. It will not do to accede to the request, for if one man goes, all have a right to go, and, moreover, the absence would probably terminate in a course of foraging or pillaging. Mindful of his duty and the orders of his superiors, the captain grimly responds, "Keep your place, sir," and trudges sufferingly on, cursing inwardly the heat, the dust, the pace and, perhaps, the orders. He knows that if his fellows are caught a mile to the rear wringing the necks of chickens, he may be sent after them; and, in view of his blisters and the fifteen miles already marched and the indefinite miles yet to go, he has no fancy for such an expedition.

Once, under Franklin, in this same soldier-trampled Teche country, I made a leisurely march which was perfect in its management. Not only were the men kept strictly in their fours, but the cooks and the Negro camp followers moved in compact order in rear of their respective regiments. In obedience to directions from headquarters, I made up every morning a dozen or so of permits, written on slips of paper, to the following effect: "The bearer, —— ——, of Company I, Twelfth Connecticut, has leave to be absent from the colors ten minutes." If a man wanted to fall out I gave him one of these slips, filling the blank with his name, and adding the hour of the day and my signature. On his return, he reported to me and delivered up the paper. It was an admirable march, orderly, soldierly, and pleasing to the military soul. But that was a campaign of demonstrations, and we rarely made above twelve miles a day.

In describing the miseries of marching, I must not forget the dust. The movement of so many thousands of feet throws up such dense and prodigious clouds that one who has not witnessed the phenomenon will find it difficult to imagine it in all its vastness and nuisance. The officers dodge from side to side of the road to escape the pulverous suffocation; and the men, bound to their fours, choke desperately along in the midst of it. The faces become grimed out of all human semblance; the eyelashes are loaded, the hair discolored, and the uniform turns to the color of the earth. It frequently happens that you cannot see the length of your regiment, and it has occurred to me that I have been unable to see the length of my own company of perhaps twenty files. Of course, this annoyance varies greatly in magnitude, according to the nature of the earth.

Rain is good or bad, according to circumstances. In hot weather it cools the skin, invigorates the muscles, and is a positive comfort, except in so far as it spoils the footing. On the second day of this advance we had a pelting shower, which soaked everybody, including General Banks—which last circumstance was a source of unmixed satisfaction to the soldiers. Enlisted men like to see officers bear their share of the troubles of war; and, moreover, our fellows held the general responsible for the tearing speed at which we were going. But rain, although pleasant to the skin in warm weather, will reach the earth and make puddles; and to infantry in march a puddle in the road is a greater nuisance than people in carriages would imagine. No man, however wet he may be, wants to step into it; he crowds his next comrade, and so gets into a growling bout; or he hangs back, and so checks the succeeding files. A large puddle always produces a tailing-off of the regiment, which must be made up presently by double-quicking, much to the fatigue and wrath of the rearmost. Oh, miserable left of the column! how many times a day it has to run in order to catch up with the right! and how heartily it hates the right in consequence! Put a regiment or a brigade "left in front," and see how it will go. The men who usually march in the rear are now in the lead, and they are sure to give the fellows at the other end of the line a race. This opening out of the column of march is a constant evil, and one which officers soon learn to struggle against with incessant watchfulness. I believe that I used to shout, "Close up, men," at least a hundred times a day, in every conceivable tone of authority, impatience, and entreaty.

But are there no comforts, no pleasures, in forced marching? Just one: stopping it. Yes, compared with the incessant anguish of going, there was a keen luxury in the act of throwing one's self at full length and remaining motionless. It was a beast's heaven; but it was better than a beast's hell—insupportable fatigue and pain. The march done, the fevered feet bare to the evening breeze, the aching limbs outstretched, the head laid on the blanket roll which had been such a burden through the day, the pipe in mouth, nature revived a little and found that life retained some sweetness. Delicious dreams, too—dreams wonderfully distinct and consecutive—made slumber a conscious pleasure. All night I was at home surrounded by loving faces. No visions of war or troubles; no calling up of the sufferings of the day, nor anticipation of those of the morrow; nothing but home, peace, and friends. I do not know why this should be, but I have always found it so when quite worn out with fatigue, and I have heard others say that it was their experience.

I have already said that we were *en bivouac*. Shelter tents were as yet unknown in the Department of the Gulf, and our wall tents, as well as every other article of not absolutely essential baggage, had been left at Brashear City. For cover, our servants made hasty wigwams or lean-tos of rails, over which we threw our rubber blankets to keep out the "heft" of the showers. If it rained we sat up with our overcoats over our heads, or perhaps slept through it without minding. Not until August, more than three months later, did we again enjoy the shelter of a tent; and during that time we had only two brief opportunities for providing ourselves with board shanties. Meantime we became as dirty and ragged as beggars, and eventually as lousy.

For some time I supposed that what I ate was the free gift of the colored population, and rejoiced in the gratitude of the emancipated slaves who shared their food with their deliverers. My man George, a sly and slippery darkey, brought in sheep, chickens and corn-dodgers, saying that they had been given to him. Given they were, but by the providence of war, and not by the willing hands of welcoming men and brethren. George, representative of hungry Mars, entered whatever dwelling came handiest, whether of white or black, and took therefrom whatever was good to eat without offering to pay or consulting the inclination of the proprietor. I soon discovered this, but I had not the stomach to stop it. To march without food was impossible, and to buy without money was equally out of the question.

Let me suggest, in passing, that the irregular payments of the army were a fruitful source of demoralization. The officer cannot draw rations, and if his money is withheld from for six or eight or twelve months, as was frequently the case, he must allow his servant to forage for him, or he must starve. If he forages, the men will follow the example, although not driven by the same necessity, inasmuch as they are provided with food and clothing. The result is widespread straggling and often atrocious plundering.

Our Negro attendants, who had come with us from New Orleans or the vicinity, seemed not to have the slightest scruple about robbing their country brethren. A large, elderly, reverend-looking follower of my company, named Prince, valet to one of my corporals, executed the following swindle upon the enfranchised population of "the green Opelousas." Mounted on a sore-backed mule, he pushed ahead of the column, entered the Negro cabins by the roadside and requested the inmates to hand over their Confederate money.

" 'Tan't wuth nothing now," he explained, "and I'se the man that General Banks has sent ahead to take it up, and when he comes along he'll give you the greenbacks fur it."

Thereupon the green Opelousans would pour their Confederate wealth into Prince's broad palms, simply enquiring how they should know General Banks when he appeared.

"Oh, you'll know him right easy," answered Prince. "He's a mighty good lookin' young man, and wears specs."

This was a sufficiently accurate description of Lieutenant Colonel Frank Peck, the handsome commandant of the Twelfth Connecticut. Accordingly, the lieutenant colonel was much puzzled by the number of Negroes who approached him on the march, knuckling their heads respectfully, and enquiring: "Massa, has you brought our money?"

Prince's rascality was exposed to me by George. Devourer of plundered chickens as I was, I felt indigant at such needless roguery and turned the venerable humbug out of camp with public approbrium. It must be understood that Confederate money was at this time worth thirty or forty cents on the dollar or, at least, could be secretly exchanged at that value among the secession brokers of New Orleans. Prince had collected a roll of it as large as my fist.

At Opelousas our pursuit of Mouton ceased for a few days. Even to this moment I am grateful for that halt and smile with pleasure over the recollection of it. Our provisions were out, and we thanked heaven for it, seeing starvation on the morrow to be pleasanter than marching today. So, until the Teche could be cleared of sunken gunboats, and the transports could come up with additional salt beef and hardtack, we rested in the green Opelousas. Oh, rest! oh, sleep! Three days and nights of solid sleep! It was better than kingdoms and the glory thereof. Except when I was on duty, or eating, I did little but lie folded in slumber. The hard ground was miraculously softened, and fitted my weary limbs like down. No one can imagine the luxury of rest to the utterly weary; it is like the first draught of water to one who has pined with thirst; it must be proven to be comprehended.

For one poor fellow of my company there was no repose, even now. Sick at Brashear City, he had voluntarily left hospital for the sake of fighting; had behaved nobly at Camp Bisland, but failed rapidly under the severities of the pursuit. During this last day he staggered along between men detailed to support him, agonized with fever and half delirious, moaning: "We never rest! Oh, when shall we ever rest?" Now, with no bedding but his blanket, he lay on the ground, quite out of his head and muttering constantly, "Fall in!" as if he were still on the march. Ambulances we had none in the army, but he was sent in a country cart to hospital, and, after a long sickness, recovered.

On the arrival of the regiment it had been placed on picket, two miles north of the town; and when, next day, an order came to relieve it, men and officers begged to be allowed to remain undisturbed. Watching and the chance of fighting were trifles compared with even two miles of marching on those unhealed blisters. The petition was granted, and the Twelfth continued its picket duty, looking contentedly out over the great bare plain which led northward. No one would have wondered at our choice who had seen the plight in which the regiment reached this blessed bivouac. Seventy-five men and officers dragged along with the colors, while four hundred others lay gasping by the roadside for miles rearward, fagged nigh unto death with speed and the scorching rays of the Louisiana sun. In the whole history of the Twelfth, before and after, there never was such another falling out—not even when it was following Early up the Shenandoah, under cavalry Sheridan. The truth is that Banks was the most merciless marcher of men that I ever knew.

Our blisters had scarcely well hardened to callosities when

orders reached Weitzel's brigade to break camp, overtake Dwight, who was five miles ahead, and push the enemy as rapidly as possible to Alexandria. I was at this time on a court-martial at Opelousas, and we might, I suspect, have remained on that duty, and so have escaped the three days of misery which followed; but, anticipating a battle, we enthusiastically deemed it our duty to adjourn to the General's headquarters and beg leave to join the column.

Starting at five in the afternoon, we reached a broken bridge about seven, made it passable by dint of several hours of labor, and then pushed on until three in the morning. Next to the stupidity and fruitless worry of night fighting comes the stupidity and fruitless worry of night marching. Except under extraordinary circumstances, the results which it achieves do not half compensate for the mischief which it works on the discipline of an army, and the morale and physique of the individual soldier. The officer cannot see his men, and they straggle in spite of him. There is constant falling, stumbling, and unrewarded waste of strength, accompanied by irritation, quarrelling, and disorderliness. Every molehill seems a mountain; every unusual darkness in the path shows like an abyss; the line is continually opening and must be closed up by laborious double-quicking. The men stagger against each other, and slumber marching. At every halt to rest, some fall asleep and are left behind in the darkness. When we bivouacked at three in the morning, ten hours from our starting point, we had made only sixteen miles, and were as exhausted as if we had gone thirty. My company was immediately sent out on picket, and this duty kept me moving and watching until sunrise. After a breakfast of hardtack and coffee, I dozed a few minutes while the fall-in call was beating, and then set off on a day's march of twenty-seven miles, coming in after nightfall well blistered.

The next day, bivouacked on rolling turf by the side of a lovely stream, we bathed and rested. Before dawn on the third morning, having as yet had less than ten hours' sleep since leaving Opelousas, I commenced the hardest day's work of my life. Starting lame, and improving from hour to hour, like foundered horses, we accomplished twenty-four miles by three in the afternoon. As usual, we had halted ten minutes in every hour, closing up, coming to a front, dressing the line, stacking arms, and dropping down by the side of the road to rest. The men had kept well together; such few as had fallen out had come up during the long pause which took place at three; and we were, so far, proud of our march and rather pleased at having done so much. But this sentiment was based on the expectation that we would presently go into bivouac. When, therefore, General Banks joined the column, and some one heard him say that we must reach Alexandria that night, and the horrible tale passed down along the line of stacks, our hearts were suddenly full of despair and growling.

For the next ten miles it was a fight against nature. Every effort was made to cheer the men onward and beguile them from a sense of their miseries. The staggering drummers were forced to beat the march for the staggering regiments. Some of the field officers dismounted and walked at the head of their commands. At one halt, Lieutenant Colonel Van Petten ran foot races in his big boots with a private, to make the soldiers laugh at the unusual buffoonery. Staff officers rode up and down the line, giving orders to yell and setting the example of uproar. The company officers carried the rifles of tottering men, and hastened from straggler to straggler, cheering, ordering, and threatening, but, I think, never striking; for no one could find it in his heart to maltreat poor fellows who were almost at the last gasp with pain and fatigue. We reeled, crawled, and almost rolled toward Alexandria. As night fell, the pace increased, and the whooping became continuous, and we seemed like a column of maniacs. But in the last two miles, in the pitchy darkness between eight and nine of the evening, a silence of despair descended upon us, and then the regiments melted like frost in sunshine. I could not see who fell out of my company, and I did not care. My whole official sentiment of honor was concentrated, under the flame of intense physical suffering, into the one little idea of getting myself to Alexandria with the colors, no matter who else dropped by the way. The few men remaining in the organization reeled on speechlessly. If they passed a dying artillery horse, they no longer shouted, with savage defiance, "Fresh horses! bring on your horses!" They had stopped muttering curses against Banks and the Confederates—those two enemies. They were at the point, morally, of unspeakable desperation and, physically, of mere movement in one direction, without a thought or a sentiment beyond what was necessary to put one foot before the other, and to lean toward Alexandria.

If the enemy had been there we could not have fought him nor run away from him. But, fortunately, there was no enemy within twenty miles of us, as there had been none from the hour we started. God alone knows why we marched thus; our commander has probably forgotten. We had nothing more to boast of than that we had accomplished thirty-four miles in one day, and eighty-seven miles in the whole burst of seventy-six hours, to which Company D of the Twelfth Connecticut had added five miles by a nocturnal foraging expedition. About one third of the regiment stacked arms in the little wood where we bivouacked, and nearly all the remainder straggled in before morning. That night I was too tired to eat, and went contentedly to sleep without supper.

It is astonishing what some men will do for chickens. I had just laid myself down when one of my privates, who had dropped out an hour before under pretence of being exhausted, made his appearance with an armful of fowls. Calling up the straggler, I confiscated his plunder and divided it among those who had stuck to the colors. The next morning I learned that this indefatigable hen hawk had been off on another hunting bout of two miles or more and had supped on a fresh dozen of chickens before lying down to his virtuous slumbers. The owls ought to hold that man in everlasting hatred; he is physically and morally capable of taking the meat out of their mouths.

Longer and more rapid forced marches than this of ours have been made, but I am glad that I was not called upon to assist at the performance. We should not have suffered so much as we did, had it not been for the heat, which not only wore out our muscular forces, but greatly increased the blistering of our feet.

Perhaps it is worth while to mention that, after two or three days of repose, we were excessively proud of our thirty-four miles in a day, and were ready to march with any other brigade in the army for a wager.

CHAPTER VII

THOUGH Union forces controlled, by 1863, the Mississippi as far south as Vicksburg and also from its mouth north to Port Hudson, there was a stretch of two hundred miles of river between the two fortresses which the South guarded and used as a communications' artery between Texas, Arkansas, and western Louisiana, and the other Confederate states. Grant began to march against Vicksburg in March, 1863. Moving rapidly and defeating the opposing forces before they could unite, he finally established himself in the rear of his objective on May 18. For nearly two months thereafter he steadily tightened his grip upon Vicksburg and at last forced it to surrender on July 4, almost simultaneously with Lee's retreat from the field of Gettysburg.

Meanwhile Banks had launched an offensive against the Confederate position at Port Hudson. Dispatching a portion of his troops down the Red River and a portion overland to Simsport, he moved on May 25 into position to attack. On the 27th an assault was made and repulsed, and a second assault at a later time was also beaten off. Though his force far outnumbered that of the enemy, Banks found the Confederate stronghold so difficult of capture by storm that he invested the position and inaugurated regular siege tactics, with sapping, mining, and the like. Despite these activities, Port Hudson continued to hold out until the surrender of Vicksburg deprived it of all strategic value. At that time further resistance seemed useless and the commander of Port Hudson surrendered his entire force of 5,500 men. De Forest saw some of the most gruelling action of the war during his participation in this campaign.

Many critics felt, as did De Forest, that Banks failed seriously in developing a co-ordinated assault on May 27. Lieutenant Colonel Peck, for instance, wrote that the Twelfth Connecticut was halted at the edge of the inner fortifications "for want of harmonious support of other corps." General Banks, however, explained weakly to the Secretary of War that "the garrison was much stronger than had been represented, and the enemy was found able to defend his works at all points." De Forest's account of the fighting and of the movement of troops during the siege is accurate and agrees with the report of commanding officer, published in *The War of the Rebellion . . . Official Records*, Ser. I, Vol. XXVI, Part I, 132 f. (Ed.)

PORT HUDSON *

THE day after our forced march ended, the brigade got itself into shape and paraded through Alexandria, settling down nearby, on the banks of the Red River. We were without tents, but we looted a prodigious quantity of lumber, and in a day or two had a little city of board shanties. Porter's gunboats were in the river, and a number of supply transports had followed them, so that there was no lack of provisions.

While we healed our blisters and made up arrears of sleep Banks meditated as to whether he should push up the river to Shreveport, or re-enforce Grant in rear of Vicksburg, or turn upon Port Hudson. Eventually, hearing that the garrison of the latter place had been weakened to help Pemberton, he decided to invest it. On the 14th of May, five days after our arrival at Alexandria, Grover's division set off southward and was followed on the 16th by Emory's. We of the Weitzel brigade held on a few days longer, and then made a movement up the Red River toward Shreveport, all for the purpose of deceiving the enemy as to the ultimate destination of the army.

The feint accomplished, we faced about and hastened after our comrades, occasionally halting to lay ambuscades. Once, while the Twelfth was acting as rear guard, it tramped in doubled column into a beautiful isolated grove, which we presently discovered to be an abandoned cemetery haunted by huge copperheads who scuttled before us in terror. We lay down among the grassy graves and waited there for an hour without entrapping the Confederates; they were following us, but they were wary of Weitzel and his brigade, which was then famous in Louisiana.

On the 19th of May we overtook the main column at Sims-

* The first draft of Chapters VII and VIII appeared in *Harper's New Monthly Magazine* for August, 1867. (Ed.)

port, traversed a considerable river on transports, and marched down the west bank of the Mississippi to a point opposite Bayou Sara. Here we crossed in the boats of the squadron, and then tramped through an undulating country to the rear of Port Hudson, where we arrived amid suffocating clouds of dust. Meantime Augur's division joined us from Baton Rouge, and on the 25th of May the place was completely invested. Our numbers at this time were barely thirty thousand effectives, and they soon began to diminish with startling rapidity.

Gardner, the commandant of Port Hudson, had about seven thousand men, with twenty siege guns and thirty fieldpieces. The fortifications were earthworks, running along the sinuous brow of an elevated bluff; they were proof against any artillery that we possessed, but they had neither bombproofs nor embrasures; in short, the place was an entrenched camp rather than a fortress. The approaches were fairly well protected against assaulting columns by natural gullies alternating with abatis of felled trees.

a. The Assault of May 27th

I think General Banks ordered the assault of May 27th in the hope that some stroke of luck might give him the victory; and perhaps a general is justified in betting lives upon such a chance, rather than settle down to the sure waste of life and time incident to a long siege. There is a great deal of accident in war, and especially in storming parties; for instance, the English carried Badajoz because the French thoughtlessly withdrew their guard from the citadel. Moreover, we did come near to capturing Port Hudson by a fluke, as I shall relate further along.

Yet I never think of that bloody day without saying to myself that we had a very small chance of winning. It is no easy job to march half a mile under a telling fire, and then climb ramparts defended by cool-headed American sharpshooters.

It was broad morning when we got into line to advance upon Port Hudson. Our brigade was then in a long, narrow clearing, with a forest in the rear and a thickly wooded rising ground in front. Two hundred yards ahead of us, and just at

Military Record of John W. De Forest, New Haven, Connecticut.

(A) Mustered in as captain Co. I, 12ᵗʰ Conn. Vols. January 1, 1862.

(A) Discharged as ditto by reason of termination of period of service, Dec. 2, 1864.

(B) Surgeon's certificate for admission to the Invalid Corps, Jan. 25, 1865.

(C) Recommended for appointment into Invalid Corps by Major Genl J. B. Fry, provost marshal general, Feb. 8, 1865.

(C) Nominated to the Senate for appointment to Invalid Corps Feb. 10, 1865, and confirmed Feb. 20, 1865.

(D) Commission as captain in Veteran Reserve Corps (lately Invalid Corps), to rank from Feb. 10, 1865, signed by Andrew Johnson & E. M. Stanton, dated May 7, 1865.

(E) Ordered by the Adjutant Genl of the Army to report to the Provost Marshal General for assignment to duty; mentioned in the order as captain of Co. I, 14ᵗʰ regiment Vet. Res. Corps, Sept. 2ᵈ, 1865. (Acted for some time as captain in the regiment, previous to this order).

(F) Assigned to duty (in sequence of the above order) as Acting Assistant Adjutant General in charge of the Veteran Reserve Corps branch of the Provost Marshal General's office, Sept. 13, 1865.

(G) Ordered to report for duty in the Freedmen's Bureau, July 18, 1866. (Subsequently on duty as officer of said Bureau under orders of Major Genl O. O. Howard, in Greenville, Pickens & Anderson districts, So. Ca.

(H) Mustered out of service as captain Vet. Reserve Corps 1ˢᵗ January 1868.

SYNOPSIS, IN HIS OWN HANDWRITING, OF DE FOREST'S
MILITARY CAREER

Commissioned as brevet major to rank from March 13, 1865; commission signed May 15, 1866.

(*Field Service*)

Battle of Georgia Landing, Oct. 27, 1862. — Destruction of gunboat Cotton, Jan. 13, 1863. — 1st Assault on Port Hudson, May 27, 1863. — Night attack on Port Hudson, June 12, 1863. — 2d Assault on Port Hudson, June 14, 1863. — Trench duty under fire at Port Hudson, 39 days. — Battle of the Opequan, Sept. 19, 1864. — Battle of Fisher's Hill, Sept. 22, 1864. — Battle of Cedar Creek, Oct. 19, 1864.

Inspector General of 1st Div. 19th Corps, winter of 1863.

Aide on staff of 19th Corps, autumn of 1864.

No promotion in lineal rank, owing to the fact that in the 12th regt Conn. Vols. I entered as 9th captain by seniority and was mustered out as 4th captain; the promotions in that regiment being entirely according to seniority.

Wounds; one, at Port Hudson; slight and not reported on muster-roll.

SECOND PAGE OF DE FOREST'S MILITARY RECORD

the base of the leafy slope, appeared the dark line of another brigade, which I believe was Paine's.

While we awaited the order to set forward I studied with interest the physiognomies of our men. They had by this time quite lost the innocent, pacific air which characterized them when they entered the service. Hardened by exposure and suffering, they had a stony, indifferent stare and an expression of surly patience, reminding me of bulldogs and bloodhounds held in leash. It was impossible to divine from their faces whether they expected battle or a peaceful march.

Presently we saw the leading brigade move into the forest, and a minute or two later we quietly followed. In five minutes more our regiment had lost its comrades and was strangely alone among the shadows of the wooded ascent. Paine's men were hidden from us by dense foliage; while the mass of our own brigade had deviated to the right and was hunting the Rebels out of some advanced works which they had built there; the regiments getting on as they could over the broken ground, and the companies charging singly in wild confusion.

Meantime we of the Twelfth climbed straight on in perfect peace, seeing nothing but trees and thickets and hearing only our own tramplings. The footing was uncertain, for our feet slipped continually in the mouldering leaves of bygone years, and we found it difficult to keep the line in shape. Everybody was red, hot and breathless, and the company officers growled about the gaps, and the colonel looked every way for a general. We must have climbed for twenty minutes in this toilsome fashion before we began to hear ahead of us a dull, sullen *pum—pum—pum* of cannon, though as yet not a ball howled near us.

At last we reached a flattish crest, shadowed by noble magnolias but free of underbrush, so that we could see about us. Here we suddenly entered upon a surprisingly clamorous battle scene. In front of us, on the further edge of the crest, were Paine's regiments just descending into a gorge beyond, faced in on the other side by a long and abrupt bluff showing a yellow line which I knew to be earthworks. The enemy's artillery at this time made a tremendous uproar; the shells howled and burst over our heads incessantly and deafeningly.

Every minute or two some lordly tree, eighteen inches or two feet in diameter, flew asunder with a roar and toppled crashing to earth. For some minutes I admired without enjoying this sublime massacre of the monarchs of the forest. All this time our position exposed us badly to the enemy's fire, for we were in marching column, end-on to the fortifications, and a well-aimed shot would have raked the entire battalion. It seemed to me that we stood in this manner for a quarter of an hour while our commander looked up a general who could tell us where to go.

Meantime a woful procession of wounded streamed rearward under our eyes. One man was borne past us with both his feet shot off about midway, and the bare spikes of bone protruding white and sharp from the bloody flesh. The loss would have been heavier if the enemy had fired lower; but they aimed quite well enough to make us very uneasy. One shell, which burst over my right shoulder, blinded and deafened me for a moment; it seemed to me that, if I had lifted my hand, I could have reached the halo of smoke and black specks; but all the fragments hummed rearward, hitting only one of my crowded soldiers. A quiet little fellow named Lane limped up to me, saluted in his usual meek way, showed me a lacerated heel, and said, "Captain, shall I go on?"

"It isn't best," I replied. "Can you get to the rear alone?"

"Oh yes, Captain; I don't need any help."

"Very well," I said, and Private Lane with another salute limped away, while Private Hunter enviously muttered, "Lord! I wish I could get off with a scratch like that."

Lane had scarcely gone when a color corporal near me dropped his musket and spun around with a broad stream of blood dribbling down his face. I supposed for a moment that he was a dead man; but the ball had merely run along the upper edge of his leathern forepiece, driving it through the skin; there was nothing worse than a shallow gash from temple to temple.

He was stunned and blinded, however, and fell against a sergeant who stood near him. The sergeant laid him down, and then suddenly reeled against me, his face as white as if he were mortally wounded. I helped him to a stump, asked him where he was hurt, and found that he was merely faint. There must be something infectious in swooning, for of a sudden everything swam around me, and I had to draw long breaths to steady myself. In all my days under fire I never but this once had such a ridiculous and contemptible moment; and even now I feel like pouring out libations to Mars when I remember my escape from fainting on the battlefield.

I had scarcely got my head clear when a charge of grape screeched over us, one shot nearly finishing our major, Lewis, who was on foot ten or twelve yards behind me. It struck him just below the collarbone and emerged under the skin in the lower part of the back, producing a wound which made him famous in the annals of American surgery.* He told me afterward that the ball glanced down at him from a branch, and that he saw it coming without being able to dodge it.

All this time the regiment was in marching column, waiting for orders. It was obvious that the suspense, the uproar of the cannonade, and the falling of the huge magnolias were producing dismay. The men stared about them with anxious faces; occasionally they had to break ranks in haste, to escape the toppling timber; then they laughed at themselves and each other, but not cheerfully. Once they shouted uproariously when a splintered tree came down with a crash and dispersed a file of stragglers who had gathered behind it. Still I saw but one fugitive, a sergeant of the First Louisiana, who dodged rearward from covert to covert, his chin shaking and his face ghastly. Braley of our regiment collared this fellow and dragged him into his own company; but the scared wretch presently slipped behind a tree, and thence continued his flight with the speed of insanity.

A little later we cleared the road for two guns of Bainbridge's regular battery, which came up the wretched cart track in gallant style and opened fire a few rods in front of us. The first sonorous *spang* of the brass twelve-pounders brought a joyous cheer from our fellows, who, naturally enough, were dead sick of being fired at without having a shot in return.

Our colonel could not find Weitzel, our own chief, but he stumbled upon Dwight who commanded the second division.

* A cane could be passed through him. He did not serve again until October, 1864.

Dwight said, "Your brigade is a mile to the right, and it doesn't need you. Better turn to the left and occupy a gap there; you can throw out skirmishers to silence the enemy's barbette pieces."

These instructions were followed. Two companies deployed into the gorge to do what sharpshooting they could; the rest of the regiment filed southward along the crest, under cover of straggling thickets. It was a great relief to have something to do besides standing up as a mark for artillery; moreover, we were almost immediately out of the fire, for the garrison seemed to have lost sight of us.

Presently a third company advanced into the valley, and, further on, a fourth deployed along the brow of the crest. The remaining six, after a march of about half a mile, halted in reserve on a bluff under some magnificent magnolias. During the rest of the day we had a tolerably easy job of sharpshooting and of lounging. The reserve sprawled at ease in the shade, rarely visited by bullets commissioned to hurt, though they whistled over us frequently. Now and then, at intervals of half an hour or more, a victim was borne away to the surgeon who had established his field hospital in a neighboring gully. But mostly we could smoke our pipes and discuss the chances of the combat with a sense of enjoyment.

Meantime the skirmishing companies, spread out over a front of nearly half a mile and sheltered behind stumps and felled trees, popped away at the gunners whenever they tried to reload the barbette pieces, or at the tents visible inside of the earthworks, or at whatever else seemed worth hitting.

At last an unpleasant moment, not unlike that in which you take your seat in a dentist's chair, came to the author of this history. When the colonel said, "Captain, take out your company and relieve Company G," I felt that heavy heart within me which man is almost always conscious of as he deliberately approaches the confines of visible death. With a smile of simulated gayety I turned to my men and shouted, "Fall in!" Five minutes thereafter, the ice of suspense broken, the blood heated with advancing and fighting, that gayety became real.

Skirmishing is not nearly so trying as charging or line fighting. In the first place, you generally have cover; in the second, if you are shot at you can also shoot. Now to fire at a person who is firing at you is somehow wonderfully consolatory and sustaining; more than that, it is exciting and produces in you the so-called joy of battle. I was presently shouting with enthusiasm, cheering my men with jokes and laughter, jumping over fallen trees instead of crawling under them, and running about regardless of exposure. Then the close whistle of bullets, or their loud *whack* as they buried themselves in the stumps near me, would drive me temporarily to shelter. Such is skirmishing when it goes nicely, or, in other words, when the enemy is not too numerous. As to being slaughtered and driven back and scared to death, you can not make it pleasant under any circumstances.

Port Hudson, as I saw it, was an immense knoll or bluff, two miles in diameter, with a rolling surface, a forest, a church, a few scattered houses, and two or three encampments of tents or shanties. The edge of the bluff was marked by a zigzag earthwork, rough in construction and by no means lofty; and from this line the ground sank on all sides into a valley which in some places was a ravine choked with felled trees.

There was a moment when it seemed as if Port Hudson was taken. A white flag showed over the rampart, and on every hand the firing died away, while a large body of men, apparently a regiment, filed through a sally port, stacked arms outside of the entrenchments, and sat down behind the stacks. To those of our skirmishers who mingled with them and asked what their movement meant the Butternuts replied, sullenly, "We suppose that we have surrendered."

Had we had on the spot an officer intelligent enough to order this force to move into the valley the fate of the place would have been decided; for the abandoned works could have been occupied by our skirmish line, which had already reached the ditch, and the example of surrender would doubtless have been followed by other regiments. Company A of the Twelfth was at the right point, but under the command of a sergeant, its only officer, Captain Brennan, having been just taken to the rear wounded. And thus this propitious moment, this chance which might have saved a long investment and thousands of men, slipped by unimproved. While both armies stood gaping, down came a mounted Confederate officer, supposed to be General

Gardner, placed the surrendering colonel under arrest, and sent the surrendered regiment inside the entrenchments. In an instant cannonade and musketry flamed forth with renewed fury, and we recommenced the siege, which was now to last six weeks instead of a single day.

It was not till after the surrender that I learned the inside history of this singular incident. It seems, according to the Rebel officers, that the colonel of a New York regiment pushed his way up to an apron which projected from the main works and fought desperately for a while, but finally found himself in a bad box, most of the men who followed him having been disabled and the remainder driven to cover behind logs and stumps. Unable to combat longer he would have been glad to get away, but could not without exposing himself to almost certain death. In this extremity he hoisted a white handkerchief on a stick and came to a parley with that part of the garrison immediately opposed to him. The Rebel colonel in front of us saw this symbol of distress, but, deceived by the distance and the lay of the ground, supposed that it was raised by his comrades of the apron, and being a regular-minded gentleman, disposed to do what was proper, immediately got out his own handkerchief. My informants added that he was still under arrest and would be tried by court-martial as soon as exchanged. They also stated that the New Yorker eventually escaped from them unhurt.

About two hours after this blundering interlude came the charge of the Twelfth Maine. A single regiment, four hundred strong, stepped forth, by whose orders I know not, to do what would have been hard work for a brigade. Under a fire from half a mile of hostile rampart it rushed with a prolonged yell through the abatis of felled trees, diminishing in numbers at every step until not a hundred reached the ditch. One nameless hero sprang upon the earthworks, bayoneted two of the garrison, and fell pierced with three bullets. Thirty or forty of his comrades seized an old shell of a building at the base of the fortifications, and held it amidst a furious spitting of musketry, until slaughtered or driven out by an overpowering fire. It was an ill-advised, unsupported, heroic, and hopeless effort. To draw attention from it I advanced my company, but with no result beyond losing a man or two, who might otherwise have escaped.

I have already intimated that skirmishing is not dangerous. Two men mortally and two severely wounded constituted my whole loss in something like three hours' fighting out of a company of forty-one muskets. Four hours after I was relieved the widespread, straggling, wavering combat died into silence and night. The day had been a defeat: Sherman had been repulsed even more bloodily than Weitzel and Grover; nineteen hundred brave men had fallen uselessly.*

With my rubber blanket for a bed, and my blouse thrown over me for a coverlet, I slept at the foot of a huge magnolia scarred by bullets. The next day there was an armistice, demanded by Banks to bury the dead. In the afternoon we received orders to leave our position in charge of the Twenty-fourth Connecticut, and to rejoin our brigade a mile or so to the right. Through some mistake, and contrary to the rules of war, we moved before the armistice ended, thus making the little march in perfect tranquillity—a circumstance which might not have happened had our route been in sight of the garrison. Threading ravines and thickets and passing regiment after regiment concealed by the forest, we arrived an hour before sundown in a short and broad gully, faintly resembling in shape an oblong wooden bowl with one end broken out.

Here, under the shade of beeches and ashes, lounged the Eighth Vermont and the Ninety-first New York. Climbing the steepest side of the gully and looking over a solid turfy knoll which served the purpose of a rampart, I saw a deep ravine a hundred and twenty yards across, and on the other brink of it the low earthwork of an apron occupied by the Second Alabama and the Fourth Arkansas. Sallow, darkly sunburnt men, in dirty reddish homespun and broad-brimmed wool hats, stared back at me in grim silence. To the left, and a little below me, the flag of the Seventy-fifth New York waved on another knoll, behind which lay the regiment. Still farther to the left, across a rugged valley and nearly half a mile distant, rose the bluff of Port Hudson, crowned with yellow earthworks, dirty tents, ragged shanties, and a forest. We were in a broad obtuse angle, between

---

* Killed, 293; wounded, 1,545; missing (at least one half killed and wounded) 157; aggregate, 1,995 (Irwin).

the main fortress and the projecting apron, and evidently exposed to a cross fire.

Our basin was crammed with the blue uniforms and bright rifles of the three regiments. The men of the Ninety-first sat on their knapsacks, ready to move to another position on the conclusion of the armistice. Prepared to open fire at the same instant, four companies of the Twelfth, relieving four of the Eighth Vermont, were ranged along the edge of the basin nearest the enemy, under cover of the bank. There was nothing cheerful about the armistice; it was merely a funereal pause in the slaughter.

A little after sunset, just as dusk was stealing into our wood, a signal gun solemnly terminated the truce. In an instant a sheet of red flashes lit up the dimness, followed by crashes of musketry and the yells of combatants. Then came the roar of artillery, the crackling of shells, and the whistling of grape. We could hear the humming, shrieking, and hissing of the projectiles as they passed over our heads; we could feel the shuddering of the trees against which we leaned, as they were struck; we were conscious of a falling of severed leaves and branches. An order was passed along to lie down, and down we dropped, wherever we might be. As yet none of us knew our exact position with regard to that of the enemy; and, astounded by the unexpectedness and violence of the explosion, we supposed that the Rebels had attacked. Gazing steadily at the spitting stream of flashes above me, I expected every moment to be called on to fight with the bayonet. All this, it must be remembered, was in darkness; for the Louisiana summer day dies almost instantaneously, and in five minutes from the opening of the musketry it was our only light.

Presently an order reached me to move my company forward. "Now for close quarters," I thought, with a gravity becoming the moment, and picked my way toward the firing over the bodies of prostrate men. But I was halted at the foot of the bank and directed to remain there as a reserve. Meantime we had begun to find out that nobody was getting hit, that the missiles were all unquestionably passing over our heads, and that the affair was only terrible considered as a racket. Presently Colonel

Thomas of the Eighth Vermont, our brigade commander, called to me.

"Captain," said he, "I don't want this sort of thing at all. I only want the men to fire as sharpshooters. This blazing away and yelling like madmen is all nonsense. I wish you would step up there and stop it."

So I stepped up there and stopped it. Thus terminated one of the most dreadful-looking skirmishes that I ever witnessed. It was sublime, until I discovered that nobody was hurt, and that probably nobody would be hurt if it should last all night. We were sheltered behind fifty feet of solid earth, and the Rebels were equally safe on the other side of the ravine. In justice to our men I must observe that they wasted their breath and ammunition under the instructions of a passing staff officer of the division, "to pitch in lively as soon as the armistice terminated."

Now came forty days and nights in the wilderness of death. Before we left that diminutive gully fifty or sixty men of the regiment had stained it with their blood, and several of the trees, which filled it with shade, had been cut asunder by cannon shot, while others were dying under the scars of innumerable bullets. The nuisance of trench duty does not consist in the overwhelming amount of danger at any particular moment, but in the fact that danger is perpetually present. The spring is always bent; the nerves never have a chance to recuperate; the elasticity of courage is slowly worn out. Every morning I was awakened by the popping of rifles and the whistling of balls; hardly a day passed that I did not hear the loud exclamations of the wounded, or see corpses borne to the rear; and the gamut of my good-night lullaby varied all the way from Minié rifles to sixty-eight pounders.

In one respect our gully was detestable. Well covered in front, it was open at one end, and this end was exposed to the enemy. I often wished that I could turn the wretched hole around. From a distance of nearly half a mile the Rebel sharpshooters drew a bead on us with a precision which deserved the highest commendation of their officers, but which made us curse the day they were born. One incident proves, I think, that they were able to hit an object farther off than they could distinguish its nature. A rubber blanket, hung over the stump of a sapling five feet high, which stood in the centre of our bivouac, was pierced by a bullet from this quarter. A minute later a second bullet passed directly over the object and lodged in a tree behind it. I ordered the blanket to be taken down, and then the firing ceased. Evidently the invisible marksman, eight hundred yards away, had mistaken it for a Yankee. Several men were hit upon this same hillock, or immediately in rear of it; and I for one never crossed it without wondering whether I should get safely to the other side.

Another fatal spot was an exposed corner in the narrow terrace which our men had made in the bank, as a standing place whence to fire over the knoll.

"Don't go there, Captain," a soldier said to me when I first approached the place. "That's Dead Man's Corner. Five men have been killed there already."

I understood that Hubbard and Wrotnowski of Weitzel's staff both received their deathshots at Dead Man's Corner, on the 27th of May. Early on my first day in the gully, just as I had risen, smirched and damp, from my bed on the brick-colored earth, a still breathing corpse was brought down from this spot of sacrifice. A brave, handsome boy of our Company D, gay and smiling with the excitement of fighting, disdaining to cover himself, was reloading his rifle when a ball traversed his head, leaving two ghastly orifices through which the blood and brains exuded, mingling with his auburn curls. He uttered strong, loud gaspings; it seemed possible, listening to them, that he might yet live; but his eyes were fast closed and his ruddy cheek paling; in a few minutes he was dead.

We lost eight or ten men during that first day, partly from not knowing these dangerous localities, and partly from excess of zeal. Our fellows attempted to advance the position, leaped the knoll without orders, and took to the trees on the outer slope, and were only driven back after sharp fighting.

"Served me right. I'd no business there," said a suddenly enlightened Irishman, as he came in with a hole through his shoulder.

As the siege drew on and we found that there was plenty of danger without running after it, we all became more or less illuminated by this philosophy. It is a remark as old as sieges, that trench duty has a tendency to unfit men for field fighting. The habit of taking cover becomes stronger than the habit of moving in unison; and, moreover, the health is enfeebled by confinement, and the nervous system shaken by incessant peril.

The Eighth Vermont was soon moved farther to the right, and we of the Twelfth Connecticut had the gully to ourselves. Our life in it fell into military routine; the rule was one day at the parapet and two days off. On duty days we popped away at the enemy, or worked at strengthening our natural rampart. We laid a line of logs along the crest of the knoll, cut notches in them, and then put on another tier of logs, thus providing ourselves with portholes. With the patience of cats watching for mice the men would peer for hours through the portholes, waiting a chance to shoot a Rebel; and the faintest show of the crown of a hat above the hostile fortification, undistinguishable to the inexperienced eye, would draw a bullet. By dint of continual practice many of our fellows became admirable marksmen. During one of the truces the Confederates called to us, "Aha, you have some sharpshooters over there!"

After the surrender an officer of the Second Alabama told me that most of their casualties were cases of shots between the brim of the hat and the top of the head; and that having once held up a hoe handle to test our marksmanship, it was struck by no less than three bullets in as many minutes. The distance from parapet to parapet was not great; our men sighted it on their Enfields as one hundred and fifty yards; but it did not look so far, and we often exchanged taunts and challenges. Any eye not absolutely short sighted could distinguish the effect of our bullets in knocking splinters from the portholes or dust from the top of the earthworks.

The garrison gave us full as good as we sent. Several of our men were shot in the face through the portholes as they were taking aim. One of these unfortunates, I remember, drew his rifle back, set the butt on the ground, leaned the muzzle against the parapet, turned around, and fell lifeless. He had fired at the moment he was hit, and two or three eye-witnesses asserted that his bullet shivered the edge of the opposite porthole, so that in all probability he and his antagonist died together. It must be understood that these openings were but just large enough to protrude the barrel of a musket and take sight along it.

During our relief days we were quite as much shot at, without the comforting excitement of shooting. There was but one spot in the hollow, and that only a few yards square, where bullets never struck; and by some awkward providence it rarely fell to the lot of my company, no matter when we came off duty. I used to look with envy and longing at this nasty but wholesome patch of gutter. It was a land of peace, a city of refuge, thirty feet long by ten feet broad. Turning my back on its charmed tranquillity, where the dying never gasped and the wounded never groaned, I spread my rubber blanket in the mud or the sun according to the weather, lighted my pipe, and wondered when my bullet would come.

It must be stated that, excepting the canopy of the heavens, there was not a tent in the regiment. I do admit indeed, on recollection, that for two weeks or more I enjoyed the shelter of a white bed-coverlet, abstracted by my colored henchman George from I know not whose shanty or palace, which, being spread cunningly, kept off much sun and some rain. But on the 14th of June, while I was engaged in the storming party, certain vagrants from another regiment caused this improvised shelter tent to disappear. Little by little we built in the treeless portions of the gully huts of branches just high enough to admit us in a sitting posture. Over these we threw our rubber blankets during the showers and tried to imagine that we were thereby the drier. Being about to occupy the bivouac of Company F, which was going up to the parapet to relieve my company, I said to the commandant, Lieutenant Clark, "What a palace you have left me!"

"It looks nice," replied Clark, smiling doubtfully at the newly built green shanty which he was about quitting. "But it isn't all my fancy painted it. I had scarcely got comfortably settled in it and commenced reading a newspaper when a bullet went through the leading editorial."

As I was sitting at dinner beside this same domicile, a large tree, fifteen feet in rear of it, flew asunder under the blow of a cannon shot, the top plunging harmlessly across the bivouac of

Company K and scaring the first sergeant out of a sound sleep, while a splinter weighing ten pounds hissed over my head and fell between the feet of one of my own sergeants, Charles Collins. A minute afterward Collins was struck by a fatal bullet, which came from very nearly the opposite direction of the cannon shot. So much for the advantages of the shanty which Lieutenant Clark had put up, after due thought as to selecting a safe location. Our brigade commander met with similar tribulations in his search after a quiet residence. A large and comfortable-looking arbor of boughs had just been erected for him, when *screech* came a 12-pounder ball, and down came a great oak, smashing the dwelling into uninhabitability.

To escape this all-searching fire one of our officers dug for himself a "gopher-hole" in a little bank, and was much laughed at for his pains when a bullet went slap into it shortly after he had finished it. He was absent at the moment; but I came very near suffering in his place, for I was just then surveying and envying his housekeeping arrangements. Two soldiers who were standing at the mouth of the hole had a still narrower escape, the shot passing between their heads not six inches from either. When the owner returned and heard my jolly story he looked slightly disgusted, but nevertheless refused to sell out, and crawled in upon his blanket with a smile of desperate resignation.

About ten o'clock one evening, when profound peace had fallen from night upon Port Hudson and all its surroundings, we were startled from our slumbers by a tremendous explosion, succeeded a few seconds afterward by another. Mighty vibrations seemed to spread outward through the atmosphere, as ripples circle over the surface of water from the plunge of a stone. In a moment our gully swarmed with men muttering and questioning in astonishment. Running up the steep bank of the rampart, I beheld a meteor of war. Out of the black line of forest which crowned the hostile bluff came a fiery spark, flying straight toward us in silent swiftness. Then followed a sonorous, majestic basso-profundo *pu—m* which made night tremble. As the spark rose above us, as we turned our eyes upward to see it, it burst with a broad glare and was gone. Now came another report, a crashing *pa—m*, sharper, angrier than the first, but also grand, vibrating, stunning.

This was a 68-pounder shell. The first explosion was that of the gun, and the second that of the projectile. In either case the flash was visible some seconds before the detonation became audible; and that brief interval, during which we awaited possible death, was a suspense of superhuman grandeur. Six shots to our left; six directly over us; six to our right; then silence. Night after night for a week or more we were bombarded in this magnificent fashion. At first it was trying; but we soon found that the gunners could not depress the piece sufficiently to hit us; and after that we did not care a hardtack for their 68-pounder except as a spectacle. It did some little damage to our second line, we understood; but that was rather an agreeable piece of information than otherwise. Men in the front are always disposed to chuckle when their comrades in the rear get a share of the slaughtering.

Once we were pounded a little by our own artillery. On the last day of June the regiment was mustered for pay in the gully, the companies being brought one by one before the commanding officer (Lieutenant Colonel Peck), and the whole ceremony made as simple as possible in order not to attract the attention of the enemy. The last company had been reached; the men stood in line silent and statue-like with supported arms; the colonel was at the front with muster roll in his hand and lieutenant commanding by his side. As each man's name was called he answered "Here," came to a shoulder, and then an order.

The roll was half finished when suddenly there was a *whish, whish* in the air, and a spent 12-pounder shot passed over the muskets and dropped twenty feet in rear. A slight dip, a kind of courtesy, wavered through the line of arms; then they returned to their military level, while a grin glanced along the war-worn faces. The colonel turned his head, gave one stare of calm surprise, and resumed his reading. *Whish, whish* once more; another shot whispered in the track of the first; but this time the men were prepared, and the arms were steady; this time, too, the projectile flew higher and fell in the bivouac of the next regiment. Deliberately and calmly the roll was called to the end.

The company shouldered arms, faced to the right, ported arms, broke ranks, and went to its quarters.

No more shots; but still we were uneasy, for this fire came direct into the open mouth of our gully; and if it should be resumed with spirit our position would be hard to hold. The next day we learned that one of our own batteries, a mile and a half distant, had been our assailant. Aiming at a projecting angle of the Rebel works, it had elevated too high and sent its missiles clean over the mark into our quarters. Oddly enough the only person injured was the regimental coward of the 114th New York, a man who had shirked every fight, and who had dug for himself a gopher-hole unattainable by the fire of the garrison. The second ball found him out in his retreat, took off a leg and sent him into the other world. Poltroons being regarded with violent disfavor in the army, this tragedy was looked upon as little less than a special providence, and diffused a general sense of satisfaction. One man offered to show the commandant of the battery two or three more gopher-holes which he thought ought to be cleaned out.

Meantime the Rebels were as much worried by constant exposure to fire as ourselves. Not only did our artillery search every corner of the fortress, but our bullets sowed it, and even went clean over it into the Mississippi. On the very summit of the bluff, within a few rods of the river batteries, a man was putting a mug of beer to his lips when he was killed by a Minié ball which must have come at least a mile to find him. In front of us an officer had finished his tour of duty at the parapet and retired to the grove in its rear to rest, when he was shot through the body with a ramrod which one of our men discharged by accident. A little to our right an 8-inch shell from one of our mortar batteries fell just inside of the earthwork. A Rebel jumped over the mound, lay on the outer slope until the huge projectile exploded, and then dodged back again. Our men, instead of firing at him, gave him a hurrah in recognition of his coolness and dexterity.

Here I am reminded of an adventure of Andrew Bartram, a private of my company. Far to the left of our gully and nearly in front of the position which we had occupied on the 27th of May, the siegeworks had been pushed so near the rampart that the fatigue party, of which this man was one, could hear the voices of the defenders in conversation. Naturally curious and adventurous, he determined to risk his skin for the sake of obtaining a close look at his antagonists; and, taking advantage of the quiet of night and a fine moonlight, he left the covered way, scaled a slope, and found himself at the base of the earthwork.

Here, as the reader may suppose, he paused, lay low and considered. The men inside would certainly shoot him if they saw him; and the men outside might also make a mark of him, supposing him to be a Rebel. The result was that he resumed his hazardous journey, climbed the sloping mound on his hands and knees and cautiously peeped over it. There they were, immediately under his nose and almost within reach of his hand, a score or so of men in dirty grey or butternut, some lounging and others apparently sleeping. The scene was remarkable, but not altogether delightful, and he was soon satisfied with it. Sliding quietly down the face of the mound, he made a run for life, reached the covered way unseen, hurried to the nearest battery and reported the position of the Rebels. A couple of shells were pitched nicely into the spot indicated; and the shrieks which answered bore witness that they had done their pitiless duty. For this feat Bartram was made lieutenant in a Negro regiment.

Such are some of my experiences and observations in the matter of duty in the trenches. The thoughtful among my readers, those who care less for objective incidents than for their effect upon the human soul, will ask me if I liked the business. With a courage which entitles me to honorable mention at the headquarters of the veracities, I reply that I did not like it, except in some expansive moments when this or that stirring success filled me with excitement. Certain military authors who never heard a bullet whistle have written copiously for the marines, to the general effect that fighting is delightful. It is not; it is just tolerable; you can put up with it; but you can't honestly praise it. Bating a few flashes of elation which come in moments of triumph or in the height of a breathless charge, when "the air is all a yell and the earth is all a flame," it is much like being in a rich cholera district in the height of the season.

Profoundly, infinitely true, true of every species and of every individual, is the copybook maxim, "Self-preservation is the first law of nature." The man who does not dread to die or to be mutilated is a lunatic. The man who, dreading these things, still faces them for the sake of duty and honor is a hero.

b. A Night Attack

Our fighting at Port Hudson was not without its spice of variety. From time to time, as a relief to the monotony of being shot at every day a little, we made an attack and were shot at a good deal. On the 10th of June General Banks ordered a nocturnal reconnoissance on a grand scale, with the object, as I understood, of discovering where the enemy's artillery was posted, so that it might be knocked out of position by our own batteries previous to delivering a general assault. The whole line, six or eight miles in length, advanced sharpshooters, with instructions to be in position by midnight and then to open vigorously.

I had noticed premonitions of mischief during the day. A cavalry orderly from division headquarters had passed through our gully with dispatches for the brigade commander. And here I will honestly clear my breast of the confession that I dreaded the sight of these orderlies for the reason that they hardly ever made their appearance among us but we were shortly engaged in some unusual high cockalorum of heroism. It must be understood that by this time we had seen as much fighting as human nature can easily absorb inside of a month. Next after the orderly came another somewhat unwelcome personage, the adjutant, going from shanty to shanty with the message, "The colonel wishes to see the company commandants."

I distinctly remember the faces of the ten men who listened to the orders for the reconnoissance. They were grave, composed, businesslike; they were entirely and noticeably without any expression of excitement; they manifested neither gloom nor exultation. When the colonel had ceased speaking three or four purely practical questions were asked, and then the officers, separating without further conversation, returned quietly to their companies.

The orders which we received were singular, and to us at the time incomprehensible. Seven companies were to be formed at midnight behind the parapet, ready to advance at a moment's notice. Three companies were to pass over the knoll, cross the ravine, carry the enemy's works, and report their success, upon which they were to be supported by the others. The companies selected for the assault were the ones whose turn it would be to mount guard the next morning.

Knowing nothing then of General Banks's purpose to make the Rebels unmask their artillery, and remembering that our companies did not average thirty men apiece while the apron to be attacked was held by two regiments, we looked upon our instructions as simple madness. Of course, however, we prepared to obey them, ordering the cartridge boxes to be replenished, the canteens and havresacks filled, and the blankets slung. That is to say, we got ready to occupy the enemy's position precisely as if we expected to carry it.

The night was warm, damp, cloudy, and almost perfectly dark. A little before the hour appointed for the attack the seven reserve companies formed line in perfect silence along the inner slope of our natural parapet. No one spoke aloud; there was a very little whispering; the suspense was sombre, heavy, and hateful. Then, as quietly as possible, but nevertheless with a tell-tale clicking of canteens against bayonets, the fighting companies climbed upon the knoll and commenced to file over it.

Suddenly there came a screech of musketry from across the ravine, a hissing of bullets in flights over our heads, a crash of cannon to our right, whistling of grape, bursting of shells, shouts of officers, and groans of wounded. The Rebels in front had caught the sound of the advance and had opened upon it instantaneously with all their power. My lieutenant, leaning against a slim sapling, felt it struck by six bullets in something like as many minutes, so thickly did the fusillade fill the air with its messengers. Now, flowing with alarming rapidity considering the small force advanced, commenced the backward stream of wounded, a halting procession of haggard men climbing painfully over the parapet and sliding down the steep bank to lie till morning upon the hard earth of the basin. In the darkness our surgeon could do nothing more than lay a little dressing upon the hurts and saturate them with water.

The clouds had by this time gathered into storm, and gleams

of lightning showed me the sufferers. A group of two brothers, one eighteen the other sixteen, the elder supporting the younger, was imprinted upon my memory by this electric photography. The wounded boy was a character well known in the regiment, a fellow of infinite mischief, perpetually in the guardhouse for petty rascalities, noisy, restless, overflowing with animal spirits, and like many such, a headlong, heroic fighter. Young Porter, as everybody called him, was firing and yelling with his usual gayety when a bullet struck him in the groin. Turning to his brother, he said, "Bill, the d—d Rebs have hit me; help me in."

As he came over the rampart one of my men, not knowing that he was wounded, laughed out, "Aha, Porter, you've come back early!"

"D—n you," he replied, "you go out there and you'll come back early."

Walking down the bank, he groaned, "Oh, my God! don't walk so fast. I can't walk so fast. This d—d thing pains me clear up to my shoulder."

On examination it was found that a second ball had actually passed through his shoulder. So severe were this lad's injuries that it was not supposed possible that he could live; but six weeks afterward, as we lay at Donaldsonville, he rejoined the regiment, having run away from hospital with a stolen tent and boat.

Within ten minutes from the commencement of the attack the three captains of the advancing companies were brought in disabled. I was leaning against the bank near the edge of the gully, thinking, I suppose, how disagreeable it was to be there and how much better it was than to be outside, when, behold! that undesired messenger, the sergeant major.

"Captain," he said, "the colonel directs that you take command of the skirmishers and push them across the ravine."

Dreading it like a toothache, but nevertheless facing it as though I liked it, I ran a little to the left in search of a spot where the bullets were not flying too thick, and went over the parapet with a light step and a heavy heart. My first adventure in the blinding darkness was to roll into a rain gulch, twenty feet deep, through the branches of a felled tree, tearing off my sword belt and losing my sabre. I groped a moment for the last-named encumbrance, deemed so essential to an officer's honor; but could not find it, and did not see it again until the end of the siege gave me a chance to seek it in safety. Parenthetically I will state that it is now hanging beside me, restored by sandpaper to something like its original brightness, but deeply pockmarked with the rust incurred in its four weeks of unprotected bivouac.

I had my revolver in my hand when I fell, and I still held fast to it at the close of my descent, as I have seen a child cling to a plaything while performing somersaults down stairs. Clambering out of the gulch and directing my steps toward a spitting of musketry, I came upon Lieutenant Smith and six men of our Company D, who had established themselves in another of the many rainways which seamed the face of the hillside.

"Forward, boys!" I shouted. "We must carry the works. Forward!"

I remember distinctly the desperate look—seen by a lightning flash—which the brave boys cast at me before they charged out of their cover. It seemed to say, "Are you, too, mad? Well, if it must be—"

In answer to our hurrah the enemy's musketry howled and the air hissed with bullets. The first who reached the edge of our gulch fell groaning; and I had five men left with whom to storm Port Hudson. Satisfied that the attempt would be futile unless I could have at least one more soldier, I allowed the survivors to take cover and wondered what General Banks would do if he were in my place.

"I don't believe the men can be led any farther," observed the lieutenant.

"This is a new thing in our regiment, flinching from fire," I remarked.

"Yes, but it has been pretty bad out here. It was tremendous when we first came over."

"Where is the rest of the storming party?" I asked.

"God knows. A great many have been carried in. The rest, I suppose, are scattered all over the hillside, fighting behind stumps."

An occasional shot from the darkness around us corroborated this supposition. Evidently our storming column of six officers and ninety men had gone to pieces, some disabled and others having taken cover as skirmishers, while many no doubt had drifted back into the regimental bivouac. There is always a great deal of skulking in night fighting; first, because darkness renders the danger doubly terrific; and second, because the officers cannot watch the line.

"Stay where you are, Lieutenant," I said. "I will report matters to the colonel and be out again with orders."

On my way in I found two men, each behind a tree with rifle ready, waiting for a flash from the hostile rampart as a target. I had not far to go to reach our headquarters, for the skirmishers had only advanced a few yards down the hillside. I felt decidedly ticklish about the legs, knowing that the muskets of our reserve were on a level with them, and not being sure that they might not break out with a volley. It was as ugly a little promenade as I ever undertook.

"Captain, the orders are explicit," said the colonel in reply to my statement. "Advance, take the enemy's works, and report the fact."

Thinks I to myself, "I wish the person who gave the order had to execute it." Back I stumbled through the midnight to my tatter of a skirmish line, pondering over my task in despair. If any other man ever had so much to do, and so little to do it with, I should like to hear his story. To charge again was out of the question; my seven heroes had had all they wanted of that. Accordingly I gave orders to separate, take such cover as could be found, crawl ahead, and fire as skirmishers.

It was all done except the crawling ahead. The men were willing enough to crawl, but not toward the enemy. I did not blame them. If any one advanced he was liable to be shot in the darkness, not only by the Rebels but by his own comrades. I don't believe that King David's first three mighty ones would have made much progress under the circumstances. What added to our discouragement was the fact that no other regiment was firing. All around Port Hudson, at least as far as we could hear, there was dumb silence, except in front of the Twelfth Connecticut. Why this was I never knew, and can only guess a diversity of orders, or perhaps a widespread influenza of self-preservation.

Presently a storm of rain burst, and both sides ceased firing. I sat on a stump with my rubber blanket over my head, suffocating under the heat of it and conscious of much moistness in the way of drippings. After an hour or so the rain stopped, and we renewed our musketry. So wore on the most uncomfortable, disgusting, irrational night that I can remember.

At last daylight appeared: not sunrise, be it understood, but faint, dusky, misty dawn: a greyish imitation of light robed in fog. Lieutenant Allen of Company K now arrived from farther down the ravine and went into the lines after the stragglers of his command. Reappearing in the course of a few minutes with a dozen men, he had to expose himself recklessly in order to shame certain demoralized ones into advancing over the fatal knoll behind us. He was admirable, as he walked slowly to and fro at his full height, saying calmly, "Come along, men; you see there is no danger." Old Putnam, galloping up and down Charlestown Neck to encourage the Provincials through the ricochetting of the British artillery, was not finer.

Now we recommenced firing with spirit and kept it up until after sunrise, thinking all the time how absurd it was and wondering that we were not recalled. Just as the fog lifted and exposed us to the view of the enemy we heard from behind our rampart a shout, "Skirmishers, retire!"

It was a good thing to hear; but it was easier said than obeyed. The Second Alabama had a clean sweep into the gulch where we had collected; and it took all the stumps and jutting banks which we could find there to cover us. We were much in the condition of the Irishman in the runaway coach, who did not jump off because he had as much as he could do to hold on. But it was necessary to be lively; the fire was growing hotter every moment; the bullets were spatting closer and closer to our lurking places.

I claim some merit for superintending the evacuation so successfully as to have only one man hit in the process; although whether the men would not have got off just as well if left to themselves is of course an open question. I ordered one fellow up an almost invisible gutter, another through a thicket of blackberry bushes, another along some tufts of high grass, and, in short, put my people on as many lines of retreat as the ground would admit. I had about fifteen soldiers, and I sent them in thirty different directions.

One fine lad, the clerk of D Company, anxious to save the ordnance stores for which his captain was responsible, undertook to carry off the muskets of five wounded men, and thereby drew upon himself an unusual amount of attention from the enemy. I ground my teeth with helpless rage and anxiety as I heard the balls strike around him like axes wielded by demons. He was lying upon his face, crawling slowly and pulling the muskets after him by a gunstrap. He had nearly reached the little log parapet when he gave a cry, "They have hit me!"

Hands were extended to help him, and he was dragged over with no other harm than a flesh wound through the thigh, but without his precious charge of ordnance stores. When I got in he was hopping about cheerfully and telling the adventures of the night to his comrades of the reserve companies. Poor, brave little Nash! Twenty months later, at Cedar Creek, he died on the field of honor.

I was now left alone with Lieutenants Allen and Smith. "Gentlemen," I said, "you are officers; you are supposed to know enough to look out for yourselves; the devil take the hindmost."

Smith disappeared among the blackberries, or perhaps went underground, for I never saw him again till I got inside. Allen, over six feet high, bounded across the knoll with a length of stride which the Rebel officers remembered after the surrender as having set them a laughing. I surveyed the ground before me and pondered to the following purpose: "Here I am, a tolerably instructed man, having read *The Book of the Indians,* all of Cooper's novels, and some of the works of Captain Mayne Reid. If I can't be as cunning as a savage or a backwoodsman I ought to be shot."

For my road of retreat I selected a faint grassy hollow, perhaps six inches deep, which wound nearly to the top of the knoll before it disappeared. From the stump which sheltered me, and which had already received one bullet and been barely missed by others, I made a spring to the foot of this hollow and dropped in it on my face at full length. I suspect that the grass

completely hid me from the view of the Rebels, for not a shot
struck near me during my tedious creep to the summit of the
hillock. And yet it was very short grass; I thought it contempt-
ibly short as I scratched through it; an alderman would have
found it no protection.

I feel certain that my escape was owing entirely to the caution and dexterity with which I effected this to me memorable
change of base; and even to this day I chuckle over my good
management, believing that if the last of the Mohicans had
been present he would have paid me his most emphatic compliments. I did not properly creep, knowing that it would not do to
raise my back; I rather swam upon the ground, catching hold
of bunches of grass and dragging myself along. My ideas meanwhile were perfectly sane and calm, but very various in character, ranging from an expectation of a ball through the spine to a
recollection of Cooper's most celebrated Indians.

About a rod from the parapet the hollow disappeared and
the herbage became diminutive. Here was the ticklish point;
the moment I rose I would be seen. I sprang to my feet, shouted,
"Out of the way!" thought of the bayonets inside, wondered if
I should be impaled, made three leaps and was safe. I have seldom felt more victorious than at that instant when I became
conscious that I had done the Rebels. The repulse of the night
seemed insignificant compared with the broad-day triumph of
my escape from scores of practiced marksmen who were on the
watch to finish me.

I immediately went to the colonel and reported the skirmishing party all in. In this, however, I was mistaken, for about half
an hour afterward an anxious voice outside informed us that
another straggler had returned thus far from his adventurings
in the ravine. A canteen of water and havresack of biscuit were
thrown out to him, and he remained all day behind a stump,
coming in safe at nightfall.

Of the ninety or one hundred officers and men engaged in this
attack thirty-eight, or about two fifths, were killed or wounded.
The affair injured the morale of the regiment, for the men
thought they had been slaughtered uselessly, and naturally concluded that there was a person somewhere above them who did

not know what orders were good to issue. Even old soldiers rarely see the sense of being pushed out merely to draw the enemy's fire.

Our artillery now went to work upon the two pieces which had been unmasked to grape us, and soon had them silenced, with their wheels in the air and their muzzles pointing backward. The next day General Banks obtained another armistice to collect the dead and wounded of his skirmishing emprise. The Rebels in our front crowded their parapet, pointing out where one of our men lay lifeless at the bottom of the ravine, and demanding news of our three wounded captains. They had learned their names during the attack from Mullen, our sergeant major, a brave little fellow who had been sent out with orders to the officers, and who, being unable to find them in the darkness, had shouted for them all over the hillside. The dead man who was brought in to us was a horrible spectacle, swollen and perfectly black with putrefaction, filling our bivouac with an insupportable odor.

Chapter VIII

PORT HUDSON (*continued*)

a. The Assault of June 14th

EVER since May 27th, or a little later, there had been
nocturnal digging in the way of preparing approaches
for a second assault. Every night details from the advanced line of regiments repaired to a winding ravine, which
led up to the hostile bluff from a wood south of Weitzel's position, and labored to convert its zigzag gulch into a covered way.
The garrison made no sallies to interrupt this work and merely
harassed the pioneer parties with casual sharpshooting, which
did little harm in the darkness.

In due time we finished nearly half a mile of trench, with an
average depth of six feet and a breadth of about ten. As it was
mostly overlooked by the fortifications, it offered very imperfect
protection to an attacking column; and moreover it stopped
eighty yards short of the parapet, at a point which was completely exposed to the musketry of the garrison. Nevertheless,
for reasons more satisfactory to Generals Banks and Grant than
to the men who had to do the storming, it was decided to risk an
assault without making a tenth part of the preparations which
enabled the French to carry the Malakoff.

About one in the morning of June 14th we of the Twelfth
were waked up and formed in column of march. Not an order
was uttered aloud; the instructions were carried to the company
commandants by the sergeant major; and we moved off stealthily while a detachment from some reserve regiment occupied our
position. Silently and in darkness we stumbled through a long
detour (it seemed like miles) of forest road, halting at last in
the grove of noble magnolias where Gardner had shelled and
graped us on the 27th of May. Here were regiments and batteries, dimly visible in the sultry gloom, and noiseless as an

army of ghosts. Our lieutenant colonel now called the captains together and murmured a brief statement of the duties before us. The Twelfth and the Seventy-fifth New York were to lead the column through the covered way, and then to spread along the base of the ramparts as skirmishers, and keep down the fire of the defenders.

Now ensued a long, darkling, solemn suspense. We sat down on the ground and talked in rare murmurs. From faraway sombre distances came a faint rattle of picket musketry, perhaps meant to deceive the garrison as to the true point of attack. An owl near us twice sent forth a prolonged, scoffing, bodeful *tu who, tu who*. It was Sunday morning, and I could hear the men muttering about it, anticipating ill luck. My belief is that they would have attacked with much greater willingness and confidence on any other day of the week.

After an hour or so came an order, whispered from company to company, to stand to arms. We rose, marched by the right flank a short distance, and were halted by some staff officer. Then followed a countermarch; then another halt and an about-face; then we stumbled onward again; all this in the darkness. The final result of this blindman's buff was that our five right companies did not observe the departure of the others and remained in place until broad daylight.

Meanwhile the left wing, groping after the Seventy-fifth New York, stumbled into the covered way, followed by the Eighth Vermont and other regiments. Here we marched very slowly, halting from time to time, I know not why. Now and then a Rebel bullet struck the shielding of the trench, or penetrated it and hissed among us with random ferocity. The men crouched a little and were clearly not in good spirits, perhaps because of our unlucky night attack of the 10th, perhaps because they had been somewhat worn down by three weeks of duty in the trenches. In my opinion it would have been wiser to head the column with fresh regiments from the reserve.

A grey dawn, all the greyer and dimmer for a thick mist, stole upon us before we neared the rampart. Of a sudden a furious roar of musketry broke forth in front, followed by the charging yell of the Seventy-fifth as it stumbled out of the covered way. Immediately we of the Twelfth surged forward; but now came unexpected causes of delay and confusion. Our unfinished trench rapidly dwindled into a mere natural rain gulch which presently ended in two branches leading in different directions. There was an inevitable hesitation and slowing in the advance; and long before we could get out of our contracted ditch, it was jammed with struggling men; for the wounded of the Seventy-fifth at once began tumbling back into it for shelter.

I had plenty of time to study these heroic sufferers, for I was captain of the rearmost of our five companies. Hurt and bloody as they were, they were temporarily in boisterous spirits, cheering us on while they impeded us. "Hurry up, boys! They want you ahead," shouted one fellow, whose face was covered with blood, excepting his huge Roman nose. He reeled against me and then staggered on rearward, repeating, "Hurry, boys! The Seventy-fifth needs you."

Some hours later I found a broad splash of blood—this man's perhaps—in the bottom of the iron cup which I carried slung to my belt.

We of the Twelfth were scarcely out of the covered way when we were broken up and misled by the mist and confusion. Our leading company, under Lieutenant Theodore Clark, filed along the right-hand gulch and made for the fortifications. But the next company, being checked by the rush of wounded, lost sight of Clark and filed to the left, blindly followed by the three others including mine. It was impossible to see or to divine that we were diverging from the fighting point. Around us was a chaos of fog and smoke, with yelling men rushing through it in various directions, officers gathering a platoon or two and then charging by guesswork, while the Southern cross fire seemed to storm in from all quarters. The fortifications were not visible, and the rattle of musketry was no guide, for it was everywhere.

I supposed that we were streaming along the skirts of the rampart with a view to take position as skirmishers and stop the parapet firing. But after marching for some minutes the noise of battle became noticeably duller. Then the head of the little column halted, and, running forward to learn the meaning of it, I discovered that we had reached the precipitous end of a deep gully and could advance no farther. Being the senior officer present, I now took command of the detachment and sent skirmishers up the banks to look for something to shoot at. One of them was killed immediately, perhaps by a Rebel sharp-shooter, perhaps by a random bullet. Meantime we heard voices, from somewhere in the fog, shouting, "Stop that firing!"

Were these cries addressed to us? Twice I opened fire, and twice I ordered it to cease, fearing lest I should damage our own people. It was a ridiculous situation, and I felt wofully ashamed of it, though unable to see my way out of it. All this while rifle balls were spatting furiously into our gully, and Port Hudson was roaring within two hundred yards of us, as invisible as if it had been in another planet. Midnight darkness would have shown the flashes of the guns, but the morning fog hid them completely.

I had lost several men in this blind, useless skirmish when our sergeant major found us and pointed out the direction of the fortifications. The colonel and adjutant, he said, were up there alone, and the right wing of the regiment was probably back in the woods. Under my orders the four companies in the gully faced about and charged on a run for a knoll which seemed to me about fifty yards from the parapet. I wonder that any of us got there unwounded, for the balls and buckshot skipped along the earth like hail. Private Hunter, as he trotted crouching by my side, looked up dolefully in my face and groaned, "Oh, Captain, ain't this awful!"

"Not a bit of it, Hunter," I laughed, not because I liked the situation, but because a captain must do his duty. Still, I was really glad to get out of our ridiculous no-thoroughfare, and I cheered my men along with a fairly honest light-heartedness, waving my rubber blanket for lack of a better flag. I learned afterward that one of Weitzel's aides, who was watching us from the head of the covered way, reported me to division head-quarters for valiant conduct. Well, I was doing the best I could; but practically it amounted to little; we soon halted.

The colonel and adjutant and many others were behind the knoll which I have mentioned. We passed them, but nobody followed us, and nobody said, "Forward." So the four companies spread out as skirmishers along the crest and opened a slow fire in response to the fire of the parapet. There was nothing to be done but sharpshooting, for the main column of assault had already gone to pieces. Some scores of men from its shattered regiments were with us; and hundreds more, I was told, had dropped back into the covered way. Dead bodies lay about in every direction, and the hospital squads were carrying off the wounded.

Meantime Lieutenant Clark had accomplished the only notable deed which fell that day to the Twelfth Connecticut. On emerging from the trenches he had filed to the right and groped his way up a bare slope to within sight of the rampart. There he was discovered by Van Petten, the brave commander of the 160th New York, who had stolen forward alone to reconnoitre.

"Lieutenant," said the colonel, "my regiment is back there in the fog. Do you jump in at once, and we will follow you."

Clark saluted and promptly moved forward, but he moved alone. Van Petten searched for his regiment in vain; either it had changed position, or he had lost his bearings. Clark reached the ditch and stealthily climbed the parapet without venturing to utter an order. But his twenty-five or thirty soldiers flinched; they did not believe that they could take Port Hudson unassisted; and they stuck fast in the ditch, staring about them for the 160th. Clark actually stood on the rampart for a few seconds without being fired at by the astonished Rebels who knelt inside. Then, giving up his hopeless emprise, he slid down to his men, and the little detachment leaked back into the fog, rejoining our regiment with trifling loss.

"The Rebs just there were not shooting much," was Clark's brief explanation of his singular escape. It would seem, therefore, that the front which he reached was weakly guarded, and that, if the 160th could have found it, a lodgement might have been effected. But this is by no means certain, for the Fourth Wisconsin and Eighth New Hampshire broke in at another point and were slaughtered out by close musketry, the former regiment being reduced to sixty-five muskets and the latter to about a hundred.

The main storming column, the one to which I belonged, had been most injudiciously directed. The covered way debouched right under a priest-cap, that is a large bastion with a re-entering angle, which delivered a murderous cross fire of buck and ball. Even our leading regiment, the admirably disciplined

Seventy-fifth New York, led by the heroic Lieutenant Colonel Babcock, had only been able to reach the ditch. Moreover, if we had got inside, we should have found a strong line there, protected by grenades attached to wires and supported by a reserve. Gardner had divined, from the direction of our trenches, that we meant to storm this bastion, and had used all his West Point science to put it in a good state of defence. A Confederate officer told me after the siege that we should have been blown out of it if we had entered it.

Cotton bags to fill the ditch and hand grenades to throw over the parapet had been furnished to two of our regiments; but they were both, I believe, nine-months' organizations, and they did not, as battalions, get near the defences. So far as could be seen where I was engaged, only one man reached the ditch and tossed his grenade into the bastion. That man lay near me, dying from a terrible wound through the abdomen, his fair face growing whiter with every laboring breath and his light blue eyes fixed vacantly on the glaring sky. He was about twenty-seven and looked to me like a respectable, intelligent American mechanic, probably a husband and father. I glanced at him pitifully from time to time as he patiently and silently drew towards his end. Such individual cases of suffering are far more moving than a broad spectacle of slaughter.

Meantime the assault, although gone to fragments, was not yet over. Detachments which had got lost during the night found their way one after the other to the front and made their unsupported, hopeless rushes. Hearing a shout on our left rear, I looked thither and saw ninety or a hundred men double-quicking toward the fortifications, led on by a tall officer who ran ten or fifteen paces in front of the swarm. The sharpshooters behind the rampart turned their fire on this slender attack with telling effect. Several men dropped; one faced about and ran twenty or thirty yards before he fell; others took to the cover of rocks or thickets. Here and there the bravest paused and fluctuated, whereupon their valiant leader would call them on with a shout, and then they would rush after him again.

But when the charge had almost reached the parapet, the thirty or forty survivors suddenly lost heart and dropped on their faces in a grassy hollow which offered some deceptive show of shelter. The officer turned angrily upon them; he cheered them and stormed at them; but his gallantry was in vain. At last, violently sheathing his sword, he turned from them with an air of contempt and strode deliberately down to the knoll where I was posted.

I never saw a more superbly heroic figure than he was in this whole affair, nor did I ever see another man who so distinctly seemed to bear a charmed life. It was impossible to understand why he should not have been pierced by a dozen bullets, unless we may suppose that the Southerners spared him out of admiration for his courage. He was a dark, handsome fellow of about thirty, with black eyes, black mustache and a dashing air. I regret to say that I cannot give his name, and merely learned that he was a captain in the 133d New York who had assumed command of one wing of the regiment, the other having gone astray in the confusion of the night.

Of course we had resumed our sharpshooting to support this forlorn hope. But presently we were obliged to crouch before our own artillery, half a mile or more to the rear, which opened fiercely upon the parapet. For a few minutes the shells screeched over us in startling proximity, some of them bursting too soon and sending down their detestable splinters among us, though without hitting any one.

Then this ended, and there came a lull. We stopped our musketry, and the defenders stopped theirs. The pitiless sun of Louisiana flamed at us until it seemed as if we should go mad. Stragglers from all quarters, men and officers from a dozen shattered regiments, drifted into the shelter of our knoll, seated themselves on the steaming earth, and waited. Our own missing five companies joined us, notwithstanding that the covered way was now crammed with dead and wounded, with hospital attendants and with skulkers. But there was nothing for the fresh men to do, and they sat down like the rest in whatever shelter they could find.

Our general purpose, I believe, was to hold on till night, or till we got orders from the rear. The ranking officer present was a colonel of a nine-months' regiment who had perhaps never been under fire before, and who certainly did not know what to do. At last, probably about ten in the forenoon, some one said, "There is the reserve."

Looking rearward, I saw a black swarm of men climbing out of the covered way near its entrance, and forming for an attack in line. There were three regiments, but I only know that two of them were the First Louisiana and the Thirteenth Connecticut, and that the whole force did not appear to be more than eight hundred strong. It was commanded by Colonel Holcomb of the First, formerly major of the Thirteenth, a good and brave officer.

Some of us were now exultant with hope of final success. But I saw that the column must climb six hundred yards in the face of musketry, and I did not expect anything from such tactics but repulse. The line pushed on steadily so long as the Confederates withheld their fire. But presently it toilsomely surmounted a low crest and made a panting effort to break forward on a double. Then the storm of bullets struck it; the gallant leader fell in sight of all his men as he mounted a stump and waved them on with his sabre; and instantaneously there came a hasty recoil down the slope. Many straggled back into the covered way, and many more ran forward along its course till they reached our position, where they joined the mixed rabble behind the knoll.

It was a discouraged and feeble effort to accomplish what seemed to me an impossibility. A more resolute push would probably have ended in murderous repulse, for by now a large part of the garrison had been concentrated on the front which we were attacking, and one man inside an earthwork is good for three outside.

The defeat of the reserve left us in a state of sullen despondency. Our fight seemed to be over; but not so that of the Rebels. Every now and then a cry or a lurching fall gave notice that some bullet had found its mark. Eight men dropped successively on a single low hillock which our knoll and its brushwood did not quite hide from the parapet. Noticing a soldier with torn clothing, I asked him if he had been hit.

"Mighty near it," he grumbled. "Those cusses jest shot my pipe square out of my trousers' pocket. Look at that hole, now!

and my time up three days ago! I wish I was in Massachusetts. Catch me again in a nine-months' regiment, or any other kind of regiment!"

A little later I witnessed another exhibition of the spirit which usually marks a short-term enlistment. One of Grover's aides came up with an order for the ranking officer present to form us all in close column, lead us over the crest on a run, and take Port Hudson. A nine-months' colonel put us in proper shape, and then looked with dismay at his pitiable army. It was composed of at least half a dozen regiments, and it numbered not more than eight hundred men, all jaded and dispirited.

"Now go back to General Grover," said the colonel to the aide. "Tell him that I have formed the column, and that, if he wants it to charge, he may come and lead it. I for my part am not going to take it into that slaughter pen."

This defiance cost him his commission, and of course properly, for while he was correct in judging that an assault would fail, he had no right to utter flat disobedience and send taunting messages to superiors. He was a tall, powerful man, with a rosy blond complexion, worried and indignant in expression, but not scared.

After this adventure we got no further behests to charge. We laid ourselves down and waited patiently for night. The hospital squads worked faithfully at their woful duty, and by latter afternoon had cleared the covered way of wounded. Then the company cooks and the officers' servants brought us our meagre supper of hardtack and coffee. It was a strange meal; not but what the fare was familiar enough; but the surroundings were unusually dismal. I remember a man seated on a stump who chewed manfully at his hard rations while a comrade tried to dig a buckshot out of his skull with a jacknife.

"G—d damn it! can't you start it?" grumbled this unsanctified sufferer. "Dig in like hell!"

When darkness came on, the Twelfth posted pickets and then fell asleep behind its bloodstained crest. We were within sixty yards of the rampart, but I slumbered promptly and without dreams. A little after midnight we were stealthily awakened and ordered to return as quietly as possible to our old position. My sergeant, Weber, shook the man next him and discovered that he was stone dead, perhaps killed in his sleep. With the utmost caution we picked our steps back to the covered way and tramped somnolently homeward to our well-known gully, reaching it about daybreak. Thus ended what I saw of the second attack on Port Hudson.

It was the only fight that I ever went into with an expectation of being hit; and perhaps the cause of the presentiment may be philosophically worthy of notice. Two days before the assault, as I was crossing a dangerous hillock just in rear of our bivouac, a Minié buzzed through the trees on my right, glanced downward from a branch to a prostrate log, and then glanced across my right leg.

The human intellect is capable of running several trains of thought at once. I heard the bullet singing hoarsely on its way and consciously sent an instantaneous malediction after it, while I hastened to pull up the leg of my trousers and see if the bone were broken, remembering what a bad thing it was to have an amputation in such hot weather. Great was my satisfaction when I found that no important harm had been done. A hole in my dirty pantaloons, a slight abrasion on the shin, and a large bruise, which soon bloomed into blue and saffron, were the only results. My main feeling so far was exultation at the escape. The cause of the presentiment of evil was yet to come.

When the accident and its harmless nature became known in my company, my veteran sergeant, Weber, muttered, "It is a warning."

"What is that, Weber?" I asked.

"Oh, it is a foolish saying, Captain. But we used to say, when a bullet merely drew blood, that it was a forerunner of another that would kill."

I am as little superstitious as a human being can well be, but Weber's speech made me very uncomfortable till the 14th of June was over. I went into the assault with a gloomy expectation of "the bullet that would kill," and hardly forgot it for a quarter of an hour together during the whole day. Even at night, while moving stealthily into the covered way, I still had a fear of the coming of that fated bullet; and when I emerged from the trenches, practically beyond the reach of hostile musketry, I experienced a distinct sense of elation at having baffled Destiny.

Moreover, this one victory knocked out the presentiment, and I never had a second.

The failure of the assault of June 14th is easily explained. The majority of assaults fail or succeed only by chance; and this is especially true when the defenders are in general good shots. An old colonel of our regular army used to say that, if an American gets into an earthwork, the devil himself can't put him out. Thus it was very unlikely that we would carry Port Hudson unless we were favored by scientific and thoroughly constructed approaches.

But this was not the case: the covered way was too narrow, it was too shallow, and it was too short: it jammed the troops, it did not protect them, and it did not take them far enough: in fact, it was more of a hindrance and nuisance than a help. We had to struggle out of it individually, gather hastily in feeble, unorganized squads, and then run a hundred yards uphill, all under a hailstorm of buck and ball.

Another cause of disaster (probably unavoidable) was the fact that we took position for the attack by night, many commands being thereby dislocated and belated, or lost altogether out of the column. Not more than six thousand troops reached the fighting line, and of these about fifteen hundred were killed or wounded, while twenty or thirty were taken prisoners inside.* Obviously the men fought well enough to win, if circumstances had favored them.

I must add that there was a strange lack of commanders at the vital points. Not a single general, and not a single regular officer that I know of, went near the ramparts during the whole day. The entire storming business was left to the management of volunteer colonels and lieutenant colonels, many of them belonging to nine-months' regiments, and none of them acquainted with the mysteries of fortifications. The ablest of these, Colonel Paine, fell at the foot of the parapet; and with him fell what little military genius we had anywhere near the parapet.†

Of course I do not pretend that Banks, or his chief of staff,

---

* Total loss, 1,805; including killed, 216; wounded, 1,401; missing, 188. In general, the class of "missing" includes some killed and wounded, frequently as many as 50 per cent, and sometimes more.

† He received the commission of brigadier general a day or two after the assault.

Weitzel, should have been up with the stormers. But there were other high officers, such as commanders of brigades and divisions, who might surely have granted us their immediate direction. It is certain that during all that bloody daybreak, while there was still a chance of success, we direly needed the guidance and encouragement of a general.

b. Closing Operations

After the assault came twenty-four days more of sharpshooting. We grew weak and nervous under the influences of summer heat, confinement, bad food, and constant exposure to danger. Men who had done well enough in battle broke down under the monotonous worry, and went to the rear invalided. From rain, perspiration, sleeping on the ground, and lack of water for washing, our clothing became stiffened and caked with inground mud. Lice appeared, increased, swarmed, infesting the entire gully, dropping upon us from the dry leaves of our bough-built shanties, and making life a disgrace as well as a nuisance. Excepting a three-days' raid into our rear to cover foragers and hunt Rebel raiders, the brigade had no relief for six weeks from the close musketry of the trenches.

Nor did we have any of those irregular truces, those mutual understandings not to fire, which were known along other portions of the line. Every day we shot at each other across the ravine from morning to night. It was a lazy, monotonous, sickening, murderous, unnatural, uncivilized mode of being. We passed our time like Comanches and New Zealanders; when we were not fighting we ate, lounged, smoked, and slept. Some of the officers tried sharpshooting, but I could never bring myself to what seemed like taking human life in pure gayety, and I had not as yet learned to play euchre. Thus I had no amusement beyond occasional old newspapers and rare walks to the position of some neighboring battery or regiment.

Meantime General Banks was preparing for another assault and offering various glories to volunteers for the forlorn hope. I observed that the regiments which had suffered most severely hitherto sent up very few names for the "roll of honor." For instance the Eighth New Hampshire, one of the most gallant organizations that I ever knew, but which had already lost more than two thirds of its numbers in our unhappy assaults, did not furnish a single officer or soldier. The thirty or forty who went from my regiment were a curious medley as to character, some of them being our very best and bravest men, while others were mere rapscallions, whose sole object was, probably, to get the whiskey ration issued to the forlorn hope. I did not volunteer; our only field officer was wounded, and I was the senior captain present; and I naturally preferred the chance of leading a regiment to the certainty of leading a company.

There was no doubt that the brigade would be put in; on what occasion had it ever been left out?

Once we were marched back to corps headquarters, formed in a hollow square, and treated to an encouraging speech from General Banks. One colonel, who admired the discourse, remarked that it was fit to be pronounced in the United States Senate. Another colonel, who did not admire it, replied that it was just fit. At the conclusion of the oratory our brigade commander called out, "Three cheers for General Banks!" whereupon the officers hurrahed loyally while the men looked on in sullen silence. Volunteers rarely believe that anybody but their commander is to blame when they are beaten, and will not make a show of enthusiasm if they do not feel it.

Finally came news that Vicksburg had surrendered, and then a mighty hurrah ran around Port Hudson, like the prophetic uproar of ramshorns around Jericho.

"What are you yelling about?" an Alabamian called to us from across the ravine.

"Vicksburg has gone up!" a score of voices shouted.

"Hell!" was the compendious reply, reminding one of Cambronne at Waterloo, as told by Victor Hugo.

Then came quiet, flags of truce, treatings for terms, and capitulation. Grand officials at headquarters got mellow together, while the lower sort mingled and prattled all along the lines. Bowie knives were exchanged for tobacco and Confederate buttons for spoonfuls of coffee. It was, "How are you, Reb?" and, "How are you, Yank?" and, "Bully for you, old boy!" and, "Now you've got us!" all through a hot summer's day. Never were fellows more friendly than the very fellows who but a few hours before were aiming bullets at each other's craniums.

I soon discovered that the Southern officers, not without good reason, were exceedingly proud of their obstinate defence. They often alluded to the fact that they had held out until they were at the point of starvation, reduced to an ear of corn a day, and such rats and mule meat as the sharpest foraging might furnish. They had surrendered, they said, because Vicksburg had; yes, they bragged not a little of having outlasted Pemberton. Nevertheless, their provisions would have been quite gone in three days more; and then they would have had to come down, Vicksburg or no Vicksburg.* One of our captains accepted an invitation to dine with these gentlemen and found broiled rat a better dish than he had expected.

"Well, you have cut the Confederacy in two," said one officer to me. "But we shall not give up the contest, and I think we shall tire you out at last."

Did he live, I wonder, to see the fate of his prophecy?

The defence of Port Hudson was stubborn, and perhaps it was valiant enough for all wise purposes, but it was not marked by venturesomeness or military genius. During the forty-five days which we passed before it, without an entrenchment and covering a line of eight miles, there was no attempt at a sally. Gardner, like Pemberton at Vicksburg, contented himself with lying behind his parapets and shooting over them. A pair of Turkish pashas would have been quite as enterprising and inventive.

On our part there was equal stubbornness, and there was also considerable audacity. Ten days before the surrender Banks knew that Taylor's column threatened New Orleans, where Emory was marching troops out by night and in by day to simulate re-enforcements. At the end of the siege we mustered about thirteen thousand effective men to hold our enormous front and cover our rear. Four thousand had been killed or wounded in the two assaults and by the incessant sharpshooting in the trenches. In the whole department there were eleven thousand men in hospital.

Yet Banks stuck fast to Port Hudson, and for this he deserves

* Vicksburg surrendered July 4th, and Port Hudson July 8th, 1863.

much credit. His prize was a strong entrenched camp, fifty-one pieces of artillery, six thousand five hundred prisoners *, and the opening of the lower Mississippi. The loss of the garrison during the siege had been about eight hundred.

* In his report to Major General H. W. Halleck, General Banks gave the total of prisoners as being "over 5,500." See *The War of the Rebellion* . . . *Official Records,* Ser. I, Vol. XXVI, Part I, 55. (Ed.)

Chapter IX

The capture of the two Confederate fortresses on the Mississippi coincided with Lee's repulse at Gettysburg. The ability Grant had shown in conducting his campaign encouraged the North to believe that it had a commander whose military skill was equal to that of the Southern generals. In addition, the winning of Tennessee in the fall of 1863 proved conclusively that the fortunes of war must eventually favor the Union cause.

When it appeared, during the summer of 1863, that her husband would remain in the field for several months, Mrs. De Forest went to Europe. Her trip was poorly timed, however, for the close of the campaign against Port Hudson presented the possibility of the captain's securing a furlough. Though she changed her plans, went immediately to London, and embarked on the *City of New York,* she arrived in the United States too late for De Forest to get a leave. By that time the regiment was so short of officers that he was in command. A detail had to go home for conscripts, he admitted in a letter to his brother, but, inasmuch as he had to make the appointments, he could not designate himself as a member of the detachment. As a result, he had to endure the heat of August in Brashear City, "one of the sickliest spots in Louisiana." "The hardy fellows" of the Twelfth Connecticut, he wrote home, became "fever-stricken fast." (Ed.)

AFTER PORT HUDSON

Port Hudson, July 10, 1863.

EXCUSE this wofully soiled paper. It is as clean as it can be after having been treasured for a week in the dirty pocket of a very dirty captain. You can hardly imagine how unclean and how ragged our regiment is, officers as well as soldiers. On all sides I can see great patches of bare skin showing through tattered shirts and trousers. I have but one suit, and so cannot wash it. My pantaloons will almost stand alone, so stiff are they with a dried mixture of dust, mud, showers and perspiration.

I look forward with longing unutterable to the day when I shall be able to substitute decent clothing for the whole foul encumbrance. I am far less out of humor with my wretched food which has consisted for weeks of little else than fried or boiled doughballs with an occasional seasoning of blackberries or of a minute slice of rusty bacon. It is rather surprising that under such circumstances we of the Twelfth are fairly healthy and show few men on the sick list compared with some other regiments. In killed and wounded we have been lucky, losing but little over a hundred out of about four hundred, while the Eighth New Hampshire and Fourth Wisconsin have been nearly exterminated.

You will have heard before this reaches you of the surrender of Port Hudson. It is reported that our brigade will sail tomorrow for Donaldsonville to hunt Taylor out of the Lafourche country. I dread this expedition because it will probably involve some hot marching. Moreover, I want my pay, now overdue for several weeks, and I want a chance to write up my company books and property returns, which are terribly behindhand. But I must not grumble; we have got Port Hudson.

I hope, with some misgivings, that you have received my letters from here. We have been surrounded by Rebel troopers who picked up stragglers and intercepted trains.

Donaldsonville, Louisiana, July 14, 1863.

WE arrived here too late to give our brigade any fighting. The Southerners had already assaulted Fort Taylor and fared as badly as we did in assaulting Port Hudson, although our garrison here numbered less than two hundred, including invalids.

They lingered in the neighborhood, however, and had a brush yesterday with Grover, getting the best of him, I believe. At any rate, we were called on to hurry to the rescue, and we met quite a number of retiring stragglers, not all of them wounded. One of these fellows paid us a compliment which made me smile.

"What troops are those?" he asked. "Weitzel's brigade, hey! Oh, *they'll* give it to 'em!" Here he cut a caper of exultation, and then continued his retreat.

We formed line in an open field confronting a forest of tall trees mingled with thickets. Then somebody's aide rode up and exhorted us not to be startled by the tactics of the enemy, who, he said, attacked with both cavalry and infantry, uttering deafening yells. A grin ran along the line of war-beaten faces at the idea of telling Weitzel's brigade not to let itself be scared by running and hallooing. We were even anxious for a field fight, remembering angrily our hopeless struggles against fortifications, and believing that we could win an easy vengeance on open ground.

But there was no attack; we sat down in rank and waited under a hot sun for hours; then we marched back to our dirty bivouac and our famine rations. For there is no foraging hereabouts, and the officers are at the point of starvation.

Brashear City, Louisiana, July 29, 1863.

WE had not been long at Donaldsonville when Banks made a call for two picked regiments for special service, and General Grover did Connecticut the honor to select the Twelfth and Thirteenth. We hurried to New Orleans in the steamer *Crescent;* lingered there a day or two, as is usual in military matters, one seldom knows why; then sailed around to this place by way of the Mississippi and the Gulf. It seems that our errand was to cut off the escape of Dick Taylor across the Atchafalaya, while a column should follow him by land from Donaldsonville through the Lafourche country. But we reached here a few hours too late and merely caught a score or two of stragglers.

You will remember that this was our station before we set out for Pattersonville and Port Hudson, and that during our absence the Rebels surprised our garrison of raw troops and captured everything. My baggage went with the rest: my dress uniform and cloak and sash: my father's venerable gold watch: your portrait and the lock of curling hair. Gone too are my books and papers, so that my company business is in almost hopeless confusion, and meanwhile the War Department is threatening to stop my pay. Those clerks seem to think that an officer can make out returns on the march or in the midst of a battle.

No money yet; our paymaster reached Donaldsonville the day after we left; and now we shall get nothing till the road is open between here and New Orleans. I came uncomfortably near starving on the *Crescent*. Two borrowed dollars were all that I had for the voyage, and the meals at the cabin table were fifty cents each. The first day I had breakfast and supper, going without dinner. The next day I had breakfast only; the third day I had dinner only. Then came twenty-four hungry hours during which I ate nothing but a slice of watermelon given me by another officer. The men were on half rations, or I might have begged some hardtack of them, though such begging is not considered proper in an officer. When I reached shore I could hardly utter an order and was in very poor condition for fighting, if we had found any. My first meal here, foraged I don't know how by my man George, was a tin plate full of fried onions, and nothing else. You can't imagine how delicious and restorative I found it.

The heat is tremendous. Flies are thicker than in Egypt, and mosquitoes thicker than in Guilford. But it is astonishing how healthy and contented our bronzed veterans are. They build themselves hovels of rails and boards, bake under them like potatoes in hot ashes, and grumble at nothing but the lack of tobacco. A soldier is not a hero in fighting alone; his patience under hardship, privation and sickness is equally heroic; sometimes I feel disposed to put him on a level with the martyrs.

Brashear City, August 25, 1863.

WE were paid ten days ago, and I wrote you the day following. I am well off for food now, but as badly off for clothing as ever, there being no tailors in Brashear City. I command the regiment in my dirty blouse, my bullet-torn Port Hudson trousers, and my knit woolen shirt patched at the elbows with blue cotton. When the lieutenant colonel returns I shall ask leave to go to New Orleans and get a decent outfit of raiment.

We have no tents as yet, but some of my soldiers have put up a board shanty for me, and I feel as if I were in a palace. It is really wonderful what a convenience a house is, and how the possession of one fosters vanity. But I am afraid that I shall catch cold sleeping under a roof, or that I shall get demoralized by so much luxury, like Hannibal's army at Capua.

Our regiment has taken a bad turn within a fortnight; the swamp fever, or country fever, is playing the mischief with it. Out of nearly four hundred men whom we brought here only about two hundred are fit for duty. At dress parade last evening (deducting the guard of course) we turned out an average of less than fourteen men per company. Two funerals yesterday, and as many today, but none of them mine. Of course I may take the fever yet, but so far I show no signs of it.

Brashear City, Louisiana, (no date).

WE have lost Lieutenant Allen who distinguished himself by his cool gallantry * during our night attack at Port Hudson. After coming off guard one morning he wandered about camp with a strange downcast air, complaining to one and another

* See page 129. (Ed.)

that people were slandering him. We thought this odd, but we suspected nothing serious till afternoon, when I was told that he had disappeared.

I turned out the regiment, deployed it in skirmish line, and started it across the plain in our rear. We soon found him lying among some tall reeds, his throat haggled with a penknife, and speech gone.* In an insane access of country fever he had committed suicide. His funeral was a pitiable and gloomy spectacle; there were but two officers to follow him, one of them with his arm in a sling; there was but one drummer, and not a single fifer, for the dead march.

Two thirds of the regiment are buried or in hospital. It is woful to see how nearly destitute of comforts and of attendance the sick are. They cannot be kept in their wretched bunks, but stagger about, jabbering and muttering insanities, till they lie down and die in their ragged, dirty uniforms. There are not enough well men to take care of them, and at the same time to perform our oppressive guard duty. The hospital has been transferred to an islet in the bay, half a mile from camp; but we can distinctly hear the screams and howls of the patients in their crazy fits. It is woful to see a battalion of four hundred choice veterans thus ruined in a few weeks. I have plenty of chance to grieve over others, for I am myself in excellent health, far better than at Camp Parapet.

One marvels what we should be able to do with the Rebels if they should attack us. They are watching us (in small numbers, I think) from the other bank of the broad Atchafalaya. As I was inspecting pickets the other day three Butternuts came out of cover, and one of them took the trouble to fire at me. I could see him aiming, but as the distance across was a full half mile, I did not believe he could hit me, and so let my horse keep on at a walk. He made a good line shot, but sighted too high, for presently a hoarse leisurely humming passed thirty feet over my head.

I pointed upward to let him know where the ball had gone, and waved my hat to signify that I entertained no hard feelings. Then, while he lazily reloaded his rifle, a wayside thicket

* He died in hospital somewhat later.

slipped between us and put an end to our curious interview. I do not know the breadth of the Atchafalaya at this point, but I did not hear the report of the Enfield nor see its puff of smoke. If my beast had guessed what kind of fun was going on, he would probably have been anxious to get out of it and would have thought me lacking in horse sense.

Algiers, Louisiana, September 6, 1863.

ALGIERS is a dirty, rascally suburb of New Orleans, separated from it by the Mississippi. Hither we came four days ago to take part in some mysterious enterprise, and here we remain sleeping on the ground and waiting for nobody knows what transport.* We marched aboard of one steamer, but it was perfectly jammed with troops, and we marched ashore again.

Many of our fellows are trying to forget their illnesses and miseries in Algerian whiskey; for swamp fever has turned our fine regiment into a sickly, dispirited, undisciplined wreck. Our service at Brashear City was not a rest; it was picket duty against an enemy within striking distance; what was far worse, it was within range of country fever. Forty-two deaths in forty-two days; barely two hundred and twenty-five men left for duty; and most of those staggering skeletons covered with fever sores; if they were at home they would be in bed and asking the prayers of the congregation.

Brashear City, Louisiana, September 16, 1863.

WE have escaped Algiers by getting sent back to Brashear City, which is something like being delivered out of purgatory into hades. The mosquitoes and other insects, including alligators,

* This was the futile expedition to Galveston.

still form the largest part of the native population, if not the worthiest.

I wonder if —— ever sent you my letter describing our tour of duty on Alligator Bayou. I was sent up there with my company to guard a bridge against a raid which was expected in our rear. We started in a hurry and with empty havresacks, expecting that rations would follow us. Then the commissary forgot us, or the transportation arrangements broke down, and we were left without food for two days. Luckily Sergeant Weber had served in the Seminole War and knew by experience that alligators' tails would make soup if they were sliced and soaked in several waters to get out the musk.

So I sent a foraging party to look up one of the innocents of the bayou and borrow his tail. Lieutenant Berry shot one who lay asleep beneath the opposite bank, blowing his skull clean off with a single ball and killing him almost instantly. Then a raft of three logs was made, and little Sweeny, our lightest man, got astride of it and paddled himself across with his paws, taking over a rope to tow back the prize. The precious tail was toted to our barracks, and for twenty-four hours we rioted on alligator soup. We pronounced it delicious; we wondered that we had never eaten it before; we would have it frequently. But as soon as we got some plain, soggy commissary bread, though without even a slice of bacon to season it, we gave up our Louisiana *potage*. There was a flavor of patchouli to it which rapidly cloyed any appetite not ravenous with hunger.—But this is an old adventure now, and you may have read of it before.

It is evident that some expedition will soon start out from here. Various Western regiments belonging to the Thirteenth Corps have joined us. We have lately received an issue of shelter tents, and shall no longer sleep like a herd of buffalo; also I hear that we may have ambulances, another new thing under the sun of Louisiana. During our furious forced marches of last spring our footsore and played-out and sunstricken men might get a lift from the quartermaster wagons, but in general were obliged to limp or crawl along as they could. As to Christian Commission stores, the custards and jellies and preserved peaches which cheer up the Army of the Potomac, they may be known to our hospitals, but not to our camps.

Vermilion Bayou, Louisiana, October 10, 1863.

As I wrote you about a fortnight ago, the army crossed the Atchafalaya without opposition. It is a large column, counting two divisions of the Nineteenth Corps, two of the Thirteenth and over two thousand cavalry, chiefly Westerners. But I cannot imagine what we are here for unless it is to make believe to carry on war, and so furnish an excuse to keep General Banks in charge of a department. We are slowly following a body of Confederate mounted infantry, who cannot be more than fifteen hundred strong, with a few light pieces, and who do nothing but burn bridges and then scamper away. It is a military promenade of the easiest and peacefullest description.

We forage like the locusts of Revelation. The Western men plunder worse than our fellows. It is pitiful to see how quickly a herd of noble cattle will be slaughtered. Our Negro servants bring in pigs, sheep and fowls, whether we bid it or forbid it. Of course, after the creatures are dead and cooked, we eat them to save them, for wasting food is prejudicial to military discipline.

It is curious how honest these looting darkeys are toward their employers; I never knew one of them to steal anything from a Union officer or soldier. They say that they used to feel free to rob their old masters, but it would be wrong to rob a man who hires them and pays them wages.

Large as our column is, it ought to be much larger. The number of men left behind in hospital and in convalescent camp is amazing. When a surgeon in the rear gets hold of a man who is handy at blacking his boots or making his coffee nice, he is very unwilling to let him go back to field duty.* One of my "absent sick" has lately rejoined me by running away from "convalescent camp," and footing it alone through sixty miles of unknown country, not over friendly. He says that many others would be glad to come if they could get away from their keepers.

Another source of feebleness in our fighting force is the enor-

---

* This passage expresses a feeling very common among officers in the field.

mous number of details for extra and special duty. Too many soldiers are used as officers' servants and as quartermasters' drudges. Fully one half of this command is now absent from the colors or is doing something besides carrying musket and sabre.

New Iberia, Louisiana, December 4, 1863.

WE are still doing nothing but attending to our health and taking wholesome exercise in the way of drill. The cold weather has had a wonderful effect in freshening up our fever-wilted constitutions. Perhaps that result was the real end and aim of our seemingly purposeless military promenade.

You would be amazed to see the swarming mulattoes and quadroons and octoroons who possess this region and call themselves Americans. Some of the richest planters, men of really great wealth, are of mixed descent. When we march through a town the people who gather to stare at us remind me of the Negro quarters of Philadelphia and New York. I understand that very few of them speak English and that they are nearly all extremely ignorant. These are not the former slaves, observe, but the former masters.

Do you remember our bumpkin lieutenant who saluted General Phelps with an applecore and was advised by him to hurry home and recommence life as a carpenter? * He turned out to be something of a sneak in fighting and was eventually court-martialed for cowardice. At Camp Bisland he was in command of his company, while Lieutenant Allen, one of our bravest officers, had charge of another. We were advancing, and the enemy was shelling us smartly, when this Jonathan Slick's pluck gave out and he decided to get behind something.

"Allen," he said, "yeou 'n' I together hain't got more'n men enough to make one respectable comp'ny. S'pose yeou take mine into the battle, 'n' dew what yeou can with 'em. As for me, I feel kinder sick to my stomach, 'n' I guess I'd better look out for a quiet, shady place. It's goin' to be a swelterin' day."

* Chapter II, letter of May 23, 1862 [pages 23–24].

Then, hastily telling his men to follow Lieutenant Allen, he turned his back on the war and disappeared till evening. For this sneaking trick and for being generally a wretched officer, he was cashiered by sentence of court-martial. But fate saved him; the judge advocate was killed at Port Hudson, and the records of the court could not be found; hence the general could not approve the sentence, and in short nothing had happened. Jonathan Slick (as I prefer to call him) retained his commission and the command of his company.

But he lately got into further trouble; he was absent without leave, though I think by accident; hence a summons to appear at division headquarters and make explanations. He went up there and, in his ignorance of military etiquette, addressed himself personally to our humorous old commander.

"Ginral," he said, "you wanted to see me 'bout suthin'."

Emory stared at him in wonder and divined that he was a greenhorn. "Yes, Lieutenant," he growled; "you are charged with cutting down the trees around General Franklin's headquarters."

Lieutenant Slick was thunderstruck. "Ginral," he protested, "I hain't struck a lick of an axe into a tree sence I was a boy."

Emory burst out laughing. "*I* don't know what you are wanted for," he replied. "Go to my adjutant general over there and ask him what is the matter."

Well, that is the whole story; the absence without leave was accounted for, after a fashion; and the Twelfth still boasts the stupidest lieutenant in the brigade.

CHAPTER X

ON January 30, 1864, the Twelfth Connecticut left New Orleans, for a furlough home, on board the steamer *Mississippi*. It arrived at New York on February 10, sailed for New Haven the following day, and landed at that city on February 12. After they had gone to Hartford to complete their re-enlistment, the troops were given leave. On March 19 came the announcement that the leave would be extended for twenty days.

In the meantime Grant, now in command of all the Union armies, began to move through the Wilderness against Richmond. Failing to defeat Lee's army north of Richmond, he decided to transfer some of his forces to the south side of the James River to flank the garrison in the Confederate capital. The Twelfth Connecticut, having returned to duty in Louisiana, was to take part in this maneuver by sailing from New Orleans to the mouth of the James; but the regiment scarcely touched shore in Virginia before it was hurried up the Potomac to help defend Washington against Early who was threatening the city from the rear. A short time later the Twelfth Connecticut joined Sheridan's army in the Shenandoah Valley.

This valley, separated from the coastal plains by the Blue Ridge Mountains, was, as De Forest remarked in Chapter VI, a side alley running parallel to the main street "wherein the heavy fighting must go on." While Lee and his various antagonists faced each other on the main street, Confederate forces would, on occasion, race up the alley and menace the Union positions from the rear. Jubal A. Early was not the first to employ this stratagem: Stonewall Jackson made a similar thrust in May, 1862. To put a stop to these threats, the Northern high command on August 7, 1864, selected Major General Philip H. Sheridan to lead the Union troops in the Shenandoah Valley. In addition to Emory's Nineteenth Corps, of which the Twelfth Connecticut was a part, this army included the Sixth Corps, commanded by Major General Horatio G. Wright, and the Eighth Corps, commanded by Brigadier General George Crook. Within three months Sheridan virtually destroyed Early's force and eliminated the possibility of Confederate operations in the valley.

Though De Forest escaped, during the summer of 1864, the heat of Louisiana, he continued to suffer the privations of field service. Since army regulations neither made arrangements for furnishing officers with rations nor honored their credit, De Forest often went hungry because he was without money. "In addition," he remarked bitterly in a letter to his brother, "many of the commissaries are scamps, who charge us a profit over and above the government price for the articles. I have known the same article to vary in price during the same day, from fifty cents to fifteen. The commissary began with charging the highest price; General Franklin found it out and issued an order; the result was there was a fall in the market. I cannot help suspecting that some generals share with the commissaries in this kind of plunder." A hard summer campaign, long marches, the prospect of half starving and of commanding half-starved men were bleak expectations even for a veteran soldier like De Forest. (Ed.)

CAMP LIFE IN VIRGINIA

DURING the winter of 1863–4 all the officers and nearly three quarters of the men of the Twelfth Connecticut re-enlisted for the war. As a reward for this bit of soldierly patriotism, it was sent home to recruit its health and numbers, while the "non-veterans," as the recusants were called, remained on continuous duty in Louisiana.

Thus the regiment escaped taking part in Banks' disastrous Red River campaign. During the latter spring it returned to Louisiana and camped for a few weeks near its old quarters at Carrollton. Meantime the Nineteenth Corps was reorganized in three divisions, and headquarters decided that one of them would suffice to guard the state. Accordingly two divisions under Major General William H. Emory, now commander of the corps, were sent to re-enforce Grant in his siege of Richmond. The second division (Grover's) landed before Petersburg. The first division (formerly Weitzel's) arrived there later, but was immediately hurried on by sea to Washington, then threatened by Early.

At this point my letters, such of them as I now find, will continue the story.

U. S. transport *Winona*, July 18, 1864.

THE Twelfth Connecticut is traveling to and fro in a quite mysterious and astonishing fashion. When I wrote you two days since, we were steaming up the Potomac to Washington; now we are steaming back to the James River or some other southerly destination.

At the landing we were met by some Sanitary Commission agents who gave the regiment a lunch of good coffee and bread (butter too!), which seemed great luxuries after the starvation on the transport, where most of the officers went hungry for lack of money. We then marched through the city and bivouacked on the western slope of Georgetown Heights near a little village called Tennallytown. Our orders were to overtake the bulk of the division which had already joined the Sixth Corps in pursuit of Early.*

But we also had orders to remain at Tennallytown until we had received and cooked four-days' rations. The wagons with the officers' baggage did not come up until two in the morning; and we found the evening air very much chillier than that of Louisiana. I went to sleep on the ground, but I had no blanket and the cold awoke me. Finally six or eight of us officers got leave of a neighboring farmer to take shelter in his barn. The hay was softer and warmer than the outside turf, and I passed the rest of the night comfortably. Next day the rations were long in coming, and the men could not fill their havresacks till about noon, the officers getting nothing. By that time another order arrived, sending us back to Washington.

It was Sunday, and as we tramped through Georgetown and down Pennsylvania Avenue, we were stared at by swarms of people. Our swarthy faces, yellow with malaria and scorched by the Southern sun, brought us not a little sympathy; and I was struck with the contrast between the friendly eyes which now surrounded us and the hostile glares which followed us

---

* Early's attack on Washington had been repulsed.

in Louisiana. At one halt, where the men rested for ten minutes or more, the ranks were invaded by citizens and children bringing ice water, cakes and fruit. A well-dressed man fanned the dusty and sweaty faces of two of our bull terriers who had seated themselves on his front steps. It was amusing to see how abashed they looked and how their comrades stared in quizzical wonder. At this halt I was lucky enough to borrow half a dollar from a brother officer and got a lunch in a corner bakeshop. It was the first food that I had had in twenty-four hours excepting one hard biscuit.

After a long wait in the broiling streets we were ordered to the Soldiers' Rest, a huge barrack for the accommodation of estrays of our profession. I had just laid down for the night on my blanket in the open court when another order came; we must pack at once, take a transport for City Point and join the army before Richmond. So here we are, cluttering the cabins and decks of the *Winona* and sleeping as much as possible in order to kill time and hunger. Let us hope that we shall be paid soon, for the officers are now all out of money, and the transports demand cash for grub. Of course I don't know whether we are to fight, nor when, nor how much. That is the general's business, and we never bother about it; we have troubles enough of our own without assuming his responsibilities.

Georgetown Heights, July 29, 1864.

BACK again, and without knowing why, in the defences of Washington. We were to have taken part in some movement at City Point,* but of a sudden we got orders to go aboard a transport, and here we are, preparing our minds and havresacks to start for Harper's Ferry. We unpaid officers would have starved at City Point if the chaplain had not begged some canned food from the Sanitary Commission. Don't come on here unless I write for you. You could sleep in a tent, you say.

* In support of the "mine attack," as appeared afterward.

Not in mine; I have none. I slept out of doors last night, lying on a blanket with my blouse for a cover.

Monocacy Junction, Maryland, August 4, 1864.

WE took cars for this place on Saturday night, going first to the Relay House and then turning west through a hilly country which reminded me pleasantly of New England. Nearing Monocacy, we moved slowly, for there were reports of Rebel cavalry ahead, and they might have torn up the track. Lying on the floor of a freight car, with no bedding but a flap of shelter tent, I got an incessant bumping and could not sleep till near morning. Five long trains of troops, with General Emory in command, followed each other. We reached here Sunday afternoon and went into position on a huge rounded hill, the field of the late battle of Monocacy.

We were still supperless, and for that matter dinnerless also, when we got orders to hurry rearward and rescue our supply train from Mosby. We had a hot and dusty march of eight miles over enormous hills, but we accomplished it in good style to save our rations. The train was unharmed, and we got something to eat, even the officers sharing. My blanket was missing, but I lay down in my dirty uniform, and when I woke the sun was shining. Then we escorted the wagons to Monocacy under a blazing sun and through clouds of dust which puffed up under our feet as though we were treading in flour.

Near us are Hunter's and Crook's troops,* both in a fagged-out and demoralized condition, ragged, famished, discouraged, sulky, and half of them in ambulances. They have been marched to tatters, they say, besides being overwhelmed and beaten. For ten days they have not had a rest of four hours at a time, and very rarely a chance to cook their rations. Crackers and raw pork have been their main diet, and hardly ever enough of

* Units in the Department of West Virginia, later organized as the Eighth Corps. (Ed.)

those abominable refreshments. Of course this is nothing strange in war; our own men meanwhile have had no meat for four days; only crackers and coffee. And the officers, being without pay and without a chance to forage, live on green apples or other such deleterious provender.

I detail these hardships to deter you from rushing on here to join me. Please understand that I am totally without money, living from hand to mouth in a wild, beggarly way, and not even able to pay the postage on this letter. My brother forwarded me a draft to Washington by express, but we were hurried through the city at such a rate that I could not stop to ask for it, and the gracious knows when I shall get it.

Monocacy Junction is said to be the key to all the neighboring passages of the Potomac. We lie here in waiting for Early, and shall jump on him if he crosses the river. You know as much about the probabilities of a battle as I do, and perhaps as much as the general. I feel pretty sure, however, that the regiment is in for a hard summer campaign of heat, dust, short rations, severe marching and possibly sharp fighting. Our present camp is the dirtiest spot, for a dry one, that I ever saw. It is an old wheat field, and the powdery soil blows incessantly through my ragged shelter tent, where I sit cross-legged on the ground, penciling this letter on my havresack. A shelter tent, by the way, is some such a figure as you make by leaning two cards against each other; it is open at the ends, about six feet square on the ground and nearly four feet high at the apex; it shelters one against the rain—sometimes. I lost mine on the train, but one of my men "picked up" another for me, and I suppose the true owner is now swearing about it.

Halltown,* Virginia, August 8, 1864.

WE are going, and that soon, but where and when I cannot say. The officers' valises, the men's knapsacks and the spare camp kettles have all been sent for storage to Harper's Ferry. Every-

* Now in West Virginia. (Ed.)

one is stripped for the march, carrying his own blanket, shelter tent, havresack and canteen, whether he be captain or private. This prophesies lively traveling, probably in the direction of Lynchburg.

A column of cavalry four or five miles long is in sight coming up the Potomac Valley. Possibly they have been hunting Mosby's guerrillas, who are said to be troubling our communications with Washington. Early with his main force is at Winchester seven miles southerly from us. You must not expect to hear much from me for some time, unless we get beaten and driven back.

The Sixth Corps, one of the best in the Army of the Potomac, is lying near us. They seem to be badly demoralized by the severe service and the disastrous battles of the campaigns in Virginia. Their guns are dirty; their camps are disorderly clutters of shelter tents; worst of all, the men are disrespectful to their officers. I heard a private say to a lieutenant, "I'll slap your face if you say that again."

These fellows lurk around our clean, orderly camps and steal our clean, bright rifles. I went over to the nearest brigade to complain of this and to recover lost ordnance stores.

"Looking for guns, Cap?" drawled a sergeant. "Well, if you find a clean gun in this camp, you claim it. We hain't had one in our brigade since Cold Harbor."

The camp astonished me by its contrast to ours, with its regular company streets, each one headed and overlooked by the tent of its officers. Here there were no boundary lines between the different regiments, all being tumbled together higgledy-piggledy, officers mixed up anyhow with the men, and the brigade commander in the middle. He was a colonel, a pleasant and gentlemanly young fellow, surrounded by young officers. Their talk about the war and our immediate military future had a tone of depression which astonished me.

"But don't you believe in Grant at all?" I finally asked.

"Yes, we believe in Grant," replied the colonel. "But we believe a great deal more in Lee and in that Army of Virginia."

"Well, I for my part predict a victory," I said as I left them.

"Let us hope you are a true prophet," they answered, smiling, but not cheerfully.

This tone of discouragement is very puzzling to us of the Nineteenth Corps. If we have not always whipped, we have at least conquered our department, and so we expect to see the conquest of this one.

Near Charles Town,* Virginia, August 21, 1864.

WELL, we tramped down the Shenandoah Valley, and we tramped back again.† If ever I volunteer again I shall remember this vale of sorrows and shall specify that I am not to make war in it. Blazing hot marches, heavy guard duty, a diet of green corn and green apples have made a rough campaign of it thus far.

In the way of scenery the valley is charming and surpasses that of the Connecticut. The mountains are lofty enough to be striking, and their contours of advance and retreat have much variety. The streams too are fine, and the many oak groves are lovely. We frequently halted in them, and once we had the luck to camp in one. Just now our Corps is posted in a long belt of forest which serves it both as shelter and as ambush. The weather has changed to rain, and on one of our late marches we got soaking wet, a circumstance which seems never to hurt anybody who wears a uniform.

Thus far General Sheridan is cautious about fighting, perhaps because of instructions from high political authority. With so many elections at hand, including the presidential, it would not do to have this army beaten and the North invaded. So, whenever Early is re-enforced, Sheridan retreats to a strong position and waits to be attacked. It is to the enemy's interest just now to take the offensive, but we doubt if Early has men enough to risk it.

An order to fall in may come at any moment. Such orders

* Now in West Virginia. (Ed.)
† This alludes to Sheridan's march to Strasburg and back; one or two letters missing here.

generally arrive at night in the awkwardest moment possible. Then we march like fury for hours; and then nothing comes of it; we march back again. Of course the general understands it all, and perhaps Omniscience does, but nobody else.

Well, this is soldiering of course, to do as we are ordered, and ask no explanations.

Halltown, Virginia, August 24, 1864.

HERE we are, nearly back to Harper's Ferry, with fieldworks all along our front, unattackable except by flanking. What the enemy amounts to I cannot say, for he only shows a line of pickets which may cover ten thousand men, or may cover thirty thousand. We hear that a detachment is crossing the Potomac above us, either to harry Maryland and Pennsylvania, or to waylay our supply trains.

We occupy two long and high parallel hills, with a narrow valley between them, and a transverse gorge which cuts the two hills into four. The ends of the valleys and the fronts of the slopes are covered by breastworks of rails filled in with earth. Behind us is the fortified height of Harper's Ferry, supported by the fortified heights of Loudoun county and of Maryland. If Early attacks us here we shall whip him dreadfully unless he is very numerous.

Having got some money at last and being settled near our base of supplies, we no longer starve on green apples and the like, but feed reasonably well on salt beef, hardtack, flour and potatoes, all purchased of the commissary. Meanwhile we are the seediest and most disreputable gang to look at that you can imagine. I have but one shirt and one pair of socks, and my coat and trousers are as ragged as a tramp's, and my shoes are innocent of blacking. What would you think of such a ragamuffin walking in upon you and claiming to be your husband?

Near Charles Town, Virginia, August 31, 1864.

YOUR latest reached me at Halltown during the evening of the 27th. Next morning at four we fell in hastily and started after Early, who was reported by our scouts to be marching up the valley. But we moved so cautiously and halted so often to reconnoitre for ambuscades that the whole day passed in making eight miles.

During the 29th our cavalry with some light artillery made a tour to the front and found the enemy an overmatch for them, I suspect, for they came back grumbling about "superior numbers." That evening our whole brigade (now in advance for the first time) was set to building fieldworks, the Twelfth working all night. By afternoon of the next day we had a strong breastwork hedged in by an abatis made of a whole grove. Then General Emory found fault with the direction of the line and had half of it thrown backward to cover our left flank.

The men are so amused with this labor that they hew and shovel in the highest spirits. And we never tire of looking at our fortification; we walk around it and discuss its merits by the hour; we are like little girls with a new baby-house. As you may lack entertainment at home, let me instruct you how to make a fieldwork. Steal all the rails that you can find in a township; then build two parallel fences four feet apart and four and a half feet high; fill in with stones, earth, and green timber, and bank up the front with earth laid at an angle of forty-five degrees; then look across it and wish the enemy would come.

Our fortifications, by the way, are not in a continuous line, but crown knolls and fill up gorges at distances of three or four-hundred yards from each other, thus covering a front of three or four miles. The ugly point of the whole business is that it will probably be labor lost. A report comes in today that part of Early's force has gone to Richmond, and that he is too feeble to attack us.

I really cannot write oftener than I do. We have had in this campaign an uncommon amount of severe guard duty, night alarums, sudden orders to fall in, and unexpected movements. If you could see me, dirty from head to foot with marching, my uniform a common soldier's blouse and trousers, my hat so ragged that it does not even keep out the sun, you would not blame your correspondent's laxity.

This letter must stop here, or I may not be able to mail it. Early has gone up the valley, and we shall be capering after him this very night, or my experience in military affairs amounts to nothing.

Near Berryville, Virginia, September 8, 1864.

I WISH you could understand how difficult I find it to write even one letter. Since mailing my last I have had no baggage but my overcoat and rubber blanket. This half-sheet of fools-cap was begged from a brother captain who begged the whole sheet from the adjutant general of our brigade. The ink was loaned me by another officer, and I hope somebody else will give me an envelope. The pen, thank Providence, is mine, and I still possess one postage stamp.

You see by my heading that we have changed position. Shortly after mailing my last letter we started in pursuit of Early, supposing that he was in full retreat, but not quite sure of it. Of a sudden, just about sundown, one of his columns stumbled upon our left wing and pitched into it at a lively rate, showing first a heavy force of skirmishers and then a line of battle.* Some of Crook's regiments were driven out of a wood where they had just begun camping; but they rallied in the open fields, charged back into the timber and recovered it in

* This was the accidental skirmish of September 3d between Anderson and Crook, incident on Sheridan's reoccupation of the Berryville position.

fine style. There was noisy musketry and cannonading for half an hour, and then the Rebels retired under cover of their artillery. We of the centre were separated from the fighting by a long knoll and did not get even a stray bullet.

Since the skirmish we have been shoveling, and now have a lovely stretch of earthworks, covering a front of three miles or more. It is uncomfortable weather, the temperature chilly for a man dressed in ragged flannel, and the heavy rain driving me away from the campfire. I lie under my shelter tent on the ground and hunch up my shoulders to keep warm. I would put on my overcoat, but I shall want it more at night. My shoes and my ragged socks have not been dry for three days. All this personal gossip is to keep you from bolting on here to join me and so making yourself miserable.

The fact is that I am not badly off just now, compared with the condition of things at times. Night before last I was on picket and splashed back to camp in the morning through a rainstorm, daubed with mud and drenched to the skin. And what a breakfast I had! Applesauce; plundered applesauce; nothing but applesauce; not even a hardtack! A perfect nutriment for heroes! but how would your ladyship like it?

By the way, I was under fire that day, for the first time since reaching Virginia. Sheridan advanced his pickets a mile or more and discovered just a little scrap of Early. A few bullets passed over my part of the line, but did not hit one out of my hundred or so of men. To the left I heard one of the Forty-seventh Pennsylvania scream, and still farther to the left there was quite a roar of musketry. But the final result was trifling; we found no real force of Rebels. It is generally believed here now that Early has divided his army and does not propose to give immediate battle.*

---

* Six days after the date of this letter, that is on the 14th of September, Early sent to Richmond Anderson's cavalry and Kershaw's infantry.

CHAPTER XI

THE slow progress of the siege forces around Petersburg and Richmond and the lack of definite victories in other theaters of operations influenced prominent groups in the North to demand, during the summer of 1864, a negotiated peace. But this despondency lifted after Farragut's blockade of the port of Mobile, and it vanished completely after Sherman's capture of Atlanta. In addition, Sheridan's brilliant maneuvers in the Shenandoah Valley nourished hopes for final success, while Grant moved toward complete victory by wearing down Lee's forces in eastern Virginia.

Having confidence in Grant and Sheridan and in the armies these two generals commanded, De Forest never doubted, even when Early's raid was at its height, the final outcome of the war. Nevertheless he was becoming weary of the privations which he had to endure during the summer campaign in the Shenandoah Valley. He was discouraged also with the little chance for promotion in the Twelfth Connecticut, and he regretted at times that he had not taken the colonelcy of the Negro regiment which had been offered to him unofficially in New Orleans. His spirits, therefore, must have risen as he shared in the series of Union victories which he describes in the following chapters. (Ed.)

SHERIDAN'S VICTORY OF THE OPEQUON

FROM the 3d of September up to the 18th we remained quietly among our fieldworks around Berryville. Early, weakened by the departure of Kershaw and Anderson, made no offer to attack us; and our activity was confined to demonstrations and reconnoissances, mostly performed by the cavalry. But meanwhile I received a curious intimation that more serious warfare might be at hand.

On the 16th of September (or was it the 17th?), as I was strolling near one of the camps of the Sixth Corps, a sergeant of the Vermont brigade eagerly called my attention to a couple of officers who were walking by themselves, engaged in grave, tranquil conversation. They were undersized men, rather squarely built, but not portly nor even heavy. The junior, who was also the shortest, had a distinctly Irish face of the puffy sort, with irregular profile and a swarthy grey complexion. He talked in a low silvery voice (the words quite inaudible to me), his elbows pressed to his sides, but gesturing slightly with his fingers. The elder man, blond and sandy-bearded, his red-oak features perfectly inexpressive, his grey eyes fixed on the ground, listened without replying.

"That youngest one is our General Sheridan," said the sergeant. "Don't you know who the other is? *That's* GRANT!"

He paused, gazed at the renowned chief with solemn eyes, and then continued pensively, "I hate to see that old cuss around. When that old cuss is around there's sure to be a big fight on hand."

I have often wondered whether that shrewd Vermonter lived through the battle which fulfilled his prophecy.

Grant knew that his constant hammering around Richmond had forced Lee to send for Anderson and Kershaw, thus reducing Early to two divisions of cavalry and four of infantry, while Sheridan had seven of infantry and four of cavalry. Consequently he had arrived to order decisive movements and had brought with him a plan for a battle to be delivered on the 20th. Sheridan declared (probably while I was looking at the two) that he could be ready to attack on the 19th, and explained in detail his project for the advance. This project so pleased Grant that he kept his own plan in his pocket and replied in substance, "Go in!"

Meanwhile Early, some ten miles to the west of us, covered Winchester with the infantry of Gordon, Ramseur, Rodes and Wharton, and the cavalry of Lomax and Fitz Hugh Lee. On the morning of the 18th he pushed Rodes and Gordon towards Martinsburg to threaten the Baltimore and Ohio Railroad, while Wharton advanced as far as Stephenson's to assure their communications with Ramseur at Winchester. Here was an opportunity for Sheridan to strike at Early's somewhat scattered army and beat it in detail. Consequently at two in the morning of the 19th, all our camps were aroused, and we set off as promptly as circumstances permitted for Winchester, Wilson's cavalry leading to clear the way, followed by Wright's infantry, then Emory's and then Crook's.

The plan seemed promising, but it was in reality not easy to execute, and it was wofully mismanaged. Our only road of advance was the Berryville and Winchester pike, which wound through a narrow gorge between picturesque hills so steep and so densely covered with forests and underbrush as to be impassable to any force but unencumbered infantry. One would have supposed that this single line of movement would have been carefully and exclusively reserved for troops and guns. But by some stupendous oversight the Sixth Corps was closely followed by its baggage train, and thus the infantry column was cut in two parts by miles of wagons.

Sheridan, Wright and Emory toiled for hours to bring order and movement out of the stupid, mischievous clutter. Eventually the Nineteenth Corps took to the woods and scrambled along on either side of the train, but not without much confusion and delay. We lost something like six hours in getting over a distance of about three miles; and the chance of attacking Early by surprise, before he could concentrate, was utterly lost.

The scene in this swarming gorge was one not easily forgotten. The road was crowded with wagons, ambulances, gun carriages and caissons, getting onward as fast as possible, but so very slowly that one might already divine that we should fight our battle almost without artillery. On the right and on the left endless lines of infantry struggled through the underbrush and stumbled over rocks and gutters. On every knoll and under every thicket, gravely watching us pass, sat the hundreds of men who belong to an army but never fight: the cooks, the officers' servants, the hospital gangs, the quartermasters' people, the "present sick" and the habitual skulkers. Here too were jammed squadrons of Wilson's cavalry, who for the present had finished their fighting, having cleared the ford of the Opequon. Presently we met litters loaded with pallid sufferers, and passed a hospital tent where I saw surgeons bending over a table, and beneath it amputated limbs lying in pools of blood.

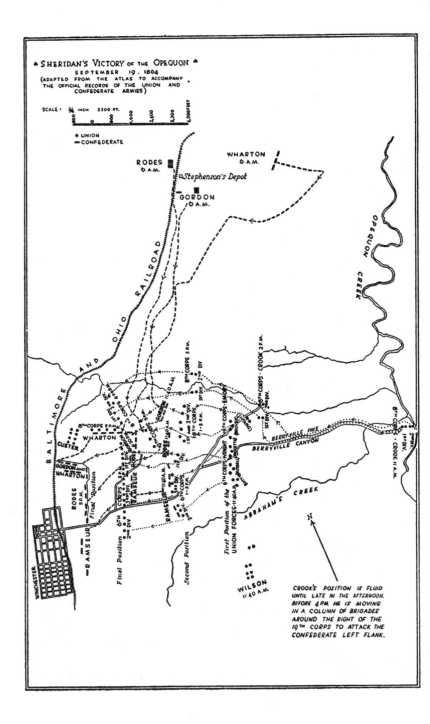

SHERIDAN'S VICTORY OF THE OPEQUON
SEPTEMBER 19. 1864
(ADAPTED FROM THE ATLAS TO ACCOMPANY
THE OFFICIAL RECORDS OF THE UNION AND
CONFEDERATE ARMIES)

SCALE: ¾ INCH 2200 FT.

● UNION
━ CONFEDERATE

CROOK'S POSITION IS FLUID
UNTIL LATE IN THE AFTERNOON.
BEFORE 4 P.M. HE IS MOVING
IN A COLUMN OF BRIGADES
AROUND THE RIGHT OF THE
19TH CORPS TO ATTACK THE
CONFEDERATE LEFT FLANK.

Ahead there was an occasional booming of cannon, deadened
to a dull *pum! pum!* by distance. Apparently Wilson's main
force had got through the defile and was trying to establish a
position for us in the irregular undulating valley east of Winchester where we were to deliver battle.

Early was not yet concentrated, but he was getting into shape
fast. The evening previous, Gordon and Rodes had rejoined
Wharton at Stephenson's, only five miles from Winchester;
and this morning, startled by Wilson's cannon, all three divisions had hastened to re-enforce Ramseur. Gordon and Wharton arrived about nine o'clock, and Rodes not more than half
an hour later.

Meantime our long column of march was dragging its slow
length through the Opequon hills. It was ten o'clock when
Wright's leading brigade began to emerge from the defile and
form line toward the left; and it was past eleven before Emory's
foremost troops could follow suit by extending toward the
right. At twenty minutes to twelve we had a line of battle which
should have been in position six hours earlier. Counting from
the right, it consisted of Grover's division of the Nineteenth
Corps, prolonged by Ricketts', Russell's and Getty's divisions
of the Sixth Corps. Dwight's division of the Nineteenth lay
echeloned behind Grover, and Crook's two divisions were still
far to the rear, penned up in the defile.

As yet we were somewhat crowded and rather ignorant of our
surroundings. Grover's division and, I believe, all of Wright's
divisions were in double lines of brigades. The extreme left of
the Sixth Corps stretched out into a region where there was
little or nothing to fight with. Moreover, we were without artillery, for the guns were tangled in the clutter on the pike, or held
back by the wooded hills behind us. Nothing remained but for
the infantry to hustle forward and make room by main force
of charging. Meanwhile we still believed that Early had been
caught unprepared and that we would find victory an easy
matter. My regimental commander, Lieutenant Colonel Peck,
said to me, "We of Dwight's division * will have no fighting today. The first line alone will take care of the enemy."

* As a result of a reorganization of the Nineteenth Corps (mentioned at the beginning of Chapter X), the Twelfth Connecticut now formed part of the second brigade

At about noon Grover and Wright commenced their advance in face of a vigorous shelling. The troops struggled over some wooded hillocks and swept down upon a stretch of broad, rolling fields, beyond which lay Early's line, sheltered in part by a wood and a rocky ledge, with the heights and fieldworks of Winchester as a support.

And now came the second great blunder, or misfortune, of the day's operations. The advance of our first line quickly became divergent, opening outward like the blades of a fan. Grover's right-hand brigade discerned a hostile line on its right front and naturally tended in that direction with pugnacious eagerness. Meanwhile his left brigade had been ordered to guide on Ricketts, who had been ordered to guide on the Winchester pike, which veered to the left instead of leading straight onward. Thus it happened that a broad gap soon appeared between Birge and Sharp in Grover's first line. This opening was temporarily filled by Molineux's brigade which Emory hurried up from the second line at double-quick in face of the hostile musketry.

All would have gone well but that another rift presently showed between Sharpe and the right of the Sixth Corps. Keifer, who commanded one of Ricketts' brigades, strove in vain to fill it with three of his regiments. Neafie, who held Sharpe's left with the 156th New York, swerved to the left without being able to keep in touch with Keifer. The gap stubbornly continued to spread, and it prophesied peril of defeat. Our general must have wished heartily at this moment that he had a single one of the Nineteenth Corps batteries which were still struggling to get out of the crowded defile behind us.

But for a time Grover's advance was triumphant. The regiments advanced rapidly, the skirmishers double-quicking at some points, and the lines following at a right-shoulder-shift with exultant yells. Three colonels, I was told, were captured by Sharpe's brigade and sent to Emory. Birge's men, breaking away from him in a wild charge, drove Evans' Georgians out of a wood and two hundred yards beyond it. The Rebel general Rodes was killed while placing a battery to check this headlong

of the first division under Brigadier General William Dwight; its brigade commander was Brigadier General James W. McMillan. (Ed.)

pursuit. For a few minutes it looked as if Early had been beaten by a single hasty and somewhat disorderly rush.

But unfortunately for us he had re-enforcements at hand. Battle's brigade of Rodes' division, five veteran regiments of Alabamians, reached the field just in time to arrest the Confederate panic; and Early promptly sent them up the pike to the point where Neafie and Keifer were vainly trying to join hands across the dangerous gap in our centre. The opening was easily seized and skilfully improved; our troops to the right and left of it were at once exposed to a flanking fire and to the chance of being enveloped; and who can wonder that they failed to hold their ground?

Up to this time Neafie, as he afterwards told me, had fought a successful battle. "We were pitted against a regiment which was giving way," he said. "There were not more than forty men left around the colors, and I was just about to order a charge when my adjutant called to me to look to the left. I looked, and behold! Ricketts' division was gone; when it went or where I don't know; but it had disappeared. In place of it there was a line in butternut sweeping past our flank and into our rear. I had no time to change front, especially as I had our enemy in front. All I could do was to retreat at once, with the hope of rallying further back. So I rushed up to my men and ordered them to double-quick to the right in order to join the rest of our brigade. But we lost some prisoners, as well as one hundred and fifteen men hit."

Such was the break in our centre which disordered fully one third of our first line and made the battle for a time uncertain. Ricketts' division, which had been severely handled at Monocacy and reduced to little over two thousand men, did not show the coolness and steadiness which had formerly distinguished it. A large part of it recoiled as soon as the enemy appeared on its flank, and swarmed confusedly back to the point whence the army had debouched from the pike. Grover's division also crumbled slowly from left to right, beginning with the brigades of Sharpe and Molineux. There was nothing strange about this; the whole Confederate line was being vigorously rallied and re-enforced; and an attack in both front and flank is pretty certainly irresistible.

Meantime Birge on our extreme right was suffering from the natural results of his hasty and tumultuous advance. Gordon brought up his whole division and recovered the wood lost by Evans, driving our fellows back to a ripple of ground about one hundred and fifty yards east of it. Altogether, but chiefly in this morning hour of the battle, Grover lost some thirteen hundred killed and wounded. The confusion for a time was considerable and seemed to threaten repulse, if not defeat. The pike was crowded with fugitives, and they dotted the adjacent fields in numbers, while hundreds had collected in the forests, where they rapidly rallied and reformed.

Russell's division of the Sixth Corps came to the rescue of the centre. Two of his brigades, Campbell's and Edwards', first cleared his own front by carrying in fine style a wooded crest which Early had occupied. Then Upton's brigade faced to the right and bore down upon the pike, pouring flanking volleys of musketry into Battle's Alabamians, killing and wounding many of them and driving the rest back in confusion. It is a curious circumstance, as showing the confusion of the battle at this moment, that one of these regiments in its retreat stumbled upon and captured some of Molineux's men who were still fighting stubbornly on their original line.

Upton's adroit attack relieved Grover's left and gave it a chance to rally. Neafie presently got his regiment together and charged back to very near the point where he had been flanked and broken. All along the rear of our right there was lively business in the way of patching up the shattered line of battle. Emory, Grover, the brigade commanders, the colonels, the staff officers galloped about after skulkers, exhorting, commanding, threatening and swearing as officers do in such cases.

One curious example of coolness and discipline contrasted oddly with the widespread panic. Captain Bradbury of Emory's staff met a captain of infantry, Rigby of the Twenty-fourth Iowa, in charge of a sergeant and twelve men, retiring as composedly as if returning from drill. At Bradbury's suggestion this little array halted, faced about and gave three cheers. The valorous note of defiance seemed to break the panic in that quarter. In a few minutes the platoon swelled to a battalion composed of men from half a dozen regiments.

Meantime two pieces of Bradbury's battery (the First Maine) had reached the field.

"Push them into that gap near the pike," said General Grover. "We *must* show a front there."

Guided by Bradbury himself, the section advanced through musketry and canister into the plain, and opened a fire which helped much toward checking the enemy. A Confederate line which tried to carry these guns was repulsed in a strange way. General Emory, after aiding to rally the 131st New York, had posted it in a narrow grove projecting from the wood which now formed Grover's base of resistance. As the Rebels passed this point they received a flanking volley and, almost immediately, another in front from the troops in the main wood. Under this double assault the charging swarm broke and fled in confusion. Shortly after this adventure Molineux pushed a line of his rallied men up to within two hundred yards of the isolated grove which Birge had won and lost. Thus bit by bit Grover's shattered division was got into passable shape again, and a large portion of the field of battle was recovered.

Up to this point I have described what I did not see. Not one incident of Grover's and Ricketts' advance and repulse was visible from the stubbly fields where Dwight's division lay in echelon behind the forest which separated it from the foremost line. The wood not only hid the contest from us, but in a measure stifled its uproar. The cannonade had not been heavy, and we heard little of the musketry. During an hour or more we supposed that all was going well; that for once the "Old First" would not be wanted; that a battle would be won without it. The supposition was not an unpleasant one.

But presently there came a call for our first brigade. Lounging in a hollow over which the Rebel shells screamed harmlessly, I watched it rise, move forward in line and disappear over the crest of a low hill in our front. Emory, it seems, had sent for Dwight, pointed out to him the breaks and staggerings in our second division, and said to him, "Have this whole nonsense stopped at once."

So the first brigade of our first division had been pushed into furious battle against Early's strong and victorious left wing; and we of the second brigade were the sole reserve of the Nineteenth Corps, for our third brigade was at Harper's Ferry, and our third division in Louisiana.

Presently a staff officer cantered up and demanded our brigadier, McMillan. We divined what was coming, and we were prepared to rise when the orders rang out, "Attention!—Left face!—Forward mar—ch!"

In ordinary marching column we draggled for perhaps half a mile through imperfectly cleared fields parallel with the as yet invisible lines of combatants. Then we halted on a high open slope, whence a scrap or two of the fighting could be seen. Far away to the left I observed a movement which may have been the advance of Russell and the storming of the wooded crest. But Grover's obstinate and bloody struggle was still hidden from us by a belt of forest. We could hear an incessant rattle of musketry not far away, and we wondered that the bullets did not hum oftener through our ranks. One man in the Twelfth fell; the random ball had passed through his head; and he was gone, and in his first battle! A recruit, and so many old soldiers tramping past him unhurt! each one glad to escape death once more, and each thinking, "Who next?"

The captain, excited and shrill, uttered wrathful lament for the loss of his soldier. "That man shot? By G—d I'm sorry that man's shot. He was a good man; I knew his folks. It's too damn bad he should be killed right off that way."

Presently fresh orders reached us. We changed direction, tramped westward for a few minutes and halted in a clearing which gave us a fairly broad view of the battling. A quarter of a mile in advance was our first brigade, the men kneeling or lying behind a long rail fence and keeping up a violent fire. Two hundred yards beyond them was the wood which Gordon had recovered, a smoke of hostile musketry now bordering its whole front, though not a Rebel was visible. While we looked the brigade rose, faced about and marched slowly toward us, the officers running to and fro to steady fluctuations in the ranks. We supposed that it would take position beside us, or that we should relieve it in the fighting line.

But presently a curious and picturesque incident occurred. Gordon's men in the wood rose in a long butternut line and raised jeering yells of exultation. Thereupon Colonel Love of

116th New York halted his regiment and double-quicked it
back to the abandoned fence, followed by the whole force from
left to right. It was a piece of insubordination in this brave
officer, and it nearly cost him a trial by court-martial. The position at the fence was practically untenable for any length of
time, in consequence of a Confederate battery on the right which
enfiladed it with great slaughter, while we had no guns wherewith to reply. It was at this point that the 114th New York offered up its glorious sacrifice of one hundred and eighty-five
killed and wounded out of less than three hundred present.

We had scarcely seen Beal resume his battle with Gordon
when our brigade was divided. The 160th New York and Forty-
seventh Pennsylvania remained to support the right, while the
Twelfth Connecticut and Eighth Vermont countermarched
toward the centre. It presently appeared that our little column
was needed in various places at once. Contradictory orders repeatedly changed our direction and position. We were countermarched, filed to the right, filed to the left, double-quicked and
halted till we thought that the generals had lost their wits. At
last we fronted upon an open knoll at the western edge of the
wood and looked out anew upon Grover's field of battle.

An obstinate and bloody struggle was still going on there; but
as a spectacle the scene would have disappointed a civilian. No
long lines or massive columns trampled those undulating fields;
the combatants on both sides were lying low in the herbage, or
behind fences and thickets. The only signs of battle were long
stretches of smoke from musketry, and graceful, rolling masses
of smoke from the batteries. Meanwhile the unseen Rebel guns
on our right still enfiladed us, sending most of their shells
screaming through the branches above our heads, but occasionally aiming low enough to do mischief.

Here we sat down for some minutes and awaited orders.
Bradbury had got up two more of his brass howitzers and was
putting them in position to repulse infantry. Generals Emory,
Grover and Dwight, surrounded by staff officers, lounged on
their horses nearby, and watched the deadlock of the battle.

Erelong the Twelfth lost its only field officer present, Lieutenant Colonel Frank Peck, a brave and able commander. He
had just received instructions to charge and had called out,

"Officers, rectify the alignment." I was leaning against a sapling hardly thicker than my wrist, and felt it shaken a yard or two above my head by a shell which screeched over me and instantly burst. The crash nearly deafened me for a moment, but the splinters whizzed forward without hitting me. In the next instant Peck dropped slowly from his plunging horse, while two of Bradbury's horses reared and fell dying, and an artilleryman staggered to one side with a ghastly face. The missile had done its ferocious work with frightful swiftness and clamor.

"This is a slaughterhouse," I heard General Emory say. "But it must be held; it is the key to the whole position."

A moment later, under command of our senior captain, Clark, afterwards major, we made our advance in company with the Eighth Vermont. Colonel Van Petten of the 160th New York, who had ridden up to the knoll to get a flesh wound bandaged, made us a friendly little speech as we started. "You have lost your commander, Twelfth," he shouted. "But do your duty all the same. You have been the model of my regiment. We should grieve greatly if you should flinch."

We would have cheered him if there had been time, for we knew him well as an officer of distinguished gallantry, and we remembered as he did that the 160th had been our junior comrade in the brigade when we were veterans. But just then we had something to do besides shouting; we had to keep line at double-quick with our old comrade regiment, the trusty Eighth Vermont; we had to meet and check Gordon's war-tried Georgians and Louisianians. Our orders were to replace a line (gathered from the shattered brigades of Molineux and Birge) which held a ripple of ground about two hundred yards from the isolated wood.

Trotting into the open, we wheeled slightly to the right and double-quicked for nearly a quarter of a mile across the meadows, pulling up occasionally for breath like Caesar's veterans at Pharsala, and then hurrying on again at the best speed possible. Of course there was soon no such thing as a battalion line; we were a loose swarm, the strongest in front and the feeble in rear.* One veteran skulker, who had cunningly dodged fate in

* It is only in pictures and civilian novels that brigades and regiments charge at the double *with even front* over any distance above sixty or eighty yards.

various battles and skirmishes, met his deserts in this advance. He slyly plunged for shelter into a hollow made by the uprooting of a tree; but his lieutenant, Mullen, promptly spanked him out of this ambush with the flat of a sabre. Right unwillingly the skulker straightened up and trotted onward to meet the bullet which was hastening to grant him a soldier's death. Not many others fell in this hasty and shapeless scramble; indeed, it seemed to me that the enemy fired at us very little. Probably they expected us to charge home, and therefore reserved their ammunition for close quarters.

Presently we reached the line indicated for us and dropped panting among the men who held it. So far as I could discover, they were mostly of the Fourteenth New Hampshire and 131st New York, the former belonging to Birge's brigade and the latter to Molineux's. They constituted a slender line, needing re-enforcement as well as ammunition, and by no means a match for the force which confronted them. We were scarcely among them when they began to leave us, running in a stooping posture for the nearest cover visible and generally making for the forest where Grover was reforming his division.

From this time forward Dwight's two brigades assumed the task of holding back the Rebel left until Crook should arrive. It was a hot job where the Eighth Vermont and Twelfth Connecticut lay. The musketry commenced with violence shortly after the two regiments reached their line. Every few seconds a groan, a sharp cry, a plunge of some bleeding wretch rearward showed how rapidly our men were being disabled. Once, by Clark's order and with the usual instructions of "Steady, men, aim low," we sprang up and delivered a crashing volley.

For a short while our antagonists were silenced; perhaps they expected to see us come on with the bayonet. Then, little by little, on our side first, the fire-at-will recommenced. The men in both lines were nearly all cool, old soldiers who knew their deadly business. They loaded on their backs, leveled through the grass *à fleur de terre,* and fired with deliberation, usually aiming at a puff of hostile smoke. For two hours the Southern bullets plumped into our prostrate ranks, or just barely whistled over us. One man was killed by a shot which pierced his blanket roll, his stuffed knapsack and the upper portion of his chest.

Another received a ball exactly through the top of his head. Corporal Whitaker of my company was smartly bounced and severely bruised by a shot which flung up the turf beneath his left shoulder. Out of three hundred and fifty present we had seventy hit, nearly all of them on this line of combat.

For the officers, who could not take part in the fighting but must "lie still and catch it," it was heavy-hearted business. Four of us crawled cautiously to a point just behind the colors and established a solemn little smoking congress there. One was Hendrick, captain of our Company C;* another was Lieutenant James Smith, adjutant of the Twelfth; another was a captain of the Fourteenth New Hampshire; the fourth was myself. How glad their eyes were when I produced from my breast pocket a stout bag of killikinick tobacco! We filled, lighted and smoked as cheerfully as might be while expecting that every puff would be the last. Smith and I were the only ones of the quartet who escaped unhurt, for Hendrick was severely wounded just after he left us to crawl over to his company, and the New Hampshire captain was killed while running to rejoin his regiment in the rear.

It seemed impossible that the enemy could hit so many of us unless they had some vantage spot from which to make out our exact distance and position. Probably every man of us occasionally glanced at the branches of the trees in our front with the expectation of discovering sharpshooters aloft there. But our adversaries were no doubt good shots, and besides they fired more continuously than we did. They must have had reserve ammunition at hand, while we were at a considerable distance from ours, and moreover the ground behind us was swept by hostile musketry. Twice the word was passed along our ranks to spare the powder. We fired down to ten cartridges apiece and stopped; then we fired down to five cartridges apiece; then we waited for the word to charge.

I was interested for a time by a recruit, a small and girlish youngster of barely sixteen, who lay directly in front of me. He dared not discharge his rifle, evidently for fear of getting a shot in return. I did not bully him; it would have made him no

* Albert C. Hendrick, according to official records, was a lieutenant in Company C until November 8, 1863, when he was promoted to captain of Company E. (Ed.)

braver. With a cheerful face (while the Rebel bullets skipped along our spines) I tried to coax him into sending the Rebels just one cartridge. Over and over he leveled, only to lose heart and lay his piece down, giving me a piteous half-smile of apology. Presently I appealed to one of my old soldiers, a heroic youngster of about twenty, who was loading and firing with steady, murderous pugnacity. "Bradley, give him a start," I said; "show him how to do it."

Bradley fired the rifle, but the muzzle was choked with turf, and the barrel burst. The recruit looked wofully scared, and Bradley gave him a vigorous "damning."

All this time our dead and wounded lay among us, barring a few of the latter who crawled rearward and found shelter in a ditch. Among us too were the dead and wounded of the regiments which we had relieved; and the ground in front of us was strewn with sufferers who had fallen there when Birge met his reverse. The situation of these last was most pitiable; the musketry of both sides whistled over them and around them; they were in danger from both friend and foe.

Ten paces from our front, in the merest shallow trifle of a ditch, lay an officer of an Iowa regiment disabled by three bullets. Private Brown, of Company C, crawled out to him and tried to give him a drink from his canteen. But as this gallant soldier raised himself on one elbow to perform his deed of charity a Southern ball rolled him over dying beside the sufferer whom he had sought to assist. Another brave volunteer followed Brown and accomplished his merciful errand. The Iowan drank and then said, "Never mind me now; give the Rebels the devil; never mind *me.*"

A curious change came over our men during this long musketry duel between them and Gordon's fellows. At first they were solemn enough; but this gloom passed away as they became wonted to the situation; eventually they joked, laughed aloud and exposed themselves recklessly. Corporal Gray, of Company C, dashed to the front and with his shelter tent beat out a flame which was kindling in the autumn grass, returning unharmed out of frightful peril. "Here's one for Corporal Gray!" shouted several men, springing up and pulling trigger. Then followed, "Here's one for Sheridan!" and, "Here's one for Lincoln!" and, "Here's one for McClelland who'll pay us off in gold!" and, "Here's one for Jeff Davis!" until the jest ended for lack of cartridges.

Lieutenant McCall had volunteered early to go to the rear and hurry up a supply of ammunition. It was a dangerous errand, but he went and came unhurt. When he returned he was laughing, although the Rebel balls were whistling. "They've got recruiting parties in those woods back there," he explained. "They are after skulkers with the flat of the sabre. I had hard work to get through without being enlisted by main force. By Gad, I never saw such spanking and ferruling since I was at school."

I have been minute in describing this experience of the Twelfth in close line-fighting because it gives an idea of what passed in various parts of the field during the central period of the battle. Along the entire front each side clung to its position, too exhausted to advance and too obstinate to recede. The business of Wright and Emory now was to hold Early desperately occupied until Crook should arrive to decide the struggle.

It had been Sheridan's first intention to pass Crook around Wright's left and cut off the retreat of the Confederates by seizing Winchester. But Early had shown great strength against our right; even now Gordon was being re-enforced by detachments from Wharton's division; the victory must be won there, and it would take Crook's command to win it; the surrounding and capturing must come later if at all. Thus it happened that the Army of West Virginia was eventually put into action on the right of Emory's well-worn line. Thoburn's and Duval's divisions were formed abreast and sent forward in combination.

I could not see this advance, but I heard it plainly enough. To our right, hidden from me by the isolated wood and some rolling land, the broad blue wave surged forward with a yell which lasted for minutes. In response there arose from the northern front of the wood a continuous, deafening wail of musketry without break or tremor. For a time I despaired of the success of the attack, for it did not seem possible that any troops could endure such a fire. But the yell came steadily on and triumphed gloriously over the fusillade. The captain of our right company, who could get a view of the charge, afterwards described it to me as grand; the long line tramping forward at the marching step and in perfect order, despite the rearward flow of wounded; only a few of the men firing, and those slowly like cool skirmishers.

Of course we of the Twelfth and Eighth longed to help, and believed that our help was needed. Our men recommenced the file firing and soon shot away their few remaining cartridges. Meanwhile Clark and I (impossible now to say which spoke first) told each other that the two regiments ought to charge. Captain Roach (under arrest for something, but present to fight) volunteered to carry the proposition to Colonel Thomas, and ran off stooping on his risky errand. It was a foregone conclusion that the Eighth Vermont and its veteran chief might be relied on for pitching in whenever there was a chance. In three minutes Roach was back unhurt with the message, "The Eighth will advance, and the Twelfth will keep touch with it."

Presently, looking to the left, we saw that the Vermonters were charging; and we jumped forward with a scream, the officers leading and the men hard after. We were all in a swarm, double-quicking for the wood and yelling like redskins, when we heard behind us stentorian shouts of "Halt! Lie down!" There on our tracks were mounted officers, our brigadier among them, sent by the gracious knows whom to stop our wild rush for victory—or repulse. But they were caught by the madness of the moment and put no zeal into their orders of recall.

"Well, never mind, boys," I heard McMillan say. "If you want to charge, I am not the man to stop you."

The Twelfth was still rocking back and forth, fluctuating between discipline and impulse, when an officer of Sheridan's staff (a dashing young fellow in embroidered blue shirt, with trousers tucked into his long boots) galloped into our front from the direction of Crook's column, and pointed to the wood with his drawn sabre. It was a superb picture of the equestrianism of battle; it was finer than any scene by Horace Vernet or Wouwerman. The whole regiment saw him and rejoiced in him; it flung orders to the winds and leaped out like a runaway horse. The wood was carried in the next minute, our men and Crook's entering it together from different sides, while Gordon's over-matched fellows rushed out of it in the direction of Winchester, many of them throwing away their rifles.

Such was the deciding movement of the battle, as the battle appeared to us of the right wing. Early had used up two divisions in striving to hold this wood and the adjacent fields. The slaughter in front of it proved the importance and bitterness of the fight which we had waged to get possession of it. Looking along the gentle slopes where our troops had charged, recoiled and charged again, we could see lines of dead and wounded amounting, as some thought, to fifteen hundred men. The grove itself contained numbers of Birge's slain, mostly stripped of at least a part of their clothing. There were wounded also, one of them a field officer seated at the foot of a tree, with a wounded Rebel on either side of him, all three ghastly and bloody.

"Courage, my friend," said Colonel Thomas to the one in blue. "We will take care of you soon; but first we must finish the enemy."

The sufferer waved his hand feebly and replied in a low voice, "Colonel, you are doing it gloriously."

Thomas started, for he now recognized in this mortally wounded man Lieutenant Colonel Babcock of the Seventy-fifth New York, formerly of our brigade.

"Don't trouble yourself about me now," continued Babcock. "But when you have done your fighting, spare me a couple of men to carry me away."

Crook's divisions now diverged to the right and moved against the heights where Early was rallying for a final stand. The Eighth Vermont and 160th New York, in conjunction with Upton's brigade of the Sixth Corps, followed Gordon's broken regiments and, flanking them with a sharp enfilading fire, drove them successively from a rail fence and a stone wall. Lieutenant Colonel Van Petten, of the 160th, already had a bullet hole through one thigh, but refused to give up the command of his regiment till the fighting was over. When Emory said to him, "You are going into a hot place and had better dismount," he replied, "Can't walk, General," and rode onward.

Our regiment halted in the grove and waited for ammunition. Twice it wheeled into column of companies to give passage to Birge's and Molineux's brigades, which were now pushed forward as supports to the general advance. I could not see that these commands bore any trace of the repulse of the morning; the ranks moved in fine order, and the air of the men was composed and resolute. They had just tramped by when a mounted officer, followed by a single orderly, galloped up to us. As he reined in his horse a Rebel shell, one of many which were now tearing through the wood, burst a little over his head, crowning him with its halo of smoke and whirring splinters. Had he come but a trifle slower, it might easily have cost him his life.

"That's all right, boys," he said with a short laugh. "No matter; we can lick them."

The men laughed also; then a murmur ran along the ranks that it was Sheridan; then came a spontaneous cheer.

"What regiment is this?" he asked. "What are you waiting for?"

"The Twelfth Connecticut; waiting for cartridges."

"Get them, and come along," he said, and dashed off in the direction of the firing.

Presently we advanced, in support of a battery, over high ground lately occupied by Early's centre. Our close fighting was at an end, and for the rest of the day we were spectators. Half a mile ahead of us, too far away for us to distinguish individuals, but near enough to make out movements and results, the last scene of the bloody drama was acted out. Crook's column (I suppose it was) carried the heights near Winchester and the works which crowned them. We could see the long, dark lines ascending the stony slope; we could see and hear the smoke and clatter of musketry on the summit; then we could hear our comrades' cheer of victory.

Early's battle was now reduced to a struggle to save himself from utter rout. His mounted force had been beaten by Torbert, Averell and Wilson. His infantry, sadly weakened by killed, wounded and prisoners, was retreating in great haste and complete confusion. I saw Custer's famous charge—a faraway, dark line of eager horsemen—fleeting over a broad grey slope of land, and dashing into a swarm of fugitives. Then came a furious cannonade—eight or ten fieldpieces banging with amazing rapidity—the enemies' reserve artillery covering their retreat. Behind the piling smoke of the guns spread a crimson autumnal sunset, partly veiled by long sombre bars of cloud. The battle of the Opequon, after seven hours of infantry fighting, had ended; and night was descending upon a field laden with near seven thousand killed and wounded.

It had turned out a very different battle tactically from what Sheridan had planned. But we must not blame him for that clutter of baggage on the Berryville pike which put off the beginning of the main struggle from six in the morning to nearly noon. He had ordered, the day before we advanced, that all regimental wagons, and all other wagons liable to inconvenience the movement of troops, should be sent back to Harper's Ferry. As to the gap which opened in our first line and led to its repulse, perhaps it was not easily avoidable in a wide deployment from one single point. All battles have more or less of the accidental and unexpected.

Three points I noted with regard to our opponents, the famed veterans of "the Army of Virginia." They aimed better than our men; they covered themselves (in case of need) more carefully and effectively; they could move in a swarm, without much care for alignment and touch of elbows. In short, they fought more like redskins, or like hunters, than we. The result was that they lost fewer men, though they were far inferior in numbers, and perhaps not half our numbers.*

* The above account of the battle of the Opequon (pronounced Opéckan) is corrected from a hasty and imperfect sketch written in the field at the time, and published in *Harper's Monthly* for January, 1865.

For comparative numbers and losses of the two armies see Pond's *History of the Campaigns of the Shenandoah Valley* and Irwin's *History of the Nineteenth Corps.* The latter gives Sheridan's loss as follows. Nineteenth Corps, 314 killed; 1,554 wounded; 206 missing; total, 2,074. Sixth Corps, total, 1,699. Crook's troops, total, 794. Cavalry, total, 451. Of the killed and wounded in the Nineteenth Corps Grover's four brigades lost 1,323, and Dwight's two brigades, 540.—Early's numbers and losses are a matter of discussion, and probably always will be, though we must admit that he had the smallest army. He left in our hands five guns, some flags and some 2,000 prisoners, of whom 1,200 were wounded.

Chapter XII

In October, 1864, De Forest was appointed aide to Brevet Major General William H. Emory. Mrs. De Forest wrote in a letter to her brother-in-law that her husband was supposed "to devote most of his time to writing accounts of the Nineteenth Army Corps for publication." The articles in *Harper's New Monthly Magazine* (January and February, 1865), "Sheridan's Battle of Winchester" and "Sheridan's Victory at Middletown," probably were the result of this assignment; they were the originals for Chapters XI, XIII, and XIV. Since his new post enabled him to observe the broad strategy of various engagements, the final part of *A Volunteer's Adventures* lost the tone of personal narrative and assumed more and more that of military history. It should be remembered also that in Louisiana De Forest had been a line officer and had lived in close contact with his men; but by the time of the Shenandoah Valley campaign an impersonal attitude had replaced the concern of the infantry captain for the soldiers in his company.

Unlike the previous chapter, "Fisher's Hill and the Pursuit" was never published in a contemporary periodical. At some time between 1868 and 1890, when he was preparing the first draft of *A Volunteer's Adventures,* De Forest wrote this account of the engagement specifically to fill a gap in the complete history of his army career. (Ed.)

FISHER'S HILL AND THE PURSUIT

THE battle of the Opequon ended about sunset on the 19th of September; and early on the following morning we set off in pursuit of the defeated Confederates. But the chase was a short one, for they had fallen back to the convenient position of Fisher's Hill, and that was not a nut to be cracked easily. Emory's engineer officer, Captain Oltmann, glanced along this imposing barrier with astonishment and respect.

"If they have prolonged their left sufficiently," he said, "they are inattackable."

Fisher's Hill is a natural fortification of lofty heights thrown across the Shenandoah Valley at a point where the Massanutten Mountain reduces it to a width of barely four miles. Its eastern flank and a long stretch of its front are covered by the winding gorge of the North Fork of the Shenandoah River. The only feasible road of attack is from the west over successive ranges of wooded hills which are themselves easily defensible. If there was any fault in Early's selection of this position, it lay in the fact that it was too big for his enfeebled army.

During the afternoon of the 20th Sheridan reconnoitred the imposing front of Fisher's Hill. One glance at its rocky and precipitous eastern angle convinced him that nothing could be done in that quarter. It was a spot for Rocky Mountain goats to fight in, though some human skirmishing was eventually tried there, merely as a feint. Sheridan promptly decided that he must turn the Rebels by a long detour from the west while he occupied their attention by an attack along their front. It was a far better plan of battle than that of the Opequon, and it was far more dexterously and happily executed.

Crook was selected for the turning business, and Wright for the operations against the centre. Nothing was left for Emory's two divisions but to make an uproar of skirmishing along Early's right wing, and so keep him from concentrating to support his imperiled left. I doubt if they fooled him much, but the Sixth Corps certainly did, for up to near sunset he considered it his only serious foe. Never was a general more completely surprised than he was when he heard the charging yell of the Eighth Corps over his left shoulder. Possibly it was the audacity and success of this flanking attack which inspired him to try the similar movement whereby he confounded us four weeks later.

I did not see and shall not describe the adroit and lively advances of Wright against the middle front of Fisher's Hill. During the 21st some of his regiments stormed an important outlying height on the western side of the North Fork, near Strasburg. On the following day a more advanced eminence was won by dint of musketry and rifle batteries. There was now barely

half a mile of ground between Wright's front and Early's fieldworks along the brow of Fisher's Hill.

From this statement of serious preliminary movements I return to my own modest part in the battle. On the morning of
the 21st the Twelfth Connecticut left its bivouac near Cedar-
ville (?) and moved forward in companies by the right flank,
ready to run into line of battle. As is usual with soldiers we did
not know where we were, nor where the enemy might be. We
tramped southward because we were ordered to tramp southward. We believed that the general knew whither we ought to
go. He had got a victory for us lately, and he would soon get us
another. We liked victories because they flattered our vanity
and helped to put down the rebellion.

Our march led over rolling ground, here and there wooded; in
front of us (though we could not see it) yawned the profound
and picturesque ravine of the North Fork; beyond that, superbly visible, rose the lofty slopes of Fisher's Hill and Massanutten Mountain.* We inferred that the enemy lay concealed
among those uplifted forests; but we did not bother our veteran
souls about it; that was the general's business.

Suddenly there flew towards us a hateful noise which we had
heard before oftener than we liked. It was the swift, loud, hoarse
warbling of a shell; one of Early's gunners was getting the
range of our column. The missile warbled over us, screeching
its cast-iron hatred, and dropped into silence far to the rear.
Only a single man in Company I paid any noteworthy attention
to it. That man was a recruit who had not appeared in the ranks
during yesterday's battle, but had dropped in to roll call this
morning with a story about a lame foot and a detention at a field
hospital. Suspicious and indignant, I had put him into one of
the left-hand files, meaning to keep a deadly watch on him.

There was no fight in Medad Jones, as I shall here call him.
As the shell yowled over him, fifty feet above his silly head, he
halted and turned up a whitening face while his rifle slid from
his hands and clattered to earth. Next he whirled rearward and
set off in wild flight, leaping ten feet at a stride with hands out-
spread in front, like a baseball player after a "flyer." Obviously
the long, gawky youngster was out of his senses with terror. But

* Often called Three-Top Mountain.

it was not my duty to sympathize with a dastard, and I angrily ordered the rearmost file to shoot him. The men faced about and cocked their rifles, but just then the caps of another regiment showed over a ripple of land behind us, and I saw that it would not do to fire. "As you were!" I called out, and the rearmost file promptly resumed its forward march, leaving Medad Jones in undisturbed flight for the Potomac.

Next morning (the morning of the battle) I had charge of four companies of the Twelfth which were posted as skirmishers on the left of the Nineteenth Corps. My command, perhaps half a mile in length, looked down into the gorge of the North Fork, well to the east of Strasburg. From here we had an enchanting view of the noble rampart of heights which for the moment barred our march southward. For hours not a human being was in sight beside ourselves. Both armies were swallowed up in the varied and forested landscape. Eventually, along in the afternoon I think, we saw a regiment or two in the valley to the east, making for the extreme right of Early's position. As I have already said, this right was nearly precipitous, and I easily inferred that the attack there was a feint. Nevertheless, it broke out in violent musketry and continued to clatter away at intervals for hours, the assailants even making show of an escalade.

Meantime I got orders to open a skirmishing fire upon the woods which confronted me on the southern side of the gorge, nearly half a mile distant. It seemed ridiculous, for we could not discern a living creature over there; and although I set my fellows at work, I was ashamed of such a waste of good cartridges. For two or three hours, and perhaps longer, we languidly fusilladed without getting above three bullets in return. At last, from the faraway confronting forest, we heard a long-drawn cry of "Wh—at the hell are you shoot—ing at?"

The men laughed, and I stopped the musketry. But presently up cantered an aide from the right to ask what the devil we had ceased firing for.

"Can't see any Rebels," I explained. "Only one man over there, and he may have gone. Mere waste of ammunition."

"Never mind," laughed the aide. "Waste all you've got. General Sheridan wants you to keep up a tip-top racket. Blaze away as though you meant to follow up with a charge."

Such was to be my part in the battle, it seems, and I played it indefatigably till near sunset, pitching some forty hundred bullets into Early's outlying woodlands. The squirrels and stray pigs over there must have wondered what we had against them. Of course the bottom purpose of this cartridge burning on the left was to aid in distracting the attention of the Southerners from our serious turning movement far away to the right. Perhaps the Twelfth Connecticut was just a bit useful in that way, although it did not get a man killed or wounded, and reported only Medad Jones "missing."

Meanwhile we could not see nor so much as guess what was being done to the west of us. Crook was tramping out his detour of fourteen miles to reach Early's vulnerable flank, without arousing a single farmer or Rebel scout to carry the news of his coming to Fisher's Hill. Averell's cavalry had taken Crook's place on the right of the Sixth Corps, which was manoeuvring westward and skirmishing vigorously southward. Emory's two divisions (all but my line and the regiment in the gorge) were creeping noiselessly and stealthily after the Sixth Corps. The army was gathering for a deadly spring upon the unsuspecting Confederates.

It was just about sunset when I discovered that the battle had suddenly commenced in earnest and was being won in the same instant. There was Satan to pay on the right, as an excited and delighted lieutenant phrased it. A volcano of cannonade and musketry played there all at once, and for some minutes a splendid semicircle of spouting fire was visible. Then a huge column of dust, rising high above the forest and sweeping southward, informed us that the enemy were in full flight. Crook's thunderbolt of a flank attack, followed promptly by an uphill scramble of Wright's and Emory's leading brigades, had broken and routed Early in a quarter of an hour. Sixteen of his guns were left in his entrenchments, and thirteen hundred of his men became prisoners, while about two hundred and fifty were killed and wounded. Sheridan's loss was a little over five hundred, nearly one half from the Sixth Corps.*

This was the victory of September 22 at Fisher's Hill, gained only about seventy-two hours after the victory of the Opequon.

* Sixth Corps, 238; Eighth, 162; Nineteenth, 114; cavalry, 14;—total, 528.

But we did not go to bed on the battlefield this time; our young general had already learned better than that. All night we tramped after Early, in great confusion at times, now and then firing into each other, perhaps oftener than into the enemy. Once the Twelfth, and doubtless the whole brigade also, was hustled off the road to let somebody's cavalry pass. Of course we dropped on the wayside turf and under the thickets, and slept till orders roused us again. Then we tramped onward—tramped and reeled onward the whole wearisome night—eager to overtake Early and finish him,—marching with singular zeal and perseverance,—making for instance one noble stretch of thirteen miles without a halt.

The cavalry were less fervent, or perhaps less fortunate, in carrying out orders. Torbert, who had been sent up the Luray Valley to intercept Early's flight, recoiled from a strong position at Milford held by Lomax's mounted riflemen. Averell, who was to have led our pursuing column, went into camp near Strasburg. It must be admitted, I think, that up to this time our troopers had not established a moral superiority over their opponents and were sometimes too cautious about fighting. A cavalry sergeant of a New York regiment explained the fact to me in the following fashion.

"At close quarters we can whip Lomax's men; they have no sabres and generally no revolvers. But at long range we are rather afraid of them; they carry Enfields which shoot farther than our carbines."

All the 23d we chased our retreating foes, picking up many leg-weary stragglers. One of them told us that their army was a completely disorganized rabble, barring perhaps a thousand men, largely officers, who formed the rear guard. Late in the afternoon, looking ahead across a broad, dusty flat, we espied Early's baggage train. We hoped to overtake it, but it quickened its pace and gained ground on us, the mules galloping and the guard double-quicking. Then our hopes and spirits failed us, and we were ready to sob with disappointment. Sheridan came up at this moment and put a stop to the fruitless chase.

"The infantry have done enough," he said. "They have done nobly. I wish others had done as well."

That very evening, if my memory serves me, I heard that he had disrated Averell and ordered him to Washington.

The pursuit finally ended, on the 26th of September, in the region of Harrisonburg and Mt. Crawford, where we remained till the 5th of October, devastating crops and devouring cattle. Meantime I was detailed as ordnance officer to the first division of our corps. I did not want the position, because of its large property responsibilities; but I had scant time to worry over it, for two days later I was appointed aide to General Emory.* At this time I was in a common soldier's blouse and trousers, both so ragged and dirty that I was ashamed to present myself at corps headquarters.

"You see the only clothes that I have at hand, General," I said. "My uniform is at Harper's Ferry."

"I am not very well dressed myself," he replied. "I think you will do."

On the 6th of October we commenced moving north, the Eighth Corps leading, then the Sixth, then the Nineteenth. Behind came the cavalry, in a broad line from mountain to mountain, burning the mills and barns and driving off the cattle and sheep. Between Mt. Crawford and Woodstock over seventy mills and two thousand barns, crammed with flour, wheat, corn and hay, were destroyed. The inhabitants were left so stripped of food that I cannot imagine how they escaped starvation. The valley was thus desolated, partly as a punishment for the frequent bushwhacking of our trains and stragglers, but mainly to prevent Early from subsisting his army in it and marching once more to the Potomac. It was a woful sight for civilized eyes; but as a warlike measure it was very effective.

Meantime Early, who had been strengthened by Kershaw's infantry and Rosser's cavalry, resumed the offensive in a cautious way and tried to worry our mounted detachments. The result was Sheridan's famous order to Torbert to "either whip or get whipped." Next day we infantrymen heard with delight that our troopers had routed Rosser and Lomax and taken eleven of their twelve fieldpieces with three hundred prisoners.

* I had been on Emory's staff as inspector general when he commanded the first division in Louisiana.

The pursuit, some people said, had continued for twenty-six miles, mostly at a gallop. Sheridan, or Torbert, or Custer, or somebody else had offered fifty dollars for that twelfth cannon. It was a fine story, and pretty nearly all true.

I was amused at the wrath of a young West Pointer from Torbert's headquarters when we congratulated him on the fact that Sheridan could make even the cavalry fight.

"Sheridan had nothing to do with it," he asserted. "Torbert was just about to pitch into the Rebs when Sheridan happened to come along. The fight would have come off just the same if he had kept away and minded his own business."

My impression is that jealousy is about as common among regular officers as it is in a singing choir or an opera troupe.

On the 10th of October, the next day after Rosser's defeat, we recrossed the Shenandoah. A single, tall wooden bridge gave passage to Crook's divisions, and then to Wright's, with their trains of artillery and baggage wagons. A herd of hundreds of cattle and an acre or two of sheep were bullied into swimming the current. The passage occupied four hours and was a picturesque spectacle, but made wearisome waiting for the Nineteenth Corps, which stood meanwhile in line of battle on a plateau south of the river, ready to repulse Early if he should be intrusive.

I noticed during these long hours that my corps commander looked impatient and worried. He was an elderly officer and no longer in perfect health; he doubtless feared lest he might have to fight there, unsupported, with his back to the gorge of the Shenandoah; he thought that Crook and Wright ought to ford the stream in solid column and make room promptly for us to advance. When the Nineteenth Corps at last got a chance to move, it went like an avalanche. Brigade abreast of brigade tramped down the slope and across the valley, dashed into the water wherever there was a shallow, and swarmed up the opposite bank. In twenty minutes we were across a river which had detained the two preceding corps for hours.

When the last regiment was over, the general turned to me and ordained the annihilation of the bridge. "Burn it to the water's edge," he said. "The 116th New York will carry out your orders. Stay here till the business is done."

It was an easier job to command than to execute. The supporting uprights were enormously thick beams which refused to take fire except superficially. Moreover, while we were still trying to start a blaze, I saw, less than a mile to the southward, descending the hillside road which we had lately traversed, a long column of Southern cavalry. This I did not care for, if they would come straight at us; we could whip in fair fight three times our weight in troopers; at least so I believed.

But the column did not come straight forward; it divided into two columns, one filing to the left and the other to the right; and I comprehended at once that my detachment was to be attacked on both flanks unless it promptly rejoined the corps. Here was a bit of deviltry that had not been included in my commander's instructions. It is too little to say that I was perplexed; I was tactically confounded and smartly scared. Should I hold on and get myself surrounded, and perhaps lose the 116th New York? I would have rejoiced greatly to have some superior officer arrive and tell me whether to fight or not. It became clear to me all at once that I had not that confidence and promptness of decision which make a great general.

The result was that I evaded a combat and spared Emory the necessity of sending back a brigade to disentangle me. The beams that would not burn were chopped; the middle planking was hastily piled and set on fire; the bridge, though not exterminated, was made impassable for the nonce. But I was very much afraid of the general for some days afterward; and I never dared tell him in detail how imperfectly I had carried out his orders. After all, the destruction of the bridge was a matter of small importance; for if we could ford the river easily and swiftly, the enemy could do it also.

That night we went into the straggling position behind Cedar Creek, out of which we were tumbled by a surprise nine days later. It is hardly necessary now to explain that Sheridan would not have occupied it if he could have found a better one without going as far north as Berryville or Halltown and so inviting the war back to the neighborhood of the Potomac.

But at this time we had no fear of a prompt and energetic resumption of hostilities on the part of Rebeldom in the valley. Grant believed that Early's army was weak and demoralized, and wanted the Sixth Corps sent to aid in the siege of Richmond. On the 12th Wright set out for Washington in order to take transports for the James River; but on the 13th, while fording the Shenandoah at Ashby's Gap, he was faced about by an order from Sheridan. Early, unluckily for himself, was already showing his renewed strength. Had he kept quiet but two days longer, he would have found only Crook and Emory in the lines at Cedar Creek, and he might easily have beaten them, barring accidents.

Let us go back to the 13th of October and its military revelations. On the morning of that day Emory made a personal reconnoissance toward Strasburg, taking along with him his staff, a brigade, and a section of the First Maine Battery. After a few miles of southing the infantry was left in a sheltered position, and we officers pushed forward with the two howitzers. I could not discover a sign of the enemy; but the general either saw, or divined, or suspected something alarming; he twice sent back word to Sheridan that Early was at Fisher's Hill in great force. I had occasion to learn afterwards that the wary veteran was very unwilling to have Wright's divisions withdrawn from the valley.

Erelong the howl of a shell, rushing toward our group and exploding behind it, let us know that we were not among friends. The shot apparently came from the other side of a strip of forest nearly half a mile in front of us. Obviously our presence was known to a Rebel reconnoitring party which like us had brought along cannon.

"Can't you hit those fellows, Bradbury?" asked the general.

Bradbury, smiling incredulously, agreed to try it. He waited for another shot from the foe; then he made an estimate of the distance between them and us; then he cut his fuse, loaded and trained his gun, and let drive. We could hear the shell warble southward, and burst with a crash softened by distance. Silence followed; the enemy did not fire another shot; the general chuckled, "Bradbury, you smashed them."

We rode on cautiously, traversed the belt of forest, and came out upon a cleared knoll, yellow with wheat stubble. There was a broken wheel of a gun carriage, and beside it a tattered leg of some unlucky greyback's trousers drenched with fresh blood.

We were amazed, and the general was full of admiration, or pretended to be.

"Bradbury, it's the best shot that ever was made," he declared. "I am an old artillerist myself, and I couldn't have equalled it."

He must have been joking, especially as he was not an old artillerist, but an old cavalryman.

Bradbury beckoned me to one side and whispered, "It was the purest accident in all history. I never was more astonished in my life. No wonder the Rebs got away as quick as they could clap on a spare wheel. They must have thought we were wizards."

Riding onward, we reached a point whence we could see one face of Hupp's Hill, an eminence well in advance of the northern front of Fisher's Hill. At that very moment a long blue line was slowly climbing the open green slope toward the wooded summit. We watched this advance, two miles or more away from us, without being able to take part in it and without knowing what it signified. Suddenly a grey frill of smoke lined the edge of the woodland and clung there silently for several minutes. Then the line of blue went to bits, staggered in groups and dots down the slope, and halted behind a low crest of earth. There it took shape again, laid down in ranks and opened a file fire, as we could make out by the frail spouts of smoke. This, as we afterwards learned, was Thoburn's unlucky attack on Kershaw's temporary position at Hupp's Hill, which cost us two or three hundred killed and wounded in about a quarter of an hour.

The events of this 13th of October indicated that Early had been re-enforced and that he was in a mood to venture the offensive. No wonder Sheridan summoned back Wright from Ashby's Gap and urged Grant not to weaken our Shenandoah army for the present. Emory, I have some reason to know, felt much easier in mind when he learned that the Sixth Corps had resumed position on his right rear.

A day or two after Thoburn's misadventure Early pushed forward a bold reconnoissance of infantry against the centre of our position. One of his brigades, in line of battle, came quietly over the open fields on the right front of the Nineteenth Corps and halted for twenty minutes on the broad crest of a gentle ridge. From the elevated natural bastion occupied by Emory's camps and earthworks we could see that the grey-clad soldiers were sitting or lying at ease, and that some of the officers were studying the landscape with field glasses. Major Wilkinson, one of my staff comrades, rode within two hundred yards of this line without attracting a hail or a bullet. We could have poured an effective plunging fire of shell and canister into it from the howitzers in our embrasures; but such a fire might have drawn a reply from masked batteries which would have wrought havoc in our crowded camps. The general evidently thought that the game would not be worth the candle.

"They are not Confederates," he cunningly insisted. "It is one of Wright's brigades returned from a reconnoissance."

One staff officer after another was sent to investigate the situation and make report of it. Thus an hour was frittered away, and eventually the greybacks took themselves off in peace, very little the wiser for their expedition and probably suspecting that either we were weak, or that we wanted to draw them into an ambush. When the general at last admitted that they were Rebels, he added, "I think we learned as much as they did."

Sheridan, who arrived later, had more combative ideas. "If they come again, go for them," he exhorted. "Pick a fight with them. Hurt them all you can."

Notwithstanding Early's hardy reconnoitrings nobody in our army believed that he contemplated a serious attack; at least, if there was any such belief afloat, I never heard of it. The intercepted bogus despatch, purporting to come from Longstreet and proposing a junction which should annihilate us, was accepted for what it was, a ruse. On the 15th of October Sheridan felt at liberty to visit Washington for a consultation with Stanton and Halleck. Wright, the senior major general present, remained in charge of the army, little suspecting how much he would have on his hands.

I do not mean to insinuate that he did not attend to his duties energetically and intelligently. On the 17th, two days before the attack upon us, he inspected our whole front in company with the other two major generals. Emory, who was an elderly man and something of an alarmist, grumbled at Crook's position, asserting that it did not command the valley in front of it. "The enemy," he said, "could march thirty thousand men through that defile, and we not know it till they were on our left flank."

Wright would not assent to this opinion; he only feared an attack on his other wing. Nevertheless, acting upon a suggestion just received from Sheridan, he brought in Moore's brigade of Powell's cavalry from Front Royal and posted it at Buckton's Ford about three miles to the left of Thoburn's brigade.

Through this gap, thirty-six hours later, marched three divisions of Southern infantry folded so safe in the spectral mist of morning that they were neither seen nor heard.

Meanwhile, that is on the 18th, the day before the attack, Crook became anxious as to the security of his position and sent forward a brigade to reconnoitre. The commander, Colonel Harris, brought back a report that he had advanced to Early's camps and had found them deserted. Of course he was mistaken, and we must suppose that he stopped at Hupp's Hill, the height which Kershaw held on the 13th when he repulsed Thoburn. This erroneous report probably aided not a little towards lulling our advanced left wing into believing that it stood in no immediate peril of an attack in force.

Chapter XIII

DURING the battle of Cedar Creek De Forest carried orders from General Emory to division commanders and from division commanders to brigade commanders. Though not entirely safe from musket and cannon fire as he galloped from unit to unit, he was in less danger than if he had been with Company I of the Twelfth Connecticut. Since his duties carried him to all parts of the battlefield, he had a position of vantage from which he could observe the movements of the various regiments. No doubt it was such an engagement as the one described in Chapters XIII and XIV that demonstrated to De Forest a vital fact about warfare: the utter confusion of actual combat. He wrote with complete truthfulness to William Dean Howells in 1887 that "nothing is more confounding, fragmentary, incomprehensible, than a battle as one sees it. And you see so little, too, unless you are a staff officer and ride about, or perhaps a general." (Ed.)

THE BATTLE OF CEDAR CREEK *

OUR infantry position at Cedar Creek was an echelon of three lines, posted on three successive crests of moderate height.

The left and most advanced crest was held by Thoburn's division of Crook's Army of West Virginia, sometimes called the Eighth Corps. The central crest, about a mile to the rear of the first and hidden from it by woods, showed the rather crowded camps of Emory's two divisions of the Nineteenth Corps. The third and right-hand crest, if a mass of hillocks and hollows deserves that name, was occupied by Wright's three divisions of the Sixth Corps.

Thoburn and Emory were partly covered by rude breast-

* The first draft of Chapters XIII and XIV appeared in *Harper's New Monthly Magazine* for February, 1865, under the title, "Sheridan's Victory of Middletown." (Ed.)

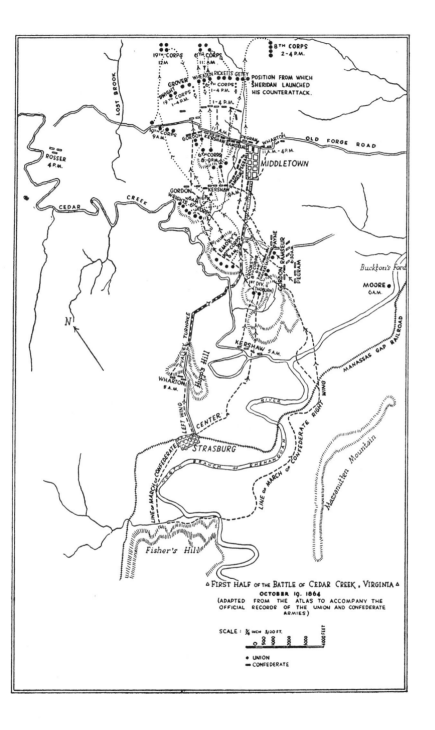

FIRST HALF OF THE BATTLE OF CEDAR CREEK, VIRGINIA

OCTOBER 19. 1864

(ADAPTED FROM THE ATLAS TO ACCOMPANY THE
OFFICIAL RECORDS OF THE UNION AND CONFEDERATE
ARMIES)

SCALE: ¾ INCH 5,120 FT.

0   500   1000   2000   3000   4000 FEET

• UNION
— CONFEDERATE

works, garnished with a few embrasures and fieldpieces. West of the Sixth Corps, spread out over a gently rolling country, lay the watchful cavalry of Torbert. The back of the echelon, toward the east, was commanded by a long eminence which bore the camps of Hayes' small division and Kitching's so-called "provisional division," both of Crook's command. Here, in seemingly complete security, stood Sheridan's headquarters and the parks of reserve ammunition and rations.

The obvious faults of the position, I then thought and still think, were the isolation of Thoburn and the lack of earthworks around Kitching and Hayes. But at that time, as I have already stated, it was not seriously suspected by our generals that Early would, without further large re-enforcements, venture a serious attack. How should he when he had not above eighteen thousand men, and we were more than twice that number?

The Confederacy, however, was in such a desperate case that its commanders were driven to risk venturesome campaigns and deliver battles which might fairly be called forlorn hopes. Like Washington just before Trenton and Princeton their only chance of success, or escape, lay in audacity. Early surely had not a rational expectation of overthrowing us in battle. But if he attacked with unexpected boldness, he might possibly astonish us into the belief that he had a strong force, thus deterring us from re-enforcing Grant against Lee, and perhaps scaring us back to the Potomac. For these important and indeed pressing reasons an assault on our superior army was hardily planned and fearlessly executed by a general whose military ability has been greatly underrated because his means were so inferior to his needs.

Early decided to attack the left and rear of our echelon because it seemed likely that we would not expect him on that side. To reach us there he would have to descend into the gorge at the base of Massanutten Mountain, ford by night the North Fork of the Shenandoah and skirt Thoburn's position for a mile or more, sometimes not four hundred yards from our pickets. Also there was a likelihood of being discovered and attacked on the other flank by Moore's brigade of cavalry at Buckton's Ford. Finally, his army would be for hours separated into four isolated columns, of course liable to isolated defeat.

The movement began during the early evening of October 18th. Nearly all the cavalry and light artillery were to deploy in front of our right with a view to occupying the attention of Torbert and the Sixth Corps until the real attack had flanked and overthrown our left. Kershaw's infantry division was to storm Thoburn's isolated camp, while Wharton's division and several batteries should push for the front of Emory. Gordon with the old Stonewall Corps, consisting of his own and Ramseur's and Pegram's divisions, was to make an assault at daybreak on the left rear of our centre and reserve. This column had as vanguard the cavalry brigade of Payne, who was instructed to surprise our general headquarters, capture Sheridan and seize our train.

Early, it will be observed, proposed a concentric movement of four columns, through hours of darkness, against a superior army. It was about as venturesome an enterprise as the nocturnal escalade of a strong fortress.. But the riskiest escalades sometimes succeed by dint of good luck and a surprise.

Just after dark the Confederates commenced their anxious and cautious descent from Fisher's Hill. The canteens were left in camp, lest they should clatter against the shanks of the bayonets; the old soldiers who formed the columns understood perfectly that their expedition was in the nature of an Indian war party; and this stealthy nocturnal advance upon a disciplined foe was accomplished with complete success.

There was a moment, indeed, when the enterprise reeled on the brink of failure. About two in the morning some of Thoburn's pickets reported to him that they had heard through the chilly fog a rustling of underbrush and a muffled trampling. He thought it sufficient to order a part of his command into the trenches, as was his regular custom at daybreak or earlier. It would have been wise to send out a reconnoissance, but probably he put faith in Harris' report * that Early had disappeared, and no doubt he shared the general belief that the enemy were too weak to venture a serious attack. He was an able and most gallant officer, and he fell that morning doing a soldier's duty.

Thus did fortune favor the seemingly mad plan of the Confederate general. An hour before dawn his shivering columns

* See page 203. (Ed.)

lay within six hundred yards of the doomed camps where thousands slumbered and unsuspicious sentries yawned. There is a story, which I can neither prove nor disprove, that some of Kershaw's men, disguised in our uniforms, regularly relieved a considerable line of Crook's pickets, thus making an opening for the advance of their division.

That morning I was in the saddle before there was light enough to let me see my white horse two rods away. Wright had ordered both Emory and Torbert to push strong reconnoissances to Fisher's Hill and find out for certain whether Early was there or not. Our Nineteenth Corps column was to consist of Molineux's brigade, followed at a short distance by the brigades of Birge and Macauley, all from Grover's division. My business was to see that the reconnoissance started on time, and to report the exact minute of its departure to my general. This is an example of the minute supervision which a veteran regular officer maintains over his command.

Thus I was at General Grover's quarters (hungry and glad to breakfast with him) at the moment when the battle opened. The "awful rose of dawn," veiled and softened by thick morning mist, had just begun to bloom over an eastern crest of hill, when, a mile away on our left front, a shrill prolonged wail of musketry broke forth, followed by scream on scream of the Rebel yell. The unexpected and astounding clamor revealed to us that Early had assaulted Thoburn's isolated position. General Grover and I silently exchanged a glance of surprise and comprehension. Then, in his usual gentle, monotonous voice, he said to his aide, "Tell the brigade commanders to move their men into the trenches"; while I tumbled into my saddle and galloped off to inform my chief of the situation.

I found him just up, coatless and hatless and uncombed, shouting for his horse and his orderlies. He was more excited and alarmed than would have seemed necessary to an ignoramus in warlike matters. As an old and trained officer he understood perfectly what a frightful mess we would be in if Early should fall upon the unfortified rear of our poorly connected echelon. Without waiting to hear my report through he answered, "Go to the commanding general with my compliments and state that the enemy have assaulted General Crook's left in force."

As I rode away I heard him grumbling, "I said so; I knew that if we were attacked, it would be there."

I found General Wright, surrounded by his staff, preparing to mount. He knew what I had to tell him, but he listened to my brief message patiently and replied with the formal courtesy of the regular army, "Give my compliments to General Emory and say that I will be with him shortly. But have you any knowledge, Captain, as to how the assault succeeded?"

I told him that I thought it had failed, because the musketry had outlasted the yelling, the latter being probably the Rebels' noise, and the former ours.

"I think so, too," he replied; but we were both mistaken. Favored by a thick fog, Kershaw's division swept through Thoburn's pickets without responding to their scattering musketry and took many of them prisoners. The few soldiers in the trenches, unable to see precisely what was coming, either fired late or not at all. There was a blind, confused, feeble scuffle of less than five minutes across the breastworks. The seven guns in the embrasures were taken before a single one of them could be discharged. The yelling assailants rapidly flooded the whole camp, shooting or capturing men just struggling out of sleep, and driving before them two or three thousand astonished fugitives who at the Opequon and Fisher's Hill had fought with dashing courage. No daybreak rush of moccasined Shawnees or Wyandots was ever more dextrous and triumphant than this charge of Kershaw's Georgians, Mississippians and South Carolinians.*

The attack on the extreme advanced left of our echelon was presently followed by another on the rear of its centre.

Returning from the Sixth Corps to General Emory's tent, I learned that he had gone to inspect the front of his position, and I was about to gallop after him at once when I heard with surprise a lively rattle of skirmishing beyond the crest of the long hill east of the pike, where stood Sheridan's headquarters and the camps of Hayes and Kitching. I paused for a few minutes to listen and thought of riding over there to find out what was happening. But as no heavy musketry ensued, I concluded that the sputtering was merely a squabble between Crook's outposts

* Two brigades of Georgians, one of Mississippians and one of South Carolinians.

and some gang of guerrillas, and I therefore pushed southward in search of my corps commander. Had I ascended the misty ridge (over which the grey daybreak was trying to reach us) I should have seen our fate stealing upon us with rapid strides. The old Stonewall Division (Ramseur on the right and Gordon on the left, with Pegram in support) was sweeping in line of battle up the bare slope, chasing in the West Virginia pickets without answering their fire.

The result of the morning's combat now depended upon the forty-five hundred men who composed Hayes' division and Kitching's "provisional division." If they gave up their commanding hill to Gordon, he would at once be on the back of the Nineteenth Corps and might easily drive it from its camp, even without the help of Kershaw and Wharton. I never could understand why Crook's usually spirited veterans went to pieces so quickly as they did that morning. One explanation is that Hayes and Kitching did not expect attack from the east, and were both in line fronting south, so that Gordon struck them on the left flank. However that may be, both divisions broke after but a few minutes of fighting and fled in such dismay as to be of no further use that day except as a reserve late in the afternoon. The entire loss of Crook's seven thousand men was only three hundred and fourteen killed and wounded to five hundred and thirty-three missing, mostly prisoners.

I think that this rout of Hayes and Kitching had not yet taken place when I found General Emory near his breastworks consulting with Generals Wright and Crook. They already knew of Thoburn's defeat; in fact, McMillan's brigade had just advanced to cover the fugitives and check Kershaw's pursuit; but of all this I was as yet ignorant and even unsuspicious. I saw, indeed, a steady flow of stragglers pouring out of a wood on our left and passing rearward; but I supposed that they were Thoburn's camp followers getting out of the range of fire, after the prudent fashion of noncombatants. Presently Emory sent me to enquire who those bummers were and whether any disaster had happened to McMillan. As I neared the wood the number of fugitives increased to a widespread swarm of twenty or twenty-five hundred, utterly without organization and many of them without arms. They were not running, not breathless and looking over their shoulders, but just trudging tranquilly rearward like a crowd hastening home from a circus.

"To the Eighth Corps," responded man after man when I asked what command they belonged to.

"Captain, what *does* this mean?" I said to the first officer whom I met.

"Why, I suppose it means that we are retreating," he replied with a bitter smile and a satirical emphasis on the final word.

"What! has Thoburn been driven from his position!" I exclaimed in amazement and dismay.

"His men have," said the captain, perhaps remembering that Thoburn lay dead in the captured camp.

Before returning to General Emory I hastily rode along McMillan's line and warned such regimental commanders as I could see that their battle was at hand. I had scarcely left the brigade when another aide galloped up with orders for it to advance; and, breasting the stream of runaways, it pushed into the tangled wood which was soon to be its slaughter pen. It was a mistake to send it forward alone, and it would have been a mistake to keep it where it was. The fact is that our Nineteenth Corps' position was already untenable, and we ought to have been getting out of it. But who could know that except the enemy?

I rejoined Emory just as he got news that Gordon had routed Crook's reserve and was in possession of the hill which overlooked our rear. He immediately ordered two of Grover's brigades to ascend the slope beyond the pike and do their best to hold back this new and most formidable peril. The remaining three brigades of the corps continued for the present at the breastworks, guarding against an expected attack in force from the south; for none of us could yet believe that Early's main body was in our rear and that our fortified plateau had become a trap, sure to ruin us if we did not skip out of it.

A roar of musketry from the wood on our left front informed us that McMillan's brigade had opened its struggle to check Kershaw's division. Within a space of barely ten minutes a sanguinary drama was enacted in that spacious thicket of trees and undergrowth. My old regiment, the Twelfth Connecticut, fired three rounds at close quarters before it was forced into the first retreat that it ever made under the assault of an enemy. The resistance of the other regiments was similarly sharp and hopeless and brief. In the mist and underbrush and in the flurry of close fighting, there was small chance to reload and there was some hand-to-hand work. After the battle we found men here who had been killed with the bayonet and others whose skulls had been dashed in with rifle butts.

Here and there the antagonists were so intermingled that they held hasty martial dialogues. Charles Wells of my company, being summoned to surrender by three Southerners, instantly shot one of them, and was shot by the two others. Lieutenant Mullen, of Company B,* called to a squad which he supposed to belong to the Eighth Vermont, "What the devil are you firing this way for?" The answer was, "Surrender, you d—d Yankee!" followed by more shooting, too hasty to be effective. Mullen, seeing now that his own men had fallen or vanished, dashed headlong into a thicket and escaped. Lieutenant Colonel Lewis, the commander of the Twelfth, got away by galloping past a swarm of Rebels and through a shower of bullets amid cries of "Kill that officer!" The fugitives were severely raked by the fire of a line drawn up across the hollow through which they had entered the wood not twenty minutes previous. During that day McMillan's regiments lost more than one third of their fighting men, the greater part on this hill of sacrifice where they suffered for the salvation of the army.

Not a battle flag fell into the enemy's hands, and the brigade rallied within two hundred yards of the wood. But this second stand was too near a victorious and advancing enemy to result in anything but a little more useless bloodshed. A semicircle of dropping musketry converged on the new position, for Early's reserve under Wharton had just got within range, and its skirmishers were raking us from the south. Our men were apparently bewildered, and did not know which way to face, and could not be brought to fire. To get another telling fight out of them here was clearly impossible, and a retreat southward along the pike was ordered by someone, probably Emory.

It was singular how few Confederates I could see at this period of the battle. We were being peppered and demoralized and

* According to official records John Mullen was a lieutenant in Company G. (Ed.)

beaten (like Braddock's and St. Clair's regulars) by an undiscoverable enemy. Our camp, overlooked as it now was by the enemy, had been changed from a fortress into a slaughter pen. Our men knew this as well as if they were all major generals, and wanted to get out of their trap before they recommenced fighting. Eventually, when Wright had established a respectable front on the plateau north of us, he sent Emory orders to join him there with all our remaining force.

But before this happened there was much to do and more to suffer. Our two brigades which had crossed the pike to recover Crook's position were forced northward by a converging fire from Kershaw and Ramseur. Meanwhile the headquarters tents and stores had been loaded and sent away under a pelting of bullets from Payne's cavalry. The train of heavy wagons and ambulances escaped by a wretched country road which forded Cedar Creek and led circuitously toward Winchester. To carry off this host of clumsy vehicles with a loss of only four or five was a feat which reflected great credit on our quartermasters and commissaries.

The general ammunition wagons had scarcely begun to file out of park when one of Payne's troopers dashed up shouting, "Here! bring that train this way."—"What the hell have you got to do with this train?" replied a guard, and sent a bullet through the bold adventurer.

Patrick, one of the Negro waiters at Emory's quarters, made a gallant attempt to save the staff cow, but was obliged to take to his heels across lots, leaving his charge mortally wounded. At a little stone house nearby, a reporter of the New York *Herald* was yelling for his blanket roll and getting it thrust out to him through the half-opened door, which was immediately slammed in his face to keep out random bullets. The occupants of this dwelling, a poor widow and her children, remained shut up in it all day, cowering below the level of the windows for safety.

The appearance of the landscape northward from this point was singular and doleful. Hundreds of noncombatants and many who should have been in the ranks, with many whose bloody clothing showed that their fighting for that day had ended, were drifting rearward confusedly, yet with curious deliberation. Over a space of a mile square the fields, long since stripped of their rail fences, were dotted with wagons, ambulances, pack mules, army followers and stray soldiers, the latter chiefly from Crook's command, none of them hurrying, but all aiming at the directest safe route to Winchester.

If Early could now have launched upon us a powerful cavalry, he would have made a great sweep of prisoners and might have converted our retreat into a rout. Our only infantry in good fighting condition was the Sixth Corps and perhaps two brigades of the Nineteenth. Fortunately our troopers were still in perfect order and kept Early's mounted tatterdemalions in awe.

About the time that our people were driven in from the hill east of the pike General Emory's horse, which was white and a tempting mark, received a fatal shot. He mounted another (which was killed later) and rode to the front of our camp to look after the brigades still in the trenches. I remained for a few minutes near the pike and aided to keep order in the retreat which had begun there. At first it required much shouting and gesticulation to prevent the worried troops from dissolving into swarms of runaways. One brigade went rearward at double-quick until the line began to fluctuate ominously, when the officers sprang to the front with drawn swords and beat back the panic, after which the men moved on at the ordinary marching step and in good order. Matters were helped somewhat by another brigade which trotted up from the camps to the pike and, hastily forming line there, gave a momentary check to the enemy.

I did not see the noble death of Lieutenant Morton, of the First Maine Battery, although it must have happened near this period of the battle. Ordered by Major Bradbury to try grape at close quarters, he galloped to the pike with two howitzers and opened fire within two hundred paces of Kershaw's line, losing his guns, half his men and his life in the hopeless struggle.

Barring these partial efforts, the left of the Nineteenth Corps was now drifting rearward, followed by a worrying shower of musketry and a gathering cannonade. Belated stragglers were running from our camps, bearing the havresacks or blankets for which they had risked their lives, and leaving behind the helpless wounded and the dead who needed no succor. Random bullets tossed up whiffets of dust from the hard-trodden earth, and their quick, spiteful *whit-whit* sang through an air acrid with the smoke of gunpowder. Here and there were splashes of blood, and zigzag trails of blood, and bodies of men and horses. I never on any other battlefield saw so much blood as on this of Cedar Creek. The firm limestone soil would not receive it, and there was no pitying summer grass to hide it.

When I rejoined General Emory he had just made his last possible disposition for resistance on his original ground by posting Birge along the reverse of our breastworks, where McMillan had already established Davis. A shallow, dry ditch on the outside of a trivial redoubt constituted the final hold of the Nineteenth Corps on its fortified camp. It was in the case of a man who has been pushed out of a window, and who desperately clings to the sill with the ends of his fingers. Behind Birge and Davis was a steep and rocky hillside, gnarled with bushes and stunted trees, where rallying was impossible and orderly retreat difficult.

At this time, I believe, we had already been directed by Wright to withdraw to a plateau north of us and form on the right of the Sixth Corps which was going into line of battle there. But Emory wanted to check Kershaw and Wharton long enough to enable us to get out of our trap without being closely followed and quite routed.

"What has the chief of artillery stopped firing for?" he demanded as soon as he saw me. "Ride over to that hill and tell him to reopen with those pieces."

Descending a rough gully and cantering up a stony height, I found Bradbury sitting his horse behind Taft's battery, and gave him the general's message.

"Our infantry is in the way," he said. "The two armies are awfully mixed up. Moreover, we ought to move; the Rebs are between us and Winchester already; and we shall lose these guns if we stop any longer."

The hill offered a broad view of the field of combat; and I could clearly see that the battle on our original line was quite lost to us; in fact, over to the eastward it was already volleying and smoking half a mile beyond our rear. Getty's division of the Sixth Corps seemed to be pushing toward the hill lately lost by

Hayes, as if with the purpose of recovering it and clearing our line of retreat. But Gordon, Ramseur and Pegram, now united in line of battle, confronted and outflanked Getty, keeping up a heavy fire. I could not hear their musketry at that distance, but I could plainly see its long ripple of smoke, like waves breaking on a distant shore. Presently we observed that Getty had halted and was volleying heavily from a plateau just west of the pike and half a mile of our camp. Obviously it was our duty and interest to join him there as promptly as might be.

It was now somewhere between eight and nine o'clock in the morning. Since the rout of Crook's divisions the Nineteenth Corps had been struggling alone for two or three hours against an enemy on its flank and at its back. It was time for us to back out of our hole, and we marched rearward sadly diminished in numbers, though not a regiment had entirely disbanded. Taft labored in vain to get his battery away from the steep and stony eminence where it was posted. His veteran artillerymen put their burly shoulders to the guns; but three out of the four were perforce left bottom up in the hillside gullies.

Birge's and Davis' brigades filed down a rugged slope, forded the insignificant current of Cedar Creek,* and mounted a plateau just north of our original position. I followed them, riding quite alone through the deserted camp and wondering if I should get out of it alive. It was the first time that I had ever taken part in a retreat under the enemy's fire. There was panic in the air; I was conscious of that strange, depressing epidemic which the ancients attributed to a god; it seemed to me that the whole army was scared. I wanted to stay in the gulch of Cedar Creek because for the moment no bullet whistled there. An old gristmill, with cobblestone walls, tempted me to lurk behind it. I cringed with fear of being ignominiously shot in the back as I cantered past this asylum and up the southern slope of the little ravine. Meantime my Pennsylvania grey, who had never been in battle before, behaved with asinine composure; though later, after he had noted the great number of dead horses about, he shied at every shell and bullet that came near him;—obviously a beast capable of drawing an inference.

On the crest of the plateau I found Birge and Davis in good

* Not Cedar Creek itself, but a tributary, Meadow Brook. (Ed.)

order, facing southward and firing at will. Other organizations were near; but what they were I did not learn; I was watching the fighting in front;—watching the men who might kill me. One of these neighboring lines showed four regimental colors and must have been a brigade, but could not have numbered more than two hundred men.

Our camp already swarmed with men in grey or butternut, some of them rummaging and plundering among the tents, others popping at us and yelping. For a few minutes the musketry was lively here, and I hoped that we had finally checked the enemy. A straggler who went by us toward the rear was equally cheerful; he bellowed to a fellow bummer, "The bloody Sixth is going in. *They'll* stop these blasted cusses. They say that, by Jesus, *they'll* hold 'em."

But the Sixth had to go, like Crook's and Emory's commands before it, only with greater deliberation and order, just in proportion as it had more time to prepare for the struggle. I was gazing with some amusement at Birge, who had lost his horse and rode a funny old wagon mule, when I saw him glance anxiously over his left shoulder and then order a retreat. Getty, overlapped on his left, was moving up the pike, and we were in danger of being enfiladed.

The Nineteenth Corps now retreated about a thousand yards, except Davis' brigade of our first division which halted near a residence called Belle Vue * and fought there alone in fine style for perhaps twenty minutes. On a crest near Middletown the whole line fronted and opened fire, supported by Chase's battery and what remained of Taft's, while the staff officers made a vain effort to halt and organize the numerous stragglers who were sauntering through the fields towards Winchester. I think it was here that the Sixth Corps repulsed and thoroughly routed an attack by Early's reserve division under Wharton. But notwithstanding this partial success, we presently resumed our retreat in search of a position less easily flanked, where our dislocated line of battle could be quietly patched together and reorganized. Both armies were at this time in a rather fragmentary condition and depleted by numerous stragglers.

Fifteen hundred yards north of Middletown we made a nearly

* Belle Grove House, according to the map accompanying the official records. (Ed.)

unmolested halt of an hour or more. The men hastily gathered rails and commenced fieldworks under a long-range fire from a few fieldpieces. A regiment of cavalry, commanded by a jolly, red-faced colonel whose name I did not learn, turned back some hundreds of bummers and sneaks, who were immediately clapped into one battalion or another.

The Nineteenth and Sixth Corps were now united in regular line of battle. We had succeeded at last in dragging our left wing out of the grasp of Early's turning column. We were in condition to wage a sturdy battle, if our men could recover their usual confidence; for Tolstoi is right in maintaining that it is largely "the spirit of the army" which wins victories. But the enemy did not attack us, for they were disquieted by the demonstrations of our cavalry, and they were as busy in reorganizing and in building rail forts as ourselves.

Chapter XIV

SHERIDAN'S victories in the autumn of 1864 rallied the North behind Lincoln in his determination to fight until the South was completely defeated. The result was that in November the people retained the President in office and, in addition, elected enough Congressmen from his party to give him the support of two thirds of the House of Representatives. After the battle of Cedar Creek De Forest engaged in no more heavy fighting. On November 7, 1864, he probably took part in the review of General Emory's corps before General Sheridan. When the approach of cold weather prevented further military operations, the Twelfth Connecticut withdrew to Kernstown, Virginia. De Forest continued as an aide until December 2 when he was discharged "by reason of expiration of term of service." (Ed.)

THE BATTLE OF CEDAR CREEK (continued)

THE lines were reorganized after a rather heterogeneous fashion. Numbers of soldiers formed up in companies and in regiments to which they did not belong. The Twelfth Connecticut, for instance, was in three detachments, one under the lieutenant colonel, one under the adjutant, and one under a sergeant. Much of this confusion resulted from the fact that the "grand guards," numbering several thousand men, had mostly been cut off in the morning from the army, and now rejoined it where they could.

An hour put the Sixth and Nineteenth Corps in fair shape; and then we made another retreat, short and our last. We had drifted considerably to the west of the pike, and General Wright was anxious to recover a hold on it. Undisturbed by our jaded and disordered enemy, we filed into columns of march by regiments and quietly retired a mile or so, veering gradually eastward. That brought us in touch with the pike, and once more we halted.

Allow me here a digression concerning fugitives, a class much misrepresented by novelists and poets. Defeated and retreating soldiers do not fly at full speed for any considerable distance. After a run of a hundred yards or less, even though the bullets are still whizzing around them, they drop into a walk, perhaps from lack of breath, perhaps from shame. Thenceforward they tramp steadily rearward, not in the least wild with fright, but discreetly selecting the best cover, slipping through hollows and woods, halting for rest and discourse behind buildings, and in short taking care of themselves with provoking intelligence. But, although they are so cool, you will find it no easy task to rally them. Try it; they will stare at you and straggle on; their faces seem to say, "We have done our best and without avail; now let somebody else face the music."

Draw your sword on them, and they will halt; but turn away, and they will begin to sidle rearward. The chief trouble with them seems to be that they have got out of their places in the military machine. If one of them finds his own company, he will probably rejoin it; he will also join another company of the same regiment; but another regiment he has no use for. An officer who loses his command appears similarly bewildered. He rarely attempts to rally any but his own men and wanders about in search of them, letting the battle go. But if a superior officer seizes upon this lost being and puts him in command of a squad of rallied men, he will lead them back among the bullets, his morale restored by the authority and responsibility which have been thrust upon him.

The talk which I heard addressed to fugitives was more or less like the following. "Halt, men! Where the devil are you going to? You will be no safer at the rear; you must fight this war out somewhere; you can't retreat forever. This is the best cover you will find. Halt and lie down and form a line. Don't be discouraged. It's all right. I tell you, boys, it's all right. We were surprised this morning; it wasn't a fair fight. But we are wide awake now; we are ready to turn the joke on them; we shall whip them sure."

"Bully for you!" exclaims one soldier, honestly pleased with this battle oration, which he probably regards as a meritorious effort to make the best of a bad case. Another man, not so burly and healthy looking as the first, smiles incredulously and says, "All right? It don't look much like it." But both fall into line, lie down behind the rude cover which has been thrown up, and recap their pieces.

From our final halting place (a considerable woodland) General Emory sent me rearward to discover and bring back a brigade which had vanished. In fifteen or twenty minutes I was in a strange country, quite alone and somewhat lost. An army of thirty thousand men had disappeared as if an earthquake had swallowed it. But presently I stumbled upon a provost guard which had been posted along a line of two or three miles for the purpose of halting and turning back fugitives. One of these troopers assured me that no stray brigade had got thus far to the rear.

"You look hungry, Captain," he said, offering me a couple of hard biscuit which I was very glad to accept. "I have plenty more. I have emptied the havresacks of two dead men this morning. We cavalry chaps ride around loose and get things."

Then he informed me that Sheridan had arrived from Winchester and was with the Sixth Corps. Away I went for the pike, hoping to find the commander in chief there and thinking that if I could bring a message from him to Emory, my failure to discover the lost brigade would be passed over. But at the pike I learned that Sheridan had gone to our wing, and thereupon I galloped thither on his trail without overtaking him. Meanwhile the missing brigade had rejoined the corps of its own accord, and I was told that I might dismount to rest my tired and hungry horse.

"I am glad Sheridan has come," said one of my brother staff officers to me. "He may help us to retrieve our character. I am perfectly ashamed of our defeat this morning. The enemy certainly had not more than eighteen thousand men."

Sheridan's arrival brought enthusiastic joy to the soldiers. They had gained two victories under his command, and now that he was with them again they hoped for another. Everybody knows the story of his eleven miles' ride from Winchester; how he came down the pike at a tearing trot, swinging his cap and shouting to the stragglers, "About face, boys! We are going back to our camps. We are going to lick them out of their boots."

For two hours, hailed everywhere by cheers of delight, he rode along the front studying the ground and occasionally addressing the men. "Boys, if I had been here, this never should have happened," he declared over and over in his animated way. "I tell you it never would have happened. And now we are going back to our camps. We are going to get a twist on those fellows. We are going to lick them out of their boots."

Sheridan reached us about half past ten in the morning, but we did not renew the battle until near four in the afternoon. There were rumors that Longstreet was at hand and that a strong Southern force was stealing around our left, all of which led to necessary but time-wasting reconnoissances by our cavalry. Meantime Emory's men threw up a long, low fieldwork of stones, rails and tree trunks in the wood where they were stationed; while, in rear of the Sixth Corps, some two thousand stragglers were hustled into line with Crook's rallied brigades, both together forming a reserve.

About three in the afternoon Emory received notice from Sheridan that a column was advancing upon our wood; and presently a violent fusillade broke out along our front line, accompanied by battle yells from our second line; though meanwhile I did not hear a hostile bullet, nor did we have a single man hit. The uproar lasted several minutes, and then I was told that the column had retreated. Was there one? I certainly did not see it, although I was posted close in rear of our centre, gazing eagerly over the prostrate ranks of volleying men. Of course the enemy may have "demonstrated" in a cautious, faraway style; but I suspected that the affair was a trick intended to test, or to encourage, our people. The generals treated it with all due seriousness, and Emory sent a report of it to Sheridan.

"That's good! That's good!" he answered gayly. "Thank God for that! Now then, tell General Emory if they attack him again to go after them, and to follow them up, and to sock it to them, and to give them the devil. We'll get the tightest twist on them yet that you ever saw. We'll have all those camps and cannon back again."

I must say that at this time many of our people needed cheering up; they were apparently somewhat dismayed at discovering that the enemy showed a willingness to renew the battle; and while the fusillade lasted I noted some ominously gloomy faces. "They are not going to fight well," said one of our staff officers sadly. "They haven't recovered their spirits. They look scared."

Toward four o'clock in the sober, weary, hungry afternoon came the long-expected orders from Sheridan. "The whole line will advance. The Nineteenth Corps will move in touch with the Sixth Corps which will be the pivot. The right of the Nineteenth will swing toward the left so as to drive the enemy down upon the pike."

It should be understood that the enemy's left, which rested upon some wooded crests, was now their strong point; while their right ran out to the pike across undulating open fields, presenting no natural line of resistance. Sheridan's plan was to push them off the crests into the plain by a turning movement of Emory's divisions, and then tumble them southward by a vigorous attack in front from the Sixth Corps and some brigades of cavalry. The major part of our troopers were in a plain west of us, looking after the weak and cautious line of Lomax and Rosser.

Not many words were uttered as we left our wood and commenced our advance. I remarked aloud, "If we beat them now, it will be magnificent." General Emory replied, "And we are very likely to do it; they will be so far from expecting us." Some of the men were heard to say, "We may as well whip them tonight; if we don't, we shall have to do it tomorrow. Sheridan will get it out of us some time."

Their eyes were grave, and their tanned faces were uplifted to look for the foe, as they tramped in line of battle out of the forest into the meadows. Then came a screeching and cracking of Rebel shells, followed some minutes later by a prolonged wail of musketry, mingled with the widespread yell of our charge. I learned afterwards from exultant brothers in arms that this first attack carried an advanced line of defence consisting of a grove, a stone wall and some half-finished works of rails and earth. The success took a load off the spirits of our men and gave them confidence to finish up the battle triumphantly.

But I had no leisure to watch this opening movement, for it

had scarcely begun when Emory sent me off with a message to Wright. "Tell him, with my compliments, that my troops are advancing, and that I hope for his support on the left."

After a gallop of some minutes I found General Wright and his staff watching the advance of his centre. They were in a little grove, all dismounted and with good reason, for Early's gunners were making the air above them hot with yowling, spitting shells which sent down showers of twigs and October leaves. Wright himself had received a gash from a slice of cast iron and had his head bound up with a bloody handkerchief. My horse, no longer the valiant beast of the morning, was so rampageous with fright that I dared not dismount lest he should break away from me. Accordingly an aide summoned the general to me out of the grove; and, after apologizing for permitting this indecorum, I delivered my message.

Wright was as composed and kindly in manner and gentle in voice as if he were "sitting in hall with ladies."

"Give General Emory my compliments," he replied, "and say that we are attacking also and shall keep in touch with him."

I saluted, he saluted, and I rode away, my steed wincing and leaping at every cannon shot. General Emory, when I found him again, was alone in an open meadow, patiently awaiting the development of the battle. His other staff officers had been sent in various directions and had not returned. He himself could not gallop about, for he had lost both his horses in the morning and now bestrode a meagre little hack, apparently a deserter from the Confederate cavalry, which could barely travel at a walk.

I could not make out at this moment that our people were gaining ground on the enemy. Four or five hundred yards south of us Grover's division occupied the crest of a long hill, exchanging a heavy fire with some force beyond it which I could not see. Dwight's division, on the extreme right, had disappeared among the forested knolls already mentioned; but it could not have gone far, for Dwight and his aide, Lieutenant Allen, were in the field this side of the woodland.

Apparently our line needed a re-enforcement or an encouragement to give it another impetus forward. Presently Emory sent me over to Dwight to enquire if artillery would help.

"Yes, artillery would help," said Dwight, who had his customary jolly air in battle. "But tell the general it is very hot up there. He would lose his horses, and might lose his guns. Perhaps he had better keep them for a pinch."

Rejoining Emory, I found him in conversation with our commander in chief, who had just arrived from the extreme right of our infantry line. Sheridan was talking of Dwight's division; he had ordered it, he said, to traverse the wood and fall upon Early's left wing in flank; he had instructed it to attack boldly and energetically.

"And I want you to see to it, General," he added earnestly. "Send a trustworthy officer there to overlook the movement. Have those men told to go in like good fellows. Tell them victory depends on it."

This duty was confided to me, and also to Captain Silsby, another of our staff who came up at the moment. It is customary to send important orders by at least two officers, in view of the fact that one alone might not make his way through the chances of battle.

Of course Silsby and I took different routes to reach the wooded knolls where we expected to find the division. He made a long circuit to the right, while I pushed diagonally across the open fields, hoping to save time and to dodge through the fire somehow. But my Quaker battle steed lost his faith in a protecting providence when we reached a gully which some of Early's guns were raking with grape, knocking about the turf and pebbles at a tempestuous rate. Taking advantage of the fact that I had lost one of my spurs, he commenced turning round and round as if upon a pivot. In a great rage, I drew my sabre and ferruled away at one flank while I dug the rowels into the other. Trembling all over, the peaceful old nag gathered himself in a bunch, like a cat about to leap at a mouse, and then made a wild scramble into the gully and up the other bank, nearly falling down in his haste and eagerness. By good luck, or as if on purpose to let us pass, the battery stopped firing just in that moment, and we got through unhurt.

Reaching the wood, I followed a cart track which ran along its edge, and presently came upon a pale sergeant seated by the roadside, supporting the head of a ghastly-faced officer. The dying man, already unconscious, was young Captain Lowell of the Twelfth Connecticut, who had fallen, shot through the body, in the charge which carried the knolls. I pitied him; but I had no time to talk of that; I simply asked, "Where is the division?"

"That way somewhere," replied the sergeant, glancing toward the western angle of the wood, and I hastily resumed my gallop. I had ridden barely a hundred yards and was approaching a point where the track turned into the timber, when I met a comrade staff officer, Lieutenant Colonel Abert. As I learned afterward, he had just escaped an ambuscade of Gordon's sharpshooters with a bruise on the right leg, caused by a bullet striking the steel scabbard of his sabre. We both pulled up, and I enquired, "Where is the first division?"

"It is beyond this wood. What do you want of it?"

"I have orders for it to attack the enemy's left."

"The orders have been delivered; besides, you can't reach the division."

"Why not?" I asked, and, as he made no answer, I repeated, "Where *is* the division?"

"I tell you that you can't reach it," he insisted impatiently.

Afterward I came to suspect that he intended to save my life, but at the moment I resented his mysterious language and peremptory manner, and therefore replied angrily, "I have the general's orders to deliver, and I shall deliver them if I can."

I dashed up the cart track and was turning at full gallop into the wood, when I saw three tall Butternuts rise behind a thicket eight or ten rods ahead and take aim at me through the upper branches. These were doubtless the men who had missed Abert, and they probably thought that I was Abert returning, for we both rode light greys. At this moment they were between Emory's two divisions and must have been pretty well isolated from their own division.

If they had fired lying down, they would have potted me easily, and as it was they came within a trifle of it. My scary nag saw them rise, and instinctively made a prodigious bound into the brushwood on the right, undoubtedly saving us both from death or wounds, for the bullets whistled very close behind us. I leaned well forward, and the horse clapped his tail as close as possible between his legs, altogether like Tam O'Shanter and his Maggie in their famous flight from the witches.

The honorable fact is that I was run away with, for my bridle was a rotten old bit of plunder, and I dared not pull hard for fear of breaking it. I had traversed perhaps sixty yards of swishing underwood, when, nearly half a mile in rear of my bushwhackers, shrilled out the long-drawn charging yell of our first division.* I knew the sound well; and no doubt the three Butternuts knew it and made haste back to their own people; and I think also that my horse knew it, for he stopped running.

Obviously Dwight, or his brigadiers McMillan and Davis, had carried out Sheridan's orders without waiting for my unnecessary oversight. The soldiers executed this charge with extraordinary spirit; they were all veterans, and understood some movements as well as if they had been West Pointers; when they came out of the wood on Gordon's flank, they knew that they had him beaten; and they went down upon him at a double-quick with a scream of delight and triumph.

In my opinion this attack decided the battle, or at least began the rout. Evan's Georgian brigade of Gordon's division (the same brigade which Birge had beaten at the Opequon) was the first to break and run. Then every regiment in that wing, from left to right, crumbled swiftly away and streamed in confusion toward the centre. Meantime Grover, the Sixth Corps, and the cavalry near the pike, all making an energetic, simultaneous push southward, promptly ended what remained of Southern resistance.

I regret that I did not witness Dwight's charge, the finest deed ever done by that noble division. But various officers who did witness it spoke of it with enthusiastic admiration. "Those men are doing all that flesh and blood can," said one of Sheridan's staff who followed up the headlong, panting rush. And, during the evening, I heard Custer say to Emory, "Your fellows on the right went in mighty pretty this afternoon. I had to sing out to my men, 'Are you going to let the infantry get ahead of you?' "

The battle ended like a dream from which one is suddenly awakened. When Emory sent me off with Sheridan's order, the

---

* *Our* yell was a long-drawn cry; the "Rebel yell" was a series of yelps.

musketry was still heavy and the fortune of the day undecided; but when I rejoined him, half an hour later, the field was deserted by the Rebels, and our infantrymen were dragging back to their camps in perfect peace.

We discovered plenty of evidences, however, that the dragon of war had lately passed that way. Dead and wounded men, dead and wounded steeds, dismounted guns, shattered caissons, broken muskets, and pools or spatters of blood bore widespread evidence to the stubborn and protracted conflict. A remarkable number of slaughtered horses showed how freely the cavalry had been used and how severely the artillery had suffered. There were so many of them in front of a stone wall east of the pike, which had been charged and carried by our troopers, that I did not stop to count them but guessed at the lot as about a hundred.

Almost every dead soldier near the road had a blanket or overcoat thrown over him by some sympathetic comrade. Of the wounded a few lay still and silent; here and there one uttered quavering cries expressive of intense agony; others groaned from time to time gently and patiently. One man, whose sky-blue trousers were ominously stained and clotted with dull crimson, called to our party in a husky voice, "Hurrah for General Emory!"

We pulled up our horses, and the general asked, "Are you badly hurt, my lad?"

"My leg is broken by a rifle shot," replied the sufferer. "I suppose I shall lose it. But I still feel able to say, 'Hurrah for General Emory.' I fought under you, General, at Sabine Cross Roads and Pleasant Hill."

His voice came in short gasps, and his wound was high up in the thigh, and I doubted if he could live an hour. The general dismounted to give him a drink of whiskey, and left a guard to see that he was put into an ambulance. Then, remounting his skeleton hack, his mind soon reverted to the battle, and turning to me, he said, "This young man, only about thirty years old, has made a great name for himself today."—Of course he was thinking of Sheridan, and obviously with admiration.

Our victorious old first division was not permitted to halt until it had occupied Hupp's Hill beside the gorge of the Shenandoah River. Grover's division, a little before dark, filed into the camp from which it had been driven in the morning, the tired and hungry ranks lying down to rest there among dead men in grey and in blue.

But there was no repose for the retreating enemy or for our cavalry. The usually gallant and elastic Southern infantry was so cowed by defeat and stupefied by fatigue that it offered scarcely any resistance to its pursuers.

Colonel Love, of the 116th New York, spurred his horse into a hurrying squad which represented the Second South Carolina, tore its battle flag out of the hands of the color sergeant and got away with it unhurt, though two or three rifles were hastily fired at him.

A grim-looking private of the Fifth New York cavalry (a Heiduc from the Balkans) overhauled a baggage wagon, sabred the driver and a man who was whipping the horses, and brought in the vehicle with three living prisoners.

Lieutenant Gray, of the First Rhode Island Artillery, rode up to a retiring battery and ordered it to face about. The sergeant in charge replied that he had been instructed to go to the rear as fast as possible.

"You don't seem to know who I am," said Gray, "I am one of those d—d Yanks. Countermarch immediately."

The battery countermarched, and Gray was leading it off alone when some of our troopers came up and took charge of it.

Lieutenant Isaacs, of the Second South Carolina, assured me after the war that he surrendered five times during this retreat, but got away after all. "Two hundred of our men," he said, "would throw down their arms to twenty or thirty of your cavalry. Then the chief of the troop would order, 'Now you stay there!' and spur off after more prisoners. Then we officers would tell our men, 'Now scatter, boys; take to the bushes and hollows; get back to Fisher's Hill.' Well, what with the nightfall and the rough country, the biggest part of us sneaked out of our scrape."

All the way to Strasburg the road was strewn with the leavings of a beaten and flying army, and the town itself soon became choked with abandoned guns and wagons and ambulances, tangled up with dead or broken-down horses. Two days later I counted near Sheridan's headquarters forty-nine field-pieces, of which twenty-four had been lost by us and retaken, while the rest were bona fide captures from Early. Also, we got fifty wagons, sixty-five ambulances, sixteen hundred rifles and twelve hundred prisoners. Although we were tired and cold and hungry at headquarters, we passed a jolly evening in listening to the news sent us by the cavalry and in bragging over a victory which came so near to being a defeat.

That night I should have gone supperless to bed, but that General Birge invited me to share a very scanty meal of fried pork and hardtack, which I was ashamed to take, yet too hungry to refuse. My bed was a board on the ground, under the beautiful, chilly stars, with no covering but my blouse thrown over my shoulders. Tents, baggage, rations and servants had all flown to Winchester and had not returned. The night was a cool one, and I turned over many times without getting any warmer. At sunrise, chilled and breakfastless, I was sent with my famished horse to Strasburg on a reconnoissance.

"But if you can find something to eat there," said our chief of staff, "I think the general will not call you to account for it."

I got a breakfast (price, one dollar before sitting down) of two fried hard biscuits, two slices of salt beef, and a cup of rye coffee. In the woods south of Strasburg Yankee soldiers and Rebel prisoners were slaughtering and roasting pigs in hungry amity. During the following morning I learned that our commissary wagons had not yet arrived, and that some of the regiments, for instance the Twelfth Connecticut, were at the point of starvation. One of my old soldiers, Quinlan, white in face and feeble in voice, said to me, "Are we *never* going to have anything to eat again?"

What with starving, freezing, swamp fever, forced marches and being shot, war is glorious fun, merely glorious, not comfortable. Perhaps the Chinese are right in holding that it is not worthy of the admiration and attention of a civilized people.

But to the great mass of mankind, cultured as well as barbarous, it has a strange fascination. Hungry as the Twelfth was, and heavily as it had suffered from the enemy, it was in good spirits because the enemy had been whipped.

"You had a tough time of it?" I said, interrogatively, to Lieutenant McCall.

"Yes, we had a tough time of it," he replied carelessly. Then, bursting into a laugh, "But, by George, it salted those non-veterans."

The "non-veterans" were men who had made themselves hated in the regiment by refusing to re-enlist for the war. A remarkably large proportion of them had been killed in the fight; and the "veterans" chuckled over the fact as a humorous bit of divine vengeance.

Presently Private Hunter came forward with a smile of satisfaction on his sunburnt mug. "Did you know, Captain, that the old company finished off under Corporal Whitaker? Lieutenant Smith was wounded right away, and that left us without an officer. Then Sergeant Stalee was captured, and Sergeant Hurlburt killed; and finally the company got down to old man Whitaker. Why, Captain, old man Whitaker ought to be promoted. He led seven charges; that is, the company had seven men for the last charge; and so I call it seven charges."

Our casualties at Cedar Creek were 569 killed, 3,425 wounded, 1,429 prisoners and 341 missing,* in all 5,764.† Early conceded a loss of 1,860 killed and wounded, and we took about 1,200 prisoners, making a total of near 3,100. It must be confessed that we bought our victory at a dear rate. For instance, we had 4,000 men hit to the enemy's 1,800, although we were fully double their number, and presumably used twice as many cartridges.

As I have said before, they were obviously the best shots, and their open-order style of fighting was an economical one. Moreover, when they retreated, they went in a swarm and at full speed, thus presenting a poor mark for musketry. We, on the contrary, sought to retire in regular order, and suffered heavily for it.‡

* Mostly, no doubt, temporary stragglers.

† These figures and the table on the following page are taken from *The Shenandoah Valley in 1864* by G. E. Pond. They are at slight variance with the figures given in the revised casualty returns published in *The War of the Rebellion . . . Official Records*, Ser. I, Vol. XLIII, Part I, 137. (Ed.)

‡ Early's loss, though still a matter of discussion, is assumed to be about as follows: killed and wounded, 1,860; prisoners, 1,200.

But Sheridan's victories were worth their cost; they helped greatly toward breaking down the already enfeebled army of Lee; and they assured the defeat of the peace-at-any-price party in the presidential election of 1864.

Sheridan's loss appears in the following table.

	Killed	Wounded	Missing	Total
Cavalry.	25	139	50	214
Sixth Corps.	255	1,666	294	2,215
Nineteenth Corps.	243	1,352	893	2,488
Eighth Corps.	46	268	533	847
	569	3,425	1,770	5,764

Of the missing Early captured 1,429. Probably the majority of the rest were temporary stragglers, while others were killed or wounded not yet reported to their company commanders.

INDEX

Smith, Lieutenant, Company D, Twelfth Connecticut, 127, 130

Smith, Lieutenant James, adjutant, Twelfth Connecticut, 82, 184

Stalee, Sergeant, Company I, Twelfth Connecticut, 231

Strong, Major, at Biloxi, 8

Sweeny, Private, Company I, Twelfth Connecticut, 65

TAYLOR, LIEUTENANT GENERAL RICHARD, in Lafourche country, 149, 150

Teche country, military importance of, 85; character of, 86

Tennallytown, 161

Thibodeaux, Confederate army at, 54; topography of, 79

Thoburn, Colonel Joseph, 186, 206, 208, 209; unlucky attack of, 201; isolated position of, 207; death of, 211

Thomas, Colonel, Eighth Vermont, 116, 187, 188

Torbert, Major General Alfred T. A., 197–198; sent to intercept Early, 196

Transports, army, 8, 162; accommodations on, 1–2, 151; armament on, 2; disembarking, 3–5, 18

See also Crescent, E. W. Farley, Fulton, Mississippi, Winona

VAN PETTEN, LIEUTENANT COLONEL, 160th New York, 137, 182, 188; on forced march, 101

Vicksburg, held by Northern forces, 103; surrender of, 145

WASHINGTON, attitude toward Northern troops, 161–162

Weber, Sergeant, in De Forest's company, 5–6, 18, 155; misfortunes of, 24–25, 29–30, 76; superstitions of, 142

Weitzel, Brigadier General Godfrey, 50, 81, 104; sketch of, 53–54; at Donaldsonville, 55–56; plan against enemy, 72, 91; in Teche country, 86

Wells, Charles, Company I, Twelfth Connecticut, 212

Whitaker, Corporal, Company I, Twelfth Connecticut, 184, 231

Wilkinson, Major, aide to Emory, 202

Wilson, Major General James Harrison, 173, 175

Winona, army transport, 162

Wright, Major General Horatio G., 159, 173, 175, 219; at Fisher's Hill, 192–193; left in charge of army in Shenandoah Valley, 202; at Cedar Creek, 208, 224